Radicalization

For Lorna

Radicalization

Kevin McDonald

polity

First published in 2018 by Polity Press

Polity Press
65 Bridge Street
Cambridge CB2 1UR, UK

Polity Press
101 Station Landing
Suite 300
Medford, MA 02155, USA

ISBN-13: 978-1-5095-2260-6
ISBN-13: 978-1-5095-2261-3(pb)

A catalogue record for this book is available from the British Library.

Library of Congress Cataloging-in-Publication Data
Names: McDonald, Kevin, 1955- author.
Title: Radicalization / Kevin McDonald.
Description: Cambridge, UK : Polity Press, 2018. | Includes bibliographical references and index.
Identifiers: LCCN 2018002843 (print) | LCCN 2018018244 (ebook) | ISBN 9781509522644 (Epub) | ISBN 9781509522606 | ISBN 9781509522606 (hardback) | ISBN 9781509522613(pbk.)
Subjects: LCSH: Radicalism--Religious aspects--Islam. | Radicalization. | Islamic fundamentalism. | Terrorism--Religious aspects--Islam. | Jihad. | Internet and terrorism. | Social media.
Classification: LCC HN49.R33 (ebook) | LCC HN49.R33 M432 2018 (print) | DDC 303.48/4--dc23
LC record available at https://lccn.loc.gov/2018002843

Typeset in 10.5 on 12 pt Plantin by Servis Filmsetting Ltd, Stockport, Cheshire
Printed and bound in the United Kingdom by Clays Ltd, Elcograf S.p.A.

The publisher has used its best endeavours to ensure that the URLs for external websites referred to in this book are correct and active at the time of going to press. However, the publisher has no responsibility for the websites and can make no guarantee that a site will remain live or that the content is or will remain appropriate.

Every effort has been made to trace all copyright holders, but if any have been inadvertently overlooked the publisher will be pleased to include any necessary credits in any subsequent reprint or edition.

For further information on Polity, visit our website: politybooks.com

Contents

Acknowledgements

While a book may be written by an individual, it almost always involves the contribution of many people. This is definitely the case with this one. Sections are based on fieldwork with 'hard to reach' groups, in some cases members of proscribed organizations or supporters of jihadism, demanding extensive periods of fieldwork and relationship building. Here my co-worker Mohammad Ilyas has been critical in nurturing relationships over several years, building on earlier work made possible by an Australian Research Council Discovery Grant and a European Union Marie Curie International Fellowship. Opportunities to explore ideas and make sense of often confusing material were fundamental to the book's construction, and here the generosity of others has been critical. Colleagues and students in the Department of Criminology and Sociology at Middlesex University in London provided invaluable opportunities to explore ideas, and it would not have been possible to complete this book without the support of my Dean, Joshua Castellino. I have been able to explore key themes at the Centre d'Analyse et d'Intervention Sociologiques at the Ecole des Hautes Etudes en Sciences Sociales in Paris, where readers will note my debt to Farhad Khosrokhavar, François Dubet, Michel Wieviorka and Alain Touraine. Research Committee 47 of the International Sociological Association, led by Geoffrey Pleyers, afforded me opportunities to make sense of material at critical points. Others have also engaged in generous dialogue, from colleagues at the Catholic University of Louvain in Belgium and Aarhus University in Denmark, to practitioners involved in the EU Radicalisation Awareness Network (RAN) and the European Expert Network on Terrorism Issues (EENeT). I have greatly benefited from advice about ethical issues, in particular that of my colleagues

Sarah Bradshaw and Philip Leach at Middlesex University. David Anderson QC, at the time the United Kingdom's Independent Reviewer of Terrorism Legislation, generously responded to ethical as well as legal questions posed by the research this book is based on. The book itself owes a great debt to the generous feedback of anonymous reviewers at Polity, and to the patient but demanding engagement of Jonathan Skerrett. Despite all this, it goes without saying that I alone am responsible for the judgements, arguments and conclusions presented in the chapters that follow.

The research upon which this book is based, whether interviewing or analysing social media material, has at times been difficult not only intellectually but personally. While sociological work can sometimes celebrate life-affirming experiences, this is not the case in this book. Undertaking this research has underlined just how much our human vulnerability and incompleteness is not a problem to be overcome but the very basis of living with others. Throughout this period, I have relied on the presence of many people constantly affirming the complexities and wonder of life – above all Lorna, to whom this book is dedicated.

1
Rethinking Radicalization

In 2012, Aqsa Mahmood was an 18-year-old living with her parents in a middle-class suburb of Glasgow, Scotland. She had completed secondary school and was making plans for the university course she would begin in the autumn. Like many young people in Europe and North America, much of her social life with her friends took place through social media. She created her first Twitter account in 2010, tweeting approximately thirty times a day, most exchanges being with a close group of friends, her 'fam'. In 2012, she created her first ask.fm account, and in it we encounter the kind of communications we would expect of an 18-year-old: chatting about her former school, her suburb, expressing pleasure at receiving compliments. She is integrated into her community; she shares opinions about local cricket teams, and her pride in the kilt that was part of her school uniform, declaring 'I'm a true Scot' (ask.fm, 13 August 2012). In November, she is tweeting pictures of steamy male film stars to her girlfriends, and screenshots of her mum's attempts to get her to pick up the phone when she calls (Twitter, 27 November 2012).

Just one year later, Aqsa Mahmood left her home in Glasgow to travel to Aleppo in Syria, where she became part of what was then known as the Islamic State of Iraq and Sham, or ISIS. There she took on an active role offering advice and strategies to other young women in the United Kingdom about how to travel successfully to Syria. On 28 September 2015, less than two years after her departure, she was deemed of sufficient importance to be added to the list of individuals subject to United Nations Security Council sanctions, named as an individual actively involved in promoting al-Qaeda-linked terrorism. This book sets out to understand how such a transformation, and others like it, is possible.

Violence, emergency, uncertainty

Aqsa Mahmood is only one of more than five thousand people estimated to have travelled from the industrialized democracies of Europe, North America and the Pacific to join jihadist groups in Syria during the period 2012 to 2017 (Europol 2017). This number reached a peak in 2016, and then began to decline as western governments made travel to Syria more difficult, and as the Islamic State began to suffer defeats and loss of territory, ultimately leading to the loss of Raqqa, its capital in Northern Syria, in October 2017. Like the majority of people who travelled to Syria during this time, Mahmood was young, the average age of those making this journey being under 25 (Europol 2017). This is very different from the age profile of those who a generation earlier travelled to join in the Afghan and Balkan wars, where the age of the majority who made this journey was over thirty. And Mahmood is not only young, but a woman, again reflecting a major transformation from two decades earlier, where those who travelled to Afghanistan were almost uniquely men.

During this period, a new potential for violence was not only evident in the numbers of people travelling to Syria. Attacks occurred across Europe, from driving vehicles into crowds and stabbings to the organized attacks in Paris in November 2015, which killed 150 and injured hundreds. Several months later there was an attack at Brussels Airport and then one on France's Bastille Day when a refrigerated lorry ran into crowds in the Riviera city of Nice, killing 86 and injuring more than four hundred. In the United Kingdom, attacks had also taken place, including a college student of Libyan origin who blew himself up with a shrapnel-filled bomb at a concert in Manchester, killing 22 people, mainly teenage girls and children. Such violence has not been confined to Europe. In the United States in 2009, a shooter killed 13 people at the Fort Worth military base and wounded a further twenty-nine. In December 2015, 14 people were killed in a shooting in San Bernadino and, in June 2016, 49 people were killed and a further 53 wounded at an LGTB nightclub in Orlando, Florida, where the killer claimed allegiance to the Islamic State. At that time, this was the largest mass killing in modern American history, and it remains the largest killing of LGTB people since the Nazi Holocaust. In September 2016, three bombs exploded in the New York City area, wounding some thirty people and, a year later in October, a 29-year-old man drove a truck down a bicycle path in Manhattan, hitting cyclists, pedestrians and a school bus, killing eight people and wounding many more. Similar radicalized violence has also emerged in Canada and Australia, including attacks with vehicles, shootings, attempted use of explosives and stabbings of police.

It is important to recognize that the scale of this violence is dwarfed by violence taking place in countries such as Syria, Iraq, Nigeria, Somalia or Libya. But these countries are all experiencing modern forms of warfare involving collapsed or compromised states, where regular military forces merge with militias, criminal groups, families and individuals, and where once clearly defined fields of battle have given way to pervasive and increasingly chaotic violence (McDonald 2013). This is not the case in Europe, North America or the industrialized countries of the Pacific.

What is striking across all these actions is the diversity of those involved. Many are very young, such as the 15-year-old schoolboy without any background of violence who, in October 2015, shot and killed a police employee in Sydney, Australia, or three schoolgirls from London who travelled to Syria in that same year. Others have backgrounds ranging from drug dealers and gang members to students and professionals or mothers with young children. This diversity has been the source of a new kind of uncertainty, a sense of disorientation and insecurity, the sense that we are living in a world that is less and less intelligible, and so less secure.

Political violence?

Interviewer:	What is jihad?
Al-Mazwagi:	Jihad is ah … , ah jihad means to ah … what's the word I'm looking for?
Interviewer:	Struggle?
Al-Mazwagi:	No, no, no, not struggle … But to kick some butt! [*giggles*] Jihad is to kick Obama's … [*laughs, then pauses*]. What's that word? There's a word [*longer pause*] Yeah, ok, jihad is to spend all your time and effort in fighting the enemies of Allah SWT'. (Ibrahim al-Mazwagi, North Syria, January 2013 (Channel 4, United Kingdom)

Ibrahim al-Mazwagi, aged 21, was the first British fighter to be killed in the Syrian civil war in February 2013. A university graduate who grew up in London, he had travelled to Syria a year earlier and joined the Katiba al Muhajireen, a brigade of foreign fighters that would eventually become part of the Islamic State. In the exchange above, he is searching to find the words to answer 'What is jihad?'. To help out, the interviewer suggests 'struggle'. Al-Mazwagi rejects this, and continues searching for a word that eludes him. Suddenly his eyes light up and he smiles; he's found what he's looking for: *kick some butt*. Laughing with relief and pleasure, he adds that it is Obama's butt to be kicked. He then pauses for several seconds, becomes more serious and offers another answer, this time with much less inflection or expression. It is as if he is repeating something that he has learnt by heart. Later in the same exchange, the interviewer asks him why he has come to Syria. Al-Mazwagi responds: 'Well, I've always known about jihad, seen the Mujahideen on TV and everything.'

This brief exchange opens up questions that will be central to this book. Al-Mazwagi offers what amounts to two accounts of what jihad means. His first answer is to 'kick some butt' which he refines as 'Obama's butt'. In this short phrase, al-Mazwagi summarizes one of the major approaches to jihadism within the social sciences today: jihad is *political violence*. He expresses a widely held view of the motivations behind jihadist violence, often associated with liberal or progressive observers. From this perspective, jihadist violence is a *response* to external events or actors. This kind of analysis is associated with influential scholars, such as the linguist and commentator on American foreign policy Noam Chomsky, who argues that terrorism needs to be fundamentally understood as a response to United States' actions. For Chomsky, the appeal of terrorism is 'primarily among young people who live under conditions of repression and humilia-tion, with little hope and little opportunity, and who seek some goal in life that offers dignity and self-realization; in this case, establishing a utopian Islamic state rising in opposition to centuries of subjuga-tion and destruction by Western imperial power' (Polychroniou and Chomsky 2015). This is a view widely defended by violent actors themselves. Michael Adebolajo and Michael Adebowale, both con-verts to Islam, murdered and then attempted to behead Lee Rigby, an off-duty soldier, as he was crossing a street in London in 2013. Adebolajo asserted to a passer-by who filmed him: 'The only reason we killed this man … is because Muslims are dying daily… . This British solider is an eye for an eye, a tooth for a tooth.'

This 'political violence' paradigm is arguably most influential in the sub-discipline of terrorism studies that developed in the 1970s, focusing on the militarized groups that emerged following the col-lapse of the western student movement, such as the Red Brigades in Italy, the Weather Underground in the United States, the Red Army Faction in Germany and more short-lived groups such as the Angry Brigade in the United Kingdom or Action Directe in France (McDonald 2013). In the years since, similarly configured separatist groups have remained a source of violence in Europe, from Corsica to Northern Ireland (Europol 2017). In such cases, violence has been structured by ideology, organization and criminality, framed by what appeared as one of the core beliefs of terrorism studies in the 1980s: 'terrorists want a lot of people watching, not a lot of people dead' (Jenkins 1975: 16).

Today's violence in North America, Europe and the industrialized countries of the Pacific takes on a very different profile. Organized and structured groups have given way to groups of friends, networks or individuals, often linked through social media. And rather than made up primarily of former university students, the new violent actors are much more diverse, with an increasing presence of people with criminal backgrounds. Those who joined violent groups in the 1970s almost always had a previous background in 'high risk' activism, often involving confrontations with police, so much so that influential approaches argued that terrorist violence was a product of competitive escalation between police and protesters (Della Porta 2013: 76). But today's situation is radically different. Rather than a long and increasingly frustrated period of activism, leading eventually to embracing violence, the great majority of today's violent actors in Europe and North America have no experience in solidarity organizations or political activism of any kind. And increasing numbers embrace jihadist violence not with a background in activism, but from involvement in criminality.

Religious violence?

In [my local] mosque there is not one person with the same mentality as me. I did not learn my jihad from the Aberdeen mosque, I learned it through my own on the Internet or whatever.

Abdul Raqib Amin, North Syria, 2014

In the mid-1990s, international relations scholars such as Samuel Huntington began to argue that, following the collapse of the Berlin Wall, the older political opposition between capitalism and communism that had dominated much of the twentieth century was giving way to what he saw as a 'clash of civilizations'. Central to this was what he saw as an emerging opposition between 'Islam' and 'the West' (Huntington 1996). From this perspective, after the collapse of communism it would be religion, rather than politics, that would be the source of major world conflicts. Influential sociologists such as Anthony Giddens argued that the pace of globalization had become so great that many people were unable to cope with a world they increasingly experienced as 'out of control' (1999: 2). Evoking a kind of 'strain theory', Giddens argued that in this world, religion was becoming one of the most important sources of security and certainty, driving what he called the growth of 'fundamentalism'. Other sociologists also used the term 'fundamentalism' to describe what they saw as a new potential for conflict and violence. The American Mark Juergensmeyer argued that religiously inspired social actors were less and less able to compromise with others, considering themselves to be the action of God in the world. Such new religious actors, he argued, were increasingly likely to see the world they were living in shaped by what he called a 'cosmic war' (Juergensmeyer 1996).

These views took on immense importance following the attacks of September 11 in 2001, not simply in academic debates, but in programmes seeking to respond to or prevent terrorist-inspired violence. In France, the political scientist Gilles Kepel argues that jihadist movements were a direct consequence of the development of Salafist religious movements in the Middle East (2015). He argues a form of radical Islam has been imported into Europe, and needs to be countered. This influential view has inspired programmes seeking to prevent radicalization through offering classes on the Qur'an and Islamic tradition. From this perspective, practices of religious piety become a source of suspicion.

This new concern with the violent potentials of religion reflects a more profound shift in the social sciences. For much of the second half of the twentieth century, the social sciences largely accepted what had come to be known as the 'secularization' paradigm, believing that religion would become more personal and have less impact on public life and culture. But from the late twentieth century, confidence in the inevitability of secularization began to wane. Michael Walzer, one of the most important American public intellectuals of the second half of the twentieth century, captures this new concern when he argues:

> I live with a generalized fear of every form of religious militancy. I am afraid of Hindutva zealots in India, messianic Zionists in Israel, and of rampaging Buddhist monks in Myanmar. But I admit that I am most

afraid of Islamist zealots because the Islamic world at this moment
in time (not always, not forever) is especially feverish and fervent... .
politically engaged Islamist zealots can best be understood as today's
crusaders. (Walzer 2015)

There is a problem with this, however. The closer we get to the
actual people involved in experiences of radicalization, the more
problematic the idea of 'religious zealots' becomes. Abdul Raqib
Amin, whom I quote in the introduction to this section, travelled
from Aberdeen to Syria in 2014 and is typical of someone who
constructs what he sees as a religious framework from sources he
discovers on the internet. Like the overwhelming majority of these
new violent actors, he demonstrates a 'born-again' profile, evident
above all in the over-representation of converts involved in jihadist
violence (current estimates suggest that 40 per cent of the Americans
who travelled to Syria to join ISIS are converts). Very often, a self-
declared embrace of Islam follows a largely secular lifestyle, in many
cases associated with drug and alcohol use or delinquency. While
often claiming a religious motivation, the majority lack any background of religious practice or history of involvement in mosques
and, as a result, possess only a rudimentary knowledge of Islamic
history or theology.

The lack of engagement with religious communities and the
superficial knowledge of Islam demonstrated by those who become
radicalized are pointed to by the French political sociologist Olivier
Roy (2017). It is not Islam that leads to radicalization, he argues,
but the opposite: angry and rebellious young people, no longer able
to believe in political ideologies, construct an impoverished version
of Islam to serve as a new ideology of protest and rupture. He insists
that radicalization is best approached not as a religious movement
but as a kind of youth movement, one where violence is not a means
but becomes an end in itself. In particular, he argues, this movement
has a generation dimension, where those who are radicalized claim
that they are embracing the 'true Islam', while their parents' beliefs
remain mired in culture and tradition. The Islam of the young radi-
cals, Roy argues, is a product of globalization: it is separated from
tradition and history, disconnected from actual religious traditions
and human communities, it is *deterritorialized* and *deculturized* (2014).
While it claims to reject globalized modernity, he insists, jihadist
radicalization is in fact one of its products. Jihadists' knowledge and
interest in the Qur'an is about as deep, Roy argues, as the knowledge of Marxism shared by the young Red Guards unleashed during

China's Cultural Revolution, whose ideology consisted of a collection of slogans from Mao's *Little Red Book*. Jihadists, argues Roy, are not religious fundamentalists who turn to violence; rather, they are violent nihilists, people without beliefs or utopias, who embrace an impoverished version of Islam (2017).

From this perspective, the paradigmatic case of jihadist radicalization is the violent criminal who embraces Islam, and who then travels to Syria to continue to enjoy a life of violence and crime. This argument certainly alerts us to the limits of the argument that sees radicalization as an extension of religious fundamentalism. But the problem with Roy's argument is that once we get closer to those who have embraced jihadism, many simply do not correspond to his account of violent nihilists, for whom violence is an end in itself. Aqsa Mahmood, who abandoned her university course in pharmacy to travel to Syria, was not a violent nihilist. Junaid Hussain, who left Britain in June 2015 to travel to Syria, was a computer hacker and gamer who in the months before his departure was wearing an Anonymous mask. His partner Sally Jones had been a digital artist promoting her works on an esoteric website and in 2012 she had been posting against all forms of organized religion, which she saw as leading inevitably to violence.

If those who embrace jihadism cannot be understood as 'fundamentalists' in search of tradition, their experience does nonetheless suggest a kind of transformative event. For many, it is an experience of conversion, in most cases constructed on the basis of material found on the internet. For others, it is a rupture with a past life. When we start to explore the ways those involved make sense of these events, certain themes emerge that reflect popular understandings of the religious: guilt and a search for purification; an encounter with something so powerful and vast that it takes one's breath away; an experience of the uncanny and déjà vu. In some cases, purification of the self appears as central to violence. Research into the background of Chérif Kouachi, who with his brother killed 12 journalists at the French satirical magazine *Charlie Hebdo* in January 2015, suggests that he possessed what he would come to consider a forbidden sexuality, his computer and mobile phone suggesting that he had at least one male sexual partner (Seelow 2016a). Kouachi's violent execution of journalists might be understandable as destroying another forbidden, in this case a magazine that had printed images of the Prophet. In other cases of horrific mass killings, Mohamed Lahouaiej-Bouhlel, author of the Nice massacre, had no connection of any kind with religious communities. But his mobile phone also indicated extensive use of online dating sites and a history of sexual encounters with both men and women (Seelow 2016a). Here, too, there may be something present relating to guilt and purification, but ideas such as 'fundamentalists' and 'religious zeal' do not help us access what is at stake.

Radicalization, vulnerability and identity?

In the years following the September 11 attacks, there was an urgent search for new ways to think about terrorism. One influential response was the publication in 2007 by the New York Police Department of *Radicalization in the West: The Homegrown Threat* (Silber and Bhatt 2007). This influential report highlighted a new approach focusing on radicalization, understood as progressing through four linear stages: 'pre-radicalization', self-identification, indoctrination and 'jihadization' – leading to a final outcome, 'attack' (2007: 20). This process was understood as 'internalizing a belief system', and its focus was 'Islamic-based terrorism' (2007: 5). A key concept embedded in this progression was the term 'indoctrination', where vulnerable people in search of meaning would be manipulated by others intent upon radicalizing them.

In the years since, this model has proved immensely influential, shaping both academic debate and policy responses. Its focus on 'indoctrination' meant that policy and prevention programmes could focus on 'counter-messaging', which increasingly came to be understood as 'counter-narratives'. In that sense, it opened up scope for action. Its use of the term 'vulnerable' allowed prevention programmes aiming at protecting, rather than criminalizing, the people they were attempting to engage with, at least in the first instance. The term 'vulnerable' was used to describe not only 'young men' but also 'Muslim diaspora communities' (Silber and Bhatt 2007: 14). Embedded within this idea of vulnerability is an account of responsibility and agency, where radicalization is something 'done to' a person. Prevention and counter-radicalization could thus be understood in terms of protecting vulnerable groups, with professional interventions increasingly drawing upon models developed in relation to 'safeguarding' other groups identified as vulnerable. If in 2007 'indoctrination' emerged as the master concept to explain radicalization, a decade later this was increasingly explained as a result of 'grooming' (Vidino and Hughes 2015: 19), where models developed in relation to internet-based child sexual abuse increasingly became a lens through which to view and prevent radicalization. In such cases, it is increasingly argued, the vulnerable person is not indoctrinated but groomed.

A second approach to radicalization also emphasizes the vulnerability of those who become radicalized, this time arguing vulnerability is a result of *social exclusion*. The 2007 NYPD report argued: 'Europe's *failure to integrate* the second and third generation of its immigrants into society, both economically and socially, has left many young Muslims torn between the secular West and their religious heritage. This inner conflict makes them especially vulnerable to extremism' (Silber and Bhatt 2007: 8; emphasis added).

For the authors of this report, while radicalization in the Middle East might be a response to oppression and suffering, 'radicalization in the West is ... a phenomenon that occurs because *the individual is looking for an identity and a cause*' (2007: 8; emphasis added). It is this loss of identity that makes the person vulnerable to indoctrination.

These are very influential arguments and became widely used by practitioners involved in the prevention of radicalization. But, while widely used, their empirical basis has been less certain. While influential in the area of child sexual abuse, there is little evidence demonstrating that 'grooming' is central to actual experiences of radicalization. Equally, it is not clear why 'looking for an identity' in itself is a form of vulnerability. We could argue that the search for an identity has become fundamental to western societies and economies, from the symbolic content of the goods we purchase (brands) to the increasing communicative dimensions of sexuality, gender, age and our bodies themselves.

The problem with these approaches is the extent they consider radicalization to be something *done to* a person. While this allows a policy response framed in terms of protection, it comes with two principal costs. The first is that we fail to understand or even explore the kinds of agency at work in experiences of radicalization. Rik Coolsaet (2016) describes what he calls 'the vulnerable youngster paradigm' in policy responses to radicalization. 'Jihadis', he insists, 'are not passive victims vulnerable to brainwashing by foreign recruiters. They are active participants in their lives, trying to make sense of their world, constructing meanings from available cultural models and making choices accordingly.' The second problem that flows from considering radicalization as something done to a person is that this isolates the person, imagining them as alone in front of a computer consuming radicalizing messages, and removed from the social relationships and world they inhabit and shape. But as we will see, radicalization is a social process, full of exchanges, communications and shared emotions.

As currently used, the term 'radicalization' *unifies* what may in fact be very different experiences, ranging from medical students motivated by humanitarianism, gang members in search of adventure or persons wishing to cleanse themselves of their guilt. As authors such as Farhad Khosrokhavar (2017) argue, pathways to such violence are associated with different forms of sociability. In many cases, such transitions take place in small, enclosed groups. The most obvious indicator is the significant incidence of 'brother' relationships, such as 2013 Boston bombers Dzlokhar and Tamerlan Tsarnaev, the Kouachi brothers who carried out the *Charlie Hebdo* massacre, brothers Brahim and Salah Abdeslam at the centre of the November 2015 Paris attacks, or the El Bakraoui brothers who undertook the March 2016 suicide attack at Brussels airport. In other cases, couple relationships are central, where risk and danger combine with erotic imaginaries of sex and death. Other types of sociability also recur, in particular associated with periods in prison or youth detention, often linked with backgrounds in different forms of street crime such as theft, assault or drug dealing. Social class occurs as a structuring principle in a significant number of cases, to the extent that different types of trajectory, for example associated with stigmatization, poverty or fractured family background, appear associated with particular forms of violence. Meanwhile, other trajectories appear more associated with what Luc Boltanski (1999) calls 'distant suffering'. Travel surfaces as a particularly important dimension, whether travelling in search of jihad or as part of humanitarian convoys to camps. In such cases, journeys are linked to an experience that allows a person to transform in a way that they become a 'foreigner in their own land' (Khosrokhavar 2017). This dimension of 'becoming a stranger' appears associated with other experiences of displacement, where the world itself becomes strange and uncanny, full of hidden meaning. Such experiences of 'strangeness' highlight the importance of conspiracy theories in trajectories to violence, something we also find in a particular openness to 'the extraordinary' that we encounter in video games and images of hidden potency, very influential in some of the earlier European movements that embraced jihadism, such as 19 HH in France, which combines support for jihadist movements with a culture of the 'epic' and the 'extraordinary'. In this case, support for jihad is constructed through a visceral experience resembling

The Lord of the Rings more than anything we might expect to find in religious or political movements. Still other paths to jihadist violence appear more shaped by the culture of computer gamers, with widespread references to games such as *Call of Duty* and its imaginary of the anti-hero and its world without norms or limits, or in Islamic State's 'Cyber Caliphate', which appears more inspired by the youth culture we encounter in Anonymous (McDonald 2015) than religious cultures or political traditions. Once we begin to explore these experiences, we do not decipher a linear path of structured stages, but a much more complex experience that appears organized more around tensions than stages.

While unifying what constitutes radicalization, much of the current debate also *separates* the violence associated with radicalization from other forms of violence that may in fact possess significant similarities but may not be regarded as significant from the perspective of terrorism studies. For example, once we begin to explore actual experiences of radicalization, we discover many that are constructed in relation to imaginaries of purity and filth and, as we will see, these manifest significant convergences with hate crime and racism. Many experiences of radicalization draw on conspiracy theories and an associated imaginary of plots and hidden meanings, mirroring important dimensions of contemporary popular culture. In other cases, jihadist violence suggests significant convergence with other forms of mass killing, most notably the school shootings that have become increasingly prevalent in North America, and to a lesser extent in Europe, over the past two decades. All this suggests that we need to break with the idea of the isolated and vulnerable person being indoctrinated and explore commonalities shared between experiences of radicalization and hate crime, rampage killings or fascination with conspiracy.

This book

This book is based on two kinds of research. The first is extensive fieldwork undertaken with members of al-Muhajiroun and its successor networks in the United Kingdom, in particular the Movement Against Crusaders (MAC). Al-Muhajiroun is a banned or proscribed group in the United Kingdom. It splintered from another radical group in the late 1990s and has come to play a role as a key channel for British young people to embrace jihadist violence. Michael Adebolajo, one of the killers of Lee Rigby, was part of this network, through which a number of people have attempted or succeeded in travelling to Syria. Al-Muhajiroun also served as a model and support for other groups such as Sharia4Belgium, the group where Abdelhamid Abaaoud, the leader of the Paris attacks of November 2015, first came across jihadist networks. The fieldwork we undertook with people involved in this group took place over a four-year period from 2009 to 2013, involving in-depth interviews and focus groups with some fifty supporters of jihadist action, including several people who were later imprisoned under UK anti-terrorism legislation.

The second type of data this book draws upon is the social media activity of British, French and American young people who either attempted to, or succeeded in, travelling to Syria to join jihadist groups, or who attempted to undertake violent action in their home country. During the period 2013–2015, there was a vast amount of jihadist material on different social media platforms while, in the period since, much has been removed. In some cases, however, there remains a significant digital 'footprint' that allows us to capture radicalization as a lived experience. In other cases the digital material is more fragmented but nonetheless offers critical insight into dimensions of a lived experience.

Much of this book is a digital ethnography seeking to bring social worlds and exchanges to life. To capture their immediacy, such exchanges have not been edited. This means errors in spelling or punctuation that may appear in posts or tweets have not been corrected, confronting and offensive language has not been filtered, and confused use of language has not been amended. This is because the closer we are to actual communications, the more we can learn: errors in spelling may capture urgent or rapid exchanges; confused use of language may be a sign of a struggle to articulate; while confronting and offensive language is central to experiences of radicalization. In writing this book, however, the aim has been to present and discuss such material in ways that do not set out to offend or shock. In some cases, where I analyse the way people in Europe respond to material they find online, links to such material are not included if there is any doubt regarding the legality of accessing it, a situation that varies greatly across countries.

Social media are not central to all pathways to radicalization, as we will see when we consider radicalization in prison. But it is so fundamental today that we have placed it at the centre of chapter 2, where we explore the radicalization experience of Aqsa Mahmood, who travelled to Syria in November 2013. While still in the United Kingdom, she encountered distant suffering, and came to invent an experiential world structured around an opposition between purity and impurity, disgust and the grotesque, where humour occupies a central place, both as a mechanism of inclusion and as a means to say what is unsayable. Many readers will find this a long chapter, but it is so for a reason. It wants to capture a life lived through social media, a world of fun and 'fam', which undergoes an extraordinary transformation in a remarkably short time. There are very few published cases of transformations such as Mahmood's, and her extraordinary social media 'footprint' allows us to explore her experience but also to identify themes and questions that will recur in other chapters as well.

Chapter 3 explores what may first appear to be a religious structure to jihadism, but which reveals itself to be of a different nature, one organized around the hidden and the revealed, closely associated with sensory regimes of vastness, risk, power and anxiety. I do so through interviews with members of al-Muhajiroun who ended up being convicted of violent offences related to radicalization; I also explore the inspiration for much of the first wave of jihadists to travel to Syria from France, the epic 19-HH videos created by Omar Diaby. In chapter 4, I explore the development of fan cultures and particular types of mass killings involving what I am calling 'revelatory violence'. This sets out to learn lessons from the experience of school shootings and the cultures that have formed around these. I complete the chapter by exploring an example of people on social media responding to atrocity, noting the ways extreme violence not only takes the life, but also the humanity, of the victim. In chapter 5, I consider the increasing importance of criminal pathways in jihadist violence, drawing on interviews with people who had conversion experiences in prison, together with social media material produced by British fighters in Syria, where we see the importance of the anti-hero and adventure. Chapter 6 explores what we can call the 'gamification' of jihad, evident not only in the recurring importance of imaginaries of video games in jihadist culture but also in the association of knowledge and power that is so important both to these games and to the jihadist imaginary. Chapter 7 focuses on the central importance of selfhood and self-transformation in jihadist violence, where we examine in more depth the purification of the self, together with the extent to which suicide–murder may increasingly link jihadist violence with depressive experience. Chapter 8 draws these themes together, considering both the extent to which we can identify different pathways present in jihadist violence and the implications for prevention programmes.

Social media: affect and embodied imagination

This book sets out to explore radicalization not as *something done to people*, but as something produced by active participants, attempting to make sense of themselves and their world. But *sense making* is not simply a question of ideas. The word *sense* underlines feelings, emotions, embodied states and sensations. It alerts us to the feeling that *something is happening* that can be lived as pleasure or shock, perturbing or traumatic (Stewart 2007: 2). Increasingly, researchers are attempting to capture this in terms of the idea of *affect*, something that involves both body and mind, where we recognize 'our power to affect the world around us and to be affected by it' (Clough 2007: ix). Kathleen Stewart argues that it is our capacity 'to affect and be affected' that allows our everyday life to be experienced as a 'continual motion of relations, scenes, contingencies, and emergences', where we find 'forms of persuasion, contagion, and compulsion, and modes of attention, attachment and agency', where we form 'publics and social worlds of all kinds' (Stewart 2007: 2). From this perspective, radicalization is not the vulnerable, isolated person consuming videos. Radicalization is the action of constructing a 'social world' shaped more by trans-personal intensities and feelings (Stewart 2007) than by membership in organizations or political programmes. Radicalization becomes a form of *embodied meaning making* (Wetherell 2012: 4), one where the ability to feel certain things makes it possible to think certain things. This is fundamentally an embodied sociality as Hilary Pilkington argues, 'practice rooted in social life and concrete activities' (2016: 202).

This is what makes social media important to contemporary radicalization. Not because it is a medium for foreign recruiters to access and brainwash vulnerable young people but rather because social media, above all in the world of young people, are a continuous flow of affect, a medium of 'networked intimacy' (Garde-Hansen and Gorton 2013). Social media are best understood as 'sensory' channels where we encounter practices of 'being' with others (Petersen 2008) and ways of 'being-in-the-world' where 'I *become* in the sensation and something *happens* through the sensation' (Deleuze 1981: 31, emphasis in original). Here, we discover immersive experiences that expand but also limit what is sensed and how it is sensed (Thrift 2011), in experiences of acceleration, urgency, displacement, distortion, pleasure, excitement or boredom.

In the 1980s, much of the sociological work on communication was influenced by thinkers such as Jürgen Habermas (1984) or

Noam Chomsky (1965) who emphasized the rationality embedded within language and linguistic structures. Today, we are much more aware that communication takes place within and constitutes what Adi Kuntsman calls 'affective fabrics': 'the lived and deeply felt everyday sociality of connections, ruptures, emotions, words, politics and sensory energies, some of which can be pinned down to words or structures; others are intense yet ephemeral' (Kuntsman 2012: 2). Once we begin to explore the 'affective fabric' that is radicalization, we find an extraordinary production and circulation of images, sounds, words, experiences of acceleration and urgency, shock, horror, strangeness, beauty or disgust. Attempting to engage with this not only involves trying to contribute to our understanding of radicalization; it also seeks to contribute to a social science able to capture the ways in which contemporary social actors interact, explore and construct meaning together.

Take, for example, an image posted to social media by a young Danish man using the *nom de guerre* or *kunya* Abu Fulan al-Muhajir, after his first few months in Syria (Figure 1.1). His photo captures an instant, one that he entitles *Sunset in Shaam, seen through my #Glock.* Many jihadist fighters take pictures of weapons that come to possess the status of a companion that they love and trust, a pattern replicating European student terrorists of the 1980s (McDonald 2013). But this image captures something more than just a trusted companion. In a moment the sun will be gone. The image captures something beautiful but ephemeral, an experience made possible through an instrument that makes him who he is. As well as the beauty of jihad, this image captures an experience of *decompression*, of a break with a world experienced as claustrophobic, a new reality offering openness and freedom. It creates a sensation, one that makes it possible to think in certain ways.

Such images continue to have an extraordinary resonance in the culture of the jihad, whether demonstrating power or capturing the ephemeral. Many fighters in Syria would film their day-to-day existence as though they were 'micro-celebrities' (Tufekci 2013) or characters in a reality television show. One of the most striking examples is Brussels-born Abdelhamid Abaaoud who returned from Syria to lead the attack in Paris in November 2015. While in Syria, he regularly wore a GoPro HD video camera around his chest or his hat and would send updates of his life to his social media followers in Belgium. He filmed himself in situations ranging from acting as a sniper to driving a four-wheel drive, dragging the corpses of executed victims to be buried in a mass grave. There is something

Abu Fulan al-Muhajir @Fulan2weet · Jan 30
Sunset in Shaam, seen through my #Glock. #NoFilter #NoMakeUp
#NaturalBeauty

61   73   •••

Figure 1.1   Sunset in Shaam. Twitter, 30 January 2014.

in such 'mediation' of the self that is of fundamental importance
to understanding radicalization. Historically, actors involved in
extreme violence have gone to great lengths to hide killings they
have perpetrated, from Nazi death camps to the executions that took
place during the Balkan wars in Europe. Some kind of transformation has occurred, where today violent actors such as Abaaoud will
film killings and upload them to social media, completely reversing
the earlier logic. This extends beyond violence in Syria. In 2015,
a young man in the British city of Reading posted images of an
improvised explosive device that he had constructed, asking his followers for advice about what to target: 'Westfield shopping centre
or London underground? Any advice would be appreciated greatly'
(Twitter, 12 May 2015). Other violent actors attempt to structure
the media reception of their action, as in the attack on an anti-
Muslim event in Garland, Texas in the same month. The two men
involved announced their action several hours before it was to take
place, creating a Twitter hashtag #texasattack to facilitate reception of their action. This is an example of what media theorists call
'pre-mediation'.

The focus of this book is radicalization, not the experience of fighters who went to Syria. However, experiences lived in Syria circulated

widely on social media, often, as with Abaaoud, largely directed at people in Europe or North America. To some extent, this parallels practices of American soldiers in Iraq who also maintained daily contact with family and friends, above all through Facebook (Silvestri 2015). It is wrong to understand this as propaganda. Many young people who travelled to Syria lived their lives through social media before departure, and the posts, tweets, images and videos they continued to produce in Syria are something they had been engaged in before leaving. One month before departing for Syria, Ifthekar Jaman was live-streaming video to social media about how to wear a turban and how to apply kohl eyeliner, engaging with his followers via Twitter as his video was streamed. In July 2016, the two young men who killed and attempted to decapitate a Catholic priest while he celebrated mass in a village church in Normandy posted about the event to social media before it happened, promising their followers that they would be live-streaming a beheading. Social media are fundamental to radicalization, not as a tool for indoctrination, but as the way to construct an experience. This is what we need to understand.

Radicalization pathways

As many observers argue, jihadism is not an organization, it is a movement (Neumann 2016). But in the contemporary world, the ways that people collaborate and constitute movements, experiencing themselves and others in the process, is undergoing profound transformation (McDonald 2006; Tufekci 2017). Scholars of social movements highlight the close association of social media with emerging forms of 'personalized politics'. Authors such as W. Lance Bennett (Bennett and Segerberg 2015) highlight the importance of networks, arguing that these are replacing older forms of membership in organizations. Others argue 'experience movements' (McDonald 2006) are replacing the kinds of social and political movements that appeared during the twentieth century. It seems clear that something of these transformations is also at work in the field of radicalization, in particular in the importance of embodied experience and imaginaries.

As we have seen, much of the research on radicalization remains framed within paradigms that developed in response to the militarized groups of the 1970s and remains shaped by scholars working in terrorism studies, a sub-discipline largely drawing on war studies and international relations. While these disciplines have much to offer to help us understand the dynamics of the Syrian civil war, a focus on propaganda and organizations may offer less insight into the social media practices of 16-year-old girls or friendship dynamics that embrace violence. But how can we meaningfully explore such practices?

This book sets out to engage with radicalization by drawing upon what has come to be known as the 'sociology of experience', an approach arising from the sociology of social movements (Dubet 1994; McDonald 1999; Touraine 2007). Its focus is not factors, but the pathways actors construct as they make sense of themselves and their worlds, where they find themselves engaged in different kinds of social relationships. The sociology of experience focuses on three such 'social fields' in particular, in each of which we encounter different kinds of radicalization.

The first of these involves the ways we live our lives in different forms of *community*. Here, action is constructed in terms of tradition, norms and identity, where actors experience themselves as 'us'. This could be a neighbourhood, an ethnic group or a social class. But community is not always benign. Action seeking to construct community can come to reject those who don't belong, defining others as 'different' or 'other'. In certain situations, the 'other' may be experienced as a threat or danger, where communities become constructed around imaginaries of purity and impurity. This is fundamental to the experience of racism, a social practice that always involves imaginaries of dirt and contamination (McDonald 1999). This kind of radicalized communitarianism can mutate into hate crime, a pathway we will see in the chapters below.

But we don't just live in communities. Many social relationships we are involved in are not based on shared community but on rules that we expect to be fair. Many forms of social interaction have within them implicit references to ideas of justice, so that even when the outcomes may differ, we are confident that these are based on ideas of fairness. Many sociologists argue that this is why sport has become such an important social practice in contemporary societies because, while the outcomes may be different, there is a sense that such outcomes are the result of just or fair competition (Ehrenberg 1991). Such social relationships take the form of competition, of winners and losers. These social relationships can also mutate in ways where shared ideas of justice become replaced by power or violence, where winning becomes an act that sets out to humiliate the 'other'. Here, too, we observe a radicalization pathway constructed around themes of winning and losing, humiliating the 'other'.

If some social practices are about 'us' (community) and others
directed towards 'you' (exchange), there are others still that are
centred on 'I'. These highlight the importance of personal subjectivity in contemporary societies, the importance of what sociologists call
'individuation'. This means not simply living according to the roles
we have available to us, nor trying to maximize our interests in relationships of competition, but it highlights the importance of creativity, autonomy, being treated with dignity. It also points to the ways
that being human means to live where we are vulnerable, where we
experience ourselves as incomplete and so open to new experiences
and ideas. We can see these three dimensions in the social experience of being a student (Dubet 1991). This involves the pleasure of
a student *community* and culture, a world of friends, an experience of
'us' where we identify with the communities we find ourselves in. But
there is also an *instrumental* dimension attached to being a student:
looking to succeed, get the highest grades one can, study at the best
school or university possible and gain access to a profession. But there
is a third dimension, one attached to the *subjective meaning* of study
as an experience of freedom and self-discovery, self-transformation.
A successful student experience will be one where the person studying succeeds in combining these three dimensions: an experience of
community, an experience where they can act instrumentally and an
experience where they are able to become more free, more creative,
more questioning about themselves and their world. The sociology of
experience thinks of these three types of relationships – with myself,
with others and with us – as being central to the different types of
social relationships in which people find themselves and which they
construct. This framework offers us a way to think about radicalization pathways.

In the chapters that follow, we will consider people and experiences. In some cases, this is through interviews, in others through
reconstructing material they have posted to social media. I will draw
extensively on exploring 'affect' and will pay particular attention to
visual material. But through all these diverse encounters, three kinds
of pathways emerge: radicalization constructed in relation to 'I', to
'you' and to 'us'. Through combining these different kinds of data
and theoretical frameworks, this book sets out to contribute to new
ways of understanding radicalization. But it also wants to explore
more broadly and construct new insights into ways of thinking
about digital media and connective action, shifting our focus from
structural models of network to a new focus on affect and embodied
experience. In the chapters that follow, we see immersive worlds con-

structed through media, in particular the ways such worlds expand and limit what is sensed, how it is sensed and, ultimately, how people experience themselves and others. In doing so, where this book explores interviews, names have been changed and information not used if it risks identifying people. Only social media material available in the public domain is discussed, and where a person under the age of 18 has posted material, even if publicly available, their names are not used.

Through identifying different pathways, this book sets out not only to help understand contemporary radicalization, but also to contribute to how we should respond to it. In addressing students and researchers, it seeks to contribute to building social sciences able to engage with the dangers, but also the possibilities, of a radically changing social world. But this book is not only aimed at social scientists. It addresses families, friends, communities and practitioners concerned by radicalization. It also addresses the very small number of young people who may find themselves becoming fascinated by the allure of jihad. In doing so, it attempts to offer a credible account of that allure and, in the process, offer resources to those seeking to combat it.

2

Distant Suffering

Aqsa Mahmood created her first Twitter account in October 2010. She ceased using the account in August 2013, and it is most likely that it was around this time that she decided to leave the United Kingdom for Syria. During this period of just under three years, she posted some 33,500 tweets, averaging more than 30 tweets per day, reflecting but also constituting the shared world of intimate exchanges that play such a central role in the lives of young people in twenty-first-century Europe. During most of this period, Mahmood's profile picture, or 'avi', was a screenshot of herself, smiling in different poses. Many of her exchanges with close friends and family members allow her to be easily identified. It is not clear whether her decision to stop using this account in the period leading up to her departure for Syria reflects a desire to leave her childhood behind when departing, or whether it was to allow her anonymity in Syria, so that she or her family would not be identified. Across her tweets, we see evidence of transformation and rupture. The first two years of these tweets largely consist of exchanges between Mahmood's 'fam' (close friends). However, by the time she ceased using it in August 2013, she had replaced the profile portrait of herself smiling at the camera with a rear shot of a man looking at a library full of books, where we, the observers, are positioned behind him, sharing his regard directed at his library. This picture is underscored with a quote from Abdullah Azzam, the founder of the Welcome Services in Afghanistan which would later develop into al-Qaeda: 'The map of Islamic history becomes coloured with two lines. One of them black, and this is what the scholar wrote with the ink of his pen and the other one red, and that is what the martyr wrote with his blood.' While there is always much that we cannot understand about the path taken by any individual person, the experiential world created by Mahmood's posts and interactions suggests a pathway. How does a schoolgirl living in an intimate world of friends come to see herself defined by what Azzam calls 'Islamic history', something produced by two elites, scholars and fighters? Mahmood is neither a scholar nor a fighter, yet somehow this world becomes hers. Her social media communications, first with her friends and then with a wider audience, help us understand how.

The fam and everybody

For the first two years of her time using Twitter, Mahmood's account illustrates the kind of exchanges and preoccupations that we would expect of any other teenager, most involving exchanges between a small group of six friends – the 'fam', or family. Made up of both young men and young women, these friends constitute the social world she calls her own. Creating and circulating images is central to how they communicate. In October 2012, one year before she would leave the United Kingdom to join ISIS, she is circulating images of pop stars, of people getting married, of someone sitting on a toilet whose face has been replaced with that of a friend; another friend's face is imposed on a monkey, with the text 'you're all fags tbh'. She comments on fashion faux pas, from a friend's fluorescent pink hijab with matching fluoro lipstick, to a 'brother' with what she considers an overly complex pattern in his beard. In November, she and her friends exchange pictures of themselves staring out from behind Japanese ninja masks. Schoolwork and study often feature. Aqsa posts a picture of a person lying on the ground – 'can't be arsed studying'. Within 30 minutes, more than ten friends respond, most posting similar advice:

DO YOUR WORK NOW OR YOU'LL END UP MARRYING A FRESHY [*a new immigrant, 'fresh' off the boat*]
FREAKING STUDY. YOU WILL MARRY MY UNCLE IN AFRICA. He's 40. Finds you fancy.
GO STUDY. U WILL MARRY A FRESHY
MY COUSIN IQBAL IS LOOKING FOR MARRIAGE ASAP. HE IS WRINKLY AND ALSO LOVES SCOTTISH PEOPLE. YOU CAN BOTH BE SHEEP SHAGGERS TOGETHER (Twitter, 9 November 2012)

These exchanges are playful and humorous, but they deal with things that matter: exploring who I am with my friends; the importance of study and profession for one's personal autonomy growing up as a woman of Pakistani origin in the United Kingdom, so as to avoid a marriage arranged to suit the family rather than oneself. Humour is fundamental to these communications: laughter constitutes a community. It is an activity we share, and it allows the group to raise questions in ways that otherwise would not be possible. Humour is also used to mark boundaries. Aqsa comes across a picture of a man in his forties on her timeline. He is looking longingly at the camera, and thus directly at the observer. She posts: '*What is this uncle doing on Instagram?* ☹' Shared humour is also a medium of social control. Aqsa posts picture of a friend wearing a hijab who is also drinking from a vodka bottle, commenting '*during her gangster days*'. A male member of the 'fam' uses an app to create four pictures of himself pointing to a message on the screen: 'For the girls that say; All guys are the same; Nobody told you to try them all; SLUT.' Aqsa retweets the image, adding as a comment: 'AMEN TO THAT BRUTHA' (27 October 2012).

The 'fam' is a refuge from the world of parents. One day, Aqsa uploads a screenshot of her phone with four separate messages from her mother, pleading to her to answer her calls. Aqsa and her friends are conscious of their impact in the wider network they are part of. Aqsa places a Twitpic image of her own face over that of a gangster with a machine gun, posting the image while adding the following text: 'Asian mafia tings < you know it fam' (16 November 2012). Another friend sends a tweet to the group: 'Fam we run this shit. Most relevant on people's timelines tbh~.' Mahmood responds, noting the claim but wanting to put it in perspective: 'so modest' (27 November 2012). Images of desire are shared and explored. Aqsa posts an image of a male television star, with the comment '*OMG~*' (14 November 2012). A girlfriend texts: 'I like Walid cos he is funny cute hot I just love him [*heart*] But don't tel him.' Aqsa promptly uploads a screenshot of this text to Twitter, directing it to the boy concerned. Attractive men are not limited to screen stars. Mahmood tweets an image of a masked Palestinian fighter to two friends, one whom had earlier warned her about the risks of marrying a 'freshie' if she didn't study (Figure 2.1). The fighter is holding his gun and looking to camera, Mahmood adds as text 'this this this this' and a smiley face with heart eyes (15 November 2012).

Fame within this community is a constant preoccupation, reflecting the place of celebrity culture within the lives of young people. Aqsa tweets a poem describing mountains she needs to climb or

Figure 2.1 this, this, this, this. Twitter, 15 November 2012.

move, an uphill battle she faces that 'sometimes I'm gonna lose'. What brings about her musing about loss and battles? Is she concerned with a major issue or challenge in her life? In fact, these poems are about 'How I feel when you quote tweet or favourite me instead of RTing [retweeting]'. This generates a putdown from one of her followers, who asks 'Do u have all of Hannah Montana's music lyrics printed out?' On another occasion, one of the group tweets about the 'Boltonian' accent of another. To which Aqsa joins in: 'Fucking shit stirrer. And stalker. And don't forget a Bengali' (23 November 2012).

How I'm feeling, atm

Across much research literature and policy response to radicalization, we meet the idea that the young person who becomes radicalized is in some way 'vulnerable'. In this case, this is clearly not so. Mahmood is central to the 'fam', and a prolific user of social media, with more than a thousand followers. There is a type of communication present in these tweets. Most are aimed less at communicating an idea or a proposition than at constructing sensation or a feeling with others. This is evident in many of what otherwise appear to be random photos circulating. They do not seek a discursive response; rather, they seek to elicit a shared feeling, often of surprise, pleasure or bemusement. In November 2012, Mahmood tweets a picture of some twenty men pushing a train in Pakistan, with the text 'Pakistani saying; as a nation if we push together we can accomplish anything ~.' She is sharing her affection for a group of people who together attempt to achieve a goal, despite what appears to be a lack of resources or any likelihood of success. A person on her timeline writes about himself 'I'm from Scottish', to which she replies: 'You're from Scotland, not "Scottish" you fucking inbred' (12 November 2012). She constantly posts photos of random, quirky objects or events – a sandal that has a mobile phone built into its sole, with the comment 'mobile robberies will now be history' (23 November 2012). She posts a picture of a man with a sun-umbrella hat speaking on the phone on a hot summer day in Pakistan – 'never before seen' (23 November 2012); another, headed 'meanwhile in Pakistan' (14 November 2012), is a picture of a group of men attempting to right a lorry that has been pulled back almost vertically onto its rear wheels, due to the excess weight it is carrying. These are all random or quirky events, transmitted to share the pleasure of living in a world full of surprises that are contingent and simultaneous.

These posts communicate an instant of what she is feeling, they are what we would call 'affective communications', the kind of communications at the centre of social media. These are ephemeral moments, but fundamental to her construction of herself, affects shared and circulated among friends. Social media communications are not principally about ideas; they are about affective states that change from one moment to the next. They are, as Mahmood herself writes, about 'how I feel atm [*at the moment*]'. What is of critical importance in these communications is that one's own affective state succeeds in generating a response from the 'other'. Failure to respond to a friend's affective state is interpreted as a slight, or as something that suggests that there is something wrong with oneself. Ifthekar Jaman, who would later travel to Syria, and Mahmood follow each other, but she has not responded to several of his tweets. He tweets to her: 'You're a pointless follower. Jokes. Actually, answer me straight. Do you even read mine? Or am I a tweeter who you just skip?' (10 November 2012). Aqsa has exams coming at the end of the year. Just beforehand, she posts a picture of all her textbooks piled on the floor in the corner of her room, with the text 'Cry for me ☺'. Images are central to these communications because they capture a moment. They allow the sender to articulate and share a sensation.

Mujahideen swag, yes pls

Mahmood and several of her friends are part of a youth culture where jihadist figures and themes are present. One of her close male friends uploads a screenshot of himself intensely reading out a statement to a video camera. She responds by humorously raising her eyebrows: 'lol ^.^. [*laughing out loud*]' He responds: 'I just wanted an excuse to tweet this pic', to which she replies 'getting ready for jihaad Akhi:')' (17 December 2012, 'Akhi' meaning 'brother'). Effectively, the style of the image replicates the suicide testaments associated with jihadists. Mahmood and other friends are in contact with Ifthekar Jaman while he is still in the United Kingdom. One friend draws a cartoon image of him, highlighting his beard. Mahmood tweets to him: 'just kohled my eyes. Because its sunnah' (9 November 2012). They play with the jihadi aesthetic. One day, Mahmood is sending pictures of men she finds on the internet to her friends. Just before sending a picture of a well-known Saudi model, she forwards to two of her girlfriends a 'band of brothers' photo of a group of Taliban fighters in a pick-up car, hanging out of windows, guns at the ready, looking into the camera. She adds 'a crew like this pls' (11 November 2012). The following day, she tweets to one of her friends involved in initiating the game of circulating images in ninja masks: 'You all ninjas get aside, its all about Mujahideen swag, Yes pls' (12 November 2012).

The term 'swag' was popularized in 2012 by the Canadian pop idol Justin Bieber and, according to his website at the time, 'swag' means 'its [*sic*] just about being yourself, you don't have to do anything special, just be yourself'. This is captured by the brooding eyes of the Palestinian fighter that Mahmood tweets to two of her girlfriends three days later, with the text 'this this this this', coupled with a smiling emoji face with hearts for eyes (15 November 2012). She retweets a similar image sent to her by another girlfriend, @smellthedeen, who has added as text 'the real men of today'. A few days later, Mahmood sends a girlfriend a widely circulated image of a group of Chechen mujahideen, again in a band-of-brothers pose, as they look directly into the camera. Mahmood adds text as if it is a message sent by the group: 'Hi, I just wanna get ta know ya x' (23 November 2012). This theme of 'real men' takes on particular importance in the first period of Mahmood's Tumblr account that she begins in January 2013. In the early months of 2013, her posts are populated by images of men riding horses or camels set against dramatic backgrounds of vast deserts or lakes, recurring images that combine romance, beauty, mystery and adventure.

These and hundreds of other exchanges like them alert us to the importance of what Mahmood calls 'Mujahideen swag': the kohl, the piercing eyes, the beards, the band of brothers, the drama, adventure and sacrifice all captured in images that these young women circulate between them in the same way that they circulate images of smouldering film stars and models. This offers us an insight into the 'post-adolescent' dimension that Khosrokhavar (2015) highlights in so many of the females who travelled to Syria, a pattern completely different from the mother and widow profiles that have been much more predominant among earlier generations of female candidates for jihadism, either in Chechnya or Palestine. Mujahideen swag points to the promise of virility and sincerity, qualities that @smellthedeen associates with what she calls 'real men'.

Pleasure and humour

The communications between Mahmood and her friends are shaped by fun and pleasure. These exchanges alert us to just how much of a role humour plays in constructing communities – *laughing together* is a powerful means through which we share, while *laughing at* is a powerful means by which a community excludes. This happens in different ways. One person sends a text to Aqsa, 'Your shit tbh' (26 November 2012). She corrects the spelling, texting back 'you're'. But she also makes sure to post a screenshot of the exchange to her Twitter feed, with title 'Uneducated'. A few days later, another person in her timeline texts her 'Your So Mean', a message Mahmood also promptly reposts to her followers (29 November 2012). She posts a series of images of an overweight Pakistani pop idol who appears to be in his forties, lying in different suggestive poses on lawns or beaches. In one image, he is lying on a lawn with his eyes shut in what appears to be an attempt at a suggestive pose. Mahmood retweets the image, attaching the remark: 'Tell me that your sexy ass ain't dead LOOOL.'

The encounter with suffering

While playing with a jihadi aesthetic, throughout this period Mahmoood demonstrates no engagement with the suffering of others or with social and political struggles. This changes dramatically for Mahmood and several of her friends with the Israeli incursion into Gaza in late 2012. A series of international campaigns began to protest Israeli bombardments, with Aqsa and her friends getting involved in the #Gaza2012Movement hashtag. While this hashtag was closer to Muslim groups and networks than to secular political groups, there was almost no presence of jihadist themes in the hundreds of posts it received; the vast majority of the flags in tweets were Palestinian, not black. The period was soon after the #Kony2012 Social Media campaign (Thomas et al. 2015) to raise awareness of the situation of child soldiers in the Lord's Resistance Army in Uganda, and visibly many of the posts are influenced by the social media culture built up around this campaign. One of Mahmood's friends posts: 'Wow #G2012M has spread really fast. Wow, wow, wow' (17 November 2012), demonstrating the extent that the *goal* of action becomes 'trending', with appeals like 'change your twitter names to #Gaz2012Movement, you can make a difference'. As part of this Twitter campaign, Mahmood photoshops a poster and tweets it with the injunction 'Print this off and hand it out to as many people as you can. Stop feeling helpless and react!' She circulates an image of a silenced Palestinian girl, imposed upon a Palestinian flag, with data about the extent of suffering. She tweets it to one of her friends, saying 'just something I made. Share this and raise awareness'. This campaign brings new people into her timeline, and she begins to explore Twitter feeds where she comes across shocking images of injured Palestinians, fathers holding children with limbs that have been blasted off, dead bodies in rubble. Her retweets indicate that she is encountering intense violence and suffering, themes that have never previously been present in her timeline.

'Stop feeling helpless and react' appears to be a phrase from Mahmood, not something she has copied and pasted from another source. It highlights a feeling experienced when confronted with what sociologists call 'distant suffering' (Boltanski 1999). A pro-Palestinian demonstration took place in Edinburgh in November 2012, and while most likely she did not attend (otherwise she would surely have posted from the demonstration), Mahmood retweets a newspaper image of the marching crowd. Above the image she writes: 'MashaAllah the support from Edinburgh is fantastic. Free Gaza. End Israeli apartheid once and for all' (17 November 2012). The march consisted of a coalition of political and human rights groups, with only Palestinian flags flying. Her pride in her support of the Palestinian people expressed in Edinburgh highlights the way collective action can be a force for integration, of discovering oneself as part of a larger shared effort.

At this time, the sources of Mahmood's Twitter protests about the violence in Gaza are largely secular. On the day following the demonstration, she retweets an image of the Palestinian flag with 'Gaza2012Movement' superimposed on it. The following day, she retweets another Palestinian flag, this time with a count of injured Palestinians and Israelis. Next day, she tweets Article 6.1 of the UN Declaration of Human Rights that affirms 'No one shall be arbitrarily deprived of his life.' Confronted with human suffering through the media, Mahmood might be becoming an activist. However, she takes a very different path. In the two-month period following the Gaza campaign, we see a fundamental transformation in Aqsa Mahmood's social media communications. New themes and preoccupations appear where they previously did not exist, new types of concern nourish and amplify each other. Two themes define this development: an engagement with the Syrian civil war; and a new focus on Shia Muslims.

This relates to me

During most of 2012, Mahmood and her friends were living the lives of carefree young people. There are tweets about jihadist kohl and images of young men with smouldering eyes, but no images of violence and suffering appear in Mahmood's timeline before the Gaza events. The first image of a martyr she uploads is of a Palestinian leader of Hamas, killed during the Gaza mobilization. Her first tweet suggesting a change is not an image of suffering but a quote from Abdullah Azzam, the founder of what would later become al-Qaeda. Significantly, the text she quotes does not concern international politics but being a student:

> You are at an age when Satan will enter upon you by way of your studies, by way of your incessant hopes ... Satan enters upon you, saying right now, you are in school. Tomorrow, when you get your degree ... you can work for Allah. [But] first of all, you do not know when you will gradu-

ate, you do not know when you will die, and you do not know when
you will meet your Lord. So, beware of having these incessant *hopes*.
(Azzam, retweeted 29 November 2012)

Mahmood captions her retweet with 'This relates to me so much
right now' (29 November 2012). An hour later, she is back to her old
self, retweeting a tweet from someone who has called her 'mean'. But
her retweet of Azzam points to something new – confronted with the
uncertainty and contingency of life (you do not know when you will
die), it is wrong to focus on study and getting a degree, even if you
intended to serve Allah with it. Such hopes for a successful future are
a sign, says Azzam, of Satan entering into you. This is the first tweet
in Mahmood's timeline to suggest a sense of the contingency and
fragility of life, a contingency that puts into doubt the moral basis of
studying for oneself, one's family or even for Allah. The future and
hopes of having a profession lose any meaning in a world full of death
and destruction, one where we can no longer plan. This may make
sense in war-torn Afghanistan, but it is foreign to the experience of
second-generation South Asian girls living in Britain, for whom, as
we saw in the humorous exchanges in Mahmood's timeline, study is
central to hopes for personal autonomy.

The initial material Mahmood tweeted in relation to Gaza had
drawn on secular themes. However, on 19 November, a week before
she posts the Azzam text about the dangers of career and study, she
retweets a photo of some thirty Muslim men praying, with crowds in
the background and smoke rising in the distance (Figure 2.2). This
image is presented as though from Gaza, with Muslim men focused
on prayer while bombs are landing around them. If they have such
courage, it asks, what excuse do we have for failing to do the same
in our own environment of comfort and safety? Framed by this text,
the image communicates a sense of detachment from bombs and
a devotion to something both more powerful and more significant.
Prayer, the image communicates, offers courage and serenity, allowing us to be the best we can be. The power of the image lies in what
it juxtaposes: calmness with chaos; silence with noise; an ordered line
of people in prayer surrounded by chaos; unity with fragmentation;
serenity with anguish; peace with violence; the sustaining presence of
God overcoming the life-denying intentions of those dropping bombs.

This image and its accompanying message was retweeted more
than 300 times, demonstrating the power of an image to communicate embodied experience in ways that written word would find
impossible. But what is important to note is that this image was not a

Figure 2.2   #Gaza. Twitter, 19 November 2012.

photo of Palestinians praying under Israeli bombs in Gaza, but one of
Egyptians at prayer in Tahrir Square, originally published by the *New
York Times* in January 2011. It is not clear whether the person who
authored the text attached to the image knew this, but it is clear that
Mahmood did not. Indeed, there is no sign that she had any knowledge at all of the events of 2011 in Cairo. But what is happening here
is clear: faced with the enormity of the violence and the presence of
God among those who are struggling, the cares of her day-to-day life
are becoming insignificant, her hopes for her future the whispering
voice of Satan.

The life of a stranger

It is possible that the peace and the power communicated by the
image she circulated was an experience that had a lasting impact upon
Mahmood. Only a week later, she tweeted the quote from Azzam
about concern with studies being an expression of the influence of

Satan. In the days following this, several other tweets also suggest a period of introspection and a break with the 'LOOOL culture' upon which her social world had been based. Two hours after her Azzam post, she tweets a quote about Paradise as a place where there is 'no worry or stress'. The same day, she uploads a photograph she has taken to Twitter of an old man eating alone in a café, the image suggesting both enjoying the moment and being alone. The next day something has happened: she posts an image from the Disney movie *Finding Nemo*, where a group of fish are judging a chastened and dejected Nemo, and she writes: 'When the moslamic side of twitter judge me ~.' She follows this with another image, a dying fish lying on its side, writing 'when my twitter account got reported ☹'. It seems her account was not cancelled, but it may have been suspended for 12 hours following a report. Two days later she is back, and posts a photoshopped image of Taliban fighters marching happily through magnificent mountains, without a care in the world (one is dancing on the back of a donkey). She writes, 'This kind of lyf pls x'. On 3 December, she tweets with a sense of relief: 'Life makes sense now.' On the same day, she tweets a long text under the title Ghurabaa (stranger). This text affirms that faithfulness to Allah means resigning oneself:

> 'to the life of a stranger among his people'... one will 'be a stranger in [one's] beliefs because his people have corrupted their beliefs. [One] will be a stranger in his religion, due to what the people have done to it. ... [One] will be a stranger in all matters of this world and the Hereafter, calling to the path of Allah and withstanding the harm of all those that go against him'.

During the next few months, there is a tension between Aqsa the high-school princess and Aqsa the stranger. A few days after this tweet, she receives a text from a friend with whom she has been involved in a friendly feud over the past months. The text message reads @_axaa ILY X. Mahmood's response involves both a reprimand that puts her friend in her place, together with an expression of friendship. She tweets the text as a screenshot, adding the following message: 'She thought I wouldn't be able to screenshot it. Wasteman. Who even is she? p.s. iLY2' (6 December 2012).

While Mahmood is still tweeting screenshots of her friends' indiscretions, a new type of tweet suggests a new sense of the contingency of human life, one that creates distance both from who she has been and who she was previously on track to become. On 8 December 2012, ten days after the Azzam tweet about Satan and study, she tweets a poem under the heading 'I love this':

O' past that has departed and is gone, I will not cry over you. You will
not see me remembering you, not even for a moment, because you have
travelled away from me never to return.
    O' future you are in the realm of the unseen, so I will not be obsessed
by your dreams. I will not be preoccupied about what is to come tomorrow because tomorrow is nothing and has not yet been create ('Don't
be Sad', Dr Â'id Al-Qarni)

Mahmood's tweets suggest a new focus on herself that will
become increasingly evident over the next few months. The poem
captures a kind of transition experience – I'm not a child any
more, and I don't know where my future will lead. There is a kind
of pathos in this poem as well, not restricted to the loss of who
one was in the past, an aloneness that was not previously part of
Mahmood's Twitter timeline. This is not a heroic poem, a call to
join with others to shape the future. It is a poem that accentuates a
kind of *individuation*; its focus is on an 'I' that is detached from both
a past and a future that are necessarily created with others. This
experience of *distancing* as part of discovering who she is becomes
increasingly articulated in the Tumblr account that Mahmood
creates in January 2013. She is aware of it, exploring it in her posts:
'My dad asked me if everything is alright, my family think I'm
weird because I prefer my own company and being alone. Lol. All
I need in this life is me and my books' (Tumblr, 8 March 2013).
'Sometimes loneliness makes you find your inner-self, perhaps the
real you. When you try to block out all those echoes and chaos'
(Tumblr, 19 April 2013).

I've got myself a new CLIQUEE

In 2012, the first aid convoys began to set off from the United
Kingdom to Syria, put together by charities and groups from
mosques, including those with previous experience of sending aid
to Gaza. Social media played a key role in publicizing these efforts,
and Mahmood begins to retweet appeals for support originating in
networks she had met in the Gaza campaign. It is in this context, in a
retweet, she posts to her timeline the word *ummah* for the first time:
'O Ummah please donate and don't stop RT for the sake of Allah.
Convoy leaves Soon 23rd of December ...' (12 December 2012).
    The term *ummah* refers to all Muslims who are faithful to Allah
and his Messenger, independent of race, class or nation. In this case,

it is an imaginary community made real through being addressed by tweeting and retweeting.

In January 2013, Mahmood created a Tumblr account, and for three weeks she does not use her Twitter timeline at all. Tumblr is a microblog site, allowing longer posts than Twitter. This shift to Tumblr is in part Mahmood redefining who she is, and to whom and why she communicates:

> Having took a break from twitter I made a tumblr acc primarily just to keep up to date and informed. However I am actually starting to prefer this over twitter simply because nobody knows who I am – the anonymity allows free speech. Also I just find it allows me to express myself without having everything I say questioned ... My little sister laughed at me today because I said 'ReTweet' (force of habit) instead of 'reblog'. (Tumblr, 23 January 2013)

This Tumblr would become central to the online profile that Mahmood constructed while in Syria, allowing her to share her personal journey as a means of promoting ISIS, in particular to young women in the United Kingdom. But when she began it in January 2013, it was not envisaged as a recruitment platform. It was a 'break from Twitter', both in terms of the types of communication and the freedom that comes with anonymity. We get some insight into what she means by a 'break with Twitter' in a tweet she posted late in 2012, about a week before creating her Tumblr account. Someone has done to her something that she takes such pleasure in doing to others: they have retweeted a communication from her. She in turn retweets this tweet, adding her own comment. In her original tweet, she evoked dissatisfaction with something that has proved a constant source of irritation throughout her Twitter timeline, namely the failure of her followers to retweet her, their preference being to simply 'favourite' her: 'GET LOST ALL YOU STINGY PAKIS ONLY FAVOURITING. USE DAT RT BUTTON OK. I AM TRYNA ENTERTAIN YOU FAGGS~.'

Mahmood's message of complaint was retweeted by one of her followers, effectively doing as she asked. Mahmood in turn retweets the original message but adds a declaration: 'I don't need you guise, I've got myself a new CLIQUEE. They get where I'm coming from' (26 December 2012). The shift foreshadowed by a 'new clique' is reflected in her Tumblr account driven by a different purpose. She will no longer be focusing on generating retweets and entertaining followers. But she does not immediately walk away

#AsianTwitterMemories2012 <3 lolz

10:11 PM - 28 Dec 2012

Figure 2.3   #AsianTwitterMemories2012. Twitter, 26 December 2012.

from 'everybody'. At the end of the year, she participates actively in #AsianTwitterMemories2012, a kind of 'best of the year celebration' involving retweets and comments, allowing 'everybody' to relive the funniest events of the past twelve months. As part of her contribution, Mahmood posts an image of herself that she had previously posted as 'Puss in Boots' (Figure 2.3).

This is not the kind of image you associate with someone who two weeks earlier had posted Abdullah Azam's musings on Satan and on being a student, and who in a year's time will have moved to Raqqa to join ISIS. At this point in late 2012, Mahmood is living in two interconnected worlds. One is the world of LOL, captured by the image of herself as 'Puss in Boots', and another is one that evokes something very different, evident in something she retweets the next day: 'We should all think of ourselves as hypocrites, it's when you think your safe you should be worried. Shaytaan uses arrogance for corruption' (Twitter, 16 December 2012).

This message about feeling unsafe and worried evokes a word that will become fundamental to Mahmood during 2013: *corruption*. But at the end 2012 she is oscillating, one day posting an image of herself as Puss in Boots, the next day warning about Shaytaan and corruption. She is aware of this herself. In March, she posts to Tumblr: 'My current self is constantly at war with my former self. The two are fighting for control of my future self.' On the same day she writes: 'I feel like I have no direction in life anymore. It's funny how things work out, once upon a time I used to be such a career-obsessed girl. Now I have no clue. I just want another fresh start and to do it right this time' (20 March 2013).

LOL

LOL culture has not been totally excluded in her Tumblr posts. On 4 February, she writes 'Lol my sister just said that "I'm going to eat so much of that cake that Mum's gonna regret making it."' On 17 March: 'Laki is the funniest. Love the stupid Bengaleez. (I'll never get over how you had a funeral for your pet fish) ded x.' On 31 March, she writes: 'My plan for today is to watch all the *Lion Kings*. Doesn't get as productive as this.' The social world constructed through Tumblr remains one of sharing humour, of anecdotes about eating too much cake, about a wacky friend's funeral for their dead fish, about a day spent watching Disney movies. Humour is central to these communications. As we saw above, humour plays a central role in creating shared experience – laughing together is a shared affect, or embodied experience, at the heart of creating a community in digital culture.

But laughter is also a way of creating borders. Mahmood and her friends do this frequently, above all when they block someone, an action regularly associated with a LOL. Difference provokes incomprehension, and this is shared and socialized through laughter. In mid-December, Mahmood is communicating through WhatsApp with a 'Niquaabi', a girl who wears the full-face veil. We do not know what question Mahmood asks, but this is the response she receives: 'My face is fitna tbh, even for the females. With so much homo Business going on I'd rather refrain. Hope you understand xxx LOOOOL (Mahmood).' Mahmood tweets a screenshot of the exchange, commenting 'Niqabbis are funneh mayn' (12 December 2012). Other groups receive similar treatment. Bengalis are described as 'the jews of India'. One of her friends sends her a humorous declaration of affection: 'I may not be the richest ... But I can still love you (: .' She replies: 'LOL Pakis are so embarrassing. Thank god I'm Arab x' (6 January 2013).

Groups and their characteristics, belonging and not-belonging, are a constant dynamic shaping the timeline shared by Mahmood and her friends. Most of these jokes focus on 'Asians', 'Desis', 'Pakis' and 'Bengalis'. For Mahmood, one of the most despicable acts possible on social media is to follow someone in order to get you to follow them in return, and once this happens, they immediately unfollow you. This is a strategy to increase one's 'fame' through increasing the number of one's followers compared to those one is following. Mahmood retweets a friend who is complaining that this has recently been done to him: 'Ha Ha this guy is such a faggot. He followed me today, as soon as I followed him he unfollowed me. Such a dick. Lol' (29 December 2012).

In late December, Mahmood tweets a screenshot of a conversation with another person who has also failed to make the grade. Mahmood has sent a 'band of brothers' image of Mujahideen fighters to her Kik contact list. One young man responds: 'So that's your strategy to turn down boys lol.' He follows this with a second message: 'Unique.' Mahmood tweets a screenshot of the exchange to her followers, commenting: 'LOOOOOL all I did was send a picture of mujahideen. Cba [*can't be arsed*] with freshys on Kik~' (27 December 2012).

It is only on Christmas Day 2012 that Mahmood retweets a communication that for the first time refers to Shia Muslims: 'Muslims [*Shia*] celebrating Christmas. I'm gonna give up on life cause this is beyond madness' (25 December 2012). This shares the same 'would you believe it' bemused spirit that also characterizes her tweets about other groups. Two weeks later, she tweets a picture of Shia Muslims marching in the street (Figure 2.4), hitting their heads with knives, blood streaming down them (7 January 2013). She attaches two hashtags to the image: #cutforbieber and #beliebers, highlighting how much she is part of social media's culture of memes and images. In 2012, an image circulated on social media platforms purporting to be Justin Bieber smoking a joint, producing widespread consternation among his fans. In this context, a spoof campaign appeared in social media. The people who created this campaign, possibly emerging from a trolling group based on the manga site 4chan (McDonald 2015), called on people to cut themselves in protest, creating a hashtag #cutforbieber for photos and messages. While this was a spoof, several young women did in fact cut themselves to share the suffering of their idol, and the hashtag #cutforbieber began trending on 7 January 2013, the day that Mahmood posted the image.

The following day, Mahmood posts a meme, this time a picture of a wide-eyed Shia mullah, with the term 'Dis guy is full of Shiite' (8 January 2013). A meme is an image with associated text that circulates in social media on the basis of retweets and reposts. A

Figure 2.4   #cutforbieber. Twitter, 7 January 2013.

meme consists of an incongruous association of image and text, one that provokes an affective response of laughter or bemusement. If a person who laughs at a meme wants to share the pleasure, they do so by circulating it.

While her Tumblr account would grow to have a different purpose, her Twitter account is still about the fans. One young woman who is followed by Mahmood tweets: '@_axaa Just followed me, am I dreaming pls I feel accepted in life now' (@SeekingTheDeen, 18 February 2013). As we would expect, Mahmood retweets, attaching a message: 'Pls the fame is getting to me I love my loyal fans ~.' Mahmood still enjoys the celebrity status she has created, but now she is able to establish an ironic distance from it.

From good and evil to innocent and guilty

Two transformations in themes being tweeted by Mahmood become increasingly evident in 2013. The first is a change in the way she responds to suffering and oppression. In January 2013, we still see the signs of the kind of secular critique of acts of oppression that

she had embraced during the Gaza campaign. On her return to
Twitter, one of her first tweets is an image of Palestinian suffering,
an Israeli demolition of a house and a distraught Palestinian boy.
She writes: 'This picture speaks a 1000 words. So much anger and
pain ☹ #Palestine.' On her Tumblr page, she posts the 2011 cover
of *Time Magazine*'s 'Person of the Year', the Protester. She posts an
image of an Anonymous activist but with a gun slung over his back.
Underneath she comments, 'liberate your mind' (23 January 2013).
She also posts images of Guantanamo detainees, focusing on the
impact on their families.

The images and language here are constructed in terms of good
and evil. But an increasing focus on 'close-up' images of suffering confronts her with the question of responsibility and personal
involvement. And here we see a transformation at work as she begins
to experience this world of mediated suffering in terms of *innocence*
and *guilt*. Innocence focuses on the experience of children suffering,
something that becomes increasingly important in particular in her
reactivated Twitter account as well as her Tumblr one, to which
she posts an increasing number of harrowing videos focusing on the
trauma and suffering of young children. These are contrasted with
a new focus on heroic men riding horses and camels, often featured
against dramatic and beautiful backgrounds. If innocence is constructed in relation to children in war, guilt is constructed through
images of the president of Syria, Bashir al Assad, and Ayatollah
Khamenei, Iran's Supreme Leader, whom she reblogs to Tumblr as
'partners in genocide' (23 January 2013).

What you aren't being told

The opposition between innocence and guilt is closely associated with
a posture of engagement, where experience is increasingly framed in
the categories of truth and falsehood. When Mahmood blogs 'liberate your minds' with an image of an Anonymous activist, or blogs a
picture of the Protester, she is engaging with a critique of controls of
information and media misrepresentation. She posts an image of a
television with a flickering screen, suggesting that the media conceal
more than they reveal. This *hidden reality* is particularly associated
with the repression of Muslims. On 20 April, she blogs an image of
the dead Boston marathon bomber in the morgue, declaring to her
followers that the truth of the circumstances surrounding his death is
being concealed by the authorities. On 24 April, she posts an image

of the surviving brother, titled 'Innocent'. The next day, she reblogs a video: 'Boston Bombings: what you aren't being told', adding 'the truth behind all this bullshit #freejahar' (Jahar being Dzhokhar Tsarnaev's nickname).

#Freejahar emerged in the period immediately after the arrest of the Boston Bomber suspect, a Twitter-based campaign grounded in fan culture and conspiracy theories that I explore in chapter 5. On the same day as blogging about the Boston bombing and 'what you aren't being told', Mahmoood reblogs, 'TV destroys families and children.' On the previous day, she posts an image of demonstrators wearing Anonymous masks and carrying a red flag. She is drawing on a popular culture of suspicion of government that is particularly strong in the United States. Mahmood evokes this critique of democracy when she blogs an image of a demonstration with a massive placard, 'Democracy is an illusion' (23 January 2013). She writes below the image, 'Democracy – the most dangerous of innovations'.

Desire and repulsion, beauty and ugliness

The Freudian tradition alerts us to the place of desire within the construction of an embodied subjectivity. It also alerts us to the place of repulsion, a visceral, embodied and sensory reaction to something, someone or some group of people. This tension becomes a significant structure shaping Mahmood's Tumblr posts in the first part of 2013. She focuses on images of beauty, which she associates with proximity to the Prophet, a core idea that she affirms as she retweets text an image from @smellthedeen, another young woman in the United Kingdom: 'The companions of our Messenger (SWT) were truly beautiful people' (5 January 2013). She posts images of classical Arabian village scenes, of men in flowing robes riding across deserts on powerful stallions or proudly seated on camels in classical poses. In this sensory world of images that Mahmood is constructing, beauty becomes increasingly juxtaposed with ugliness, and this opposition will be central for a critical transformation, as innocence and guilt become reformatted into purity and impurity.

At the centre of this transformation is the relationship Mahmood builds with Shia Muslims during 2013. As we saw above, Shia Muslims do not figure among the groups that populate her tweets before the end of 2012 – these are Asians, Desis, Bengalis and Pakistanis. The main affect though which Mahmood positions herself in relation to these groups is humour, either as a means of inclusion (laughing *with*) or exclusion/othering (laughing *at*). References to 'Shias' as a group only appears in her timeline at the end of 2012 with the image of Shia Muslims celebrating Christmas. In early January 2013, she starts to post images that aim at 'othering': the image of Shia penitents that she describes as #beliebers or a wide-eyed image of an ayatollah. In both cases, these images are located within LOL culture. She posts a mocking image of a Sufi politician in Pakistan, and retweets text and image from a new follower who is dedicated to stopping Ahmadiyyas claiming to be Muslims. All these reposts and images are framed in terms of humour, often with an explicit 'LOL' attached. She reblogs a photoshopped image of the second Iranian supreme leader, Ayatollah Khamenei, as a rapper, the text of the rap claiming that he worships Satan, he smokes weed and is a pagan. Mahmood adds to the page: 'OMG OMG LOOOOOOOOOOOOOOOOOOOOOOOOOOL nah man. I Need Oxygen.'

Disgust

From January 2013, we encounter a new theme running parallel to the LOL response to difference. Mahmood's friend @smellthedeen blogs a link to a video of a celebration taking place at a Sufi mosque in Manchester. The video captures a group of men singing at a lively celebration, with chanting and music. Near the centre of the group is a participant dancing in what appears to be a trance-like state. @smellthedeen writes 'look at what our deen has become. This video actually sickened me.' Mahmood reblogs the post and link, commenting 'LOL he's having an epileptic seizure.' Here, we have the first entry in Mahmood's timeline where difference framed in a new way: as *sickness*, that is, sickening to watch (Tumblr, 23 January 2013).

She radicalizes this theme over the coming months. She posts an image of Shia religious and political leaders eating together from a plate of lamb and rice, attaching text which claims that the religious leader of the 1979 Iranian revolution, Ayatollah Khomeini, has declared that it is lawful for 'Shia rejectionists' to enter into temporary marriage (*mutah*) relationships with animals, including sheep, provided that they do not eat the meat of an animal they have had intercourse with. Mahmood asks whether the men in the image eating lamb and rice can be certain that they are eating food from a village other than their own (14 February 2013).

This combination of image and text produces a kind of visceral disgust and revulsion. Four days later, she returns to this theme on

Umm Muʿāwiyah
@_axaa

Follow ∨

I wonder how many Kabbas have been killed due to stupid Ayatoilets...

Kabba = how sacred the blood of a Muslim is

LIKE
1

6:15 PM - 22 Feb 2013

Figure 2.5 Ayatollah Khamenei. Twitter, 22 February 2013.

her Tumblr, quoting a Shia proverb 'Every day is Ashura, Every land is Karbala', rebuking its originator by tweeting back 'Every night is mutah.' She then tweets a screenshot of her message, with the comment 'I am dead. LOOOOOOOOOL.' Later in the month, she posts a photoshopped image of Ayatollah Khamenei wearing a diamond ear-stud (Twitter, 21 February 2013), and later an image of a Shia political leader photoshopped wearing a woman's wig and make-up, along with the text 'You are a hypocrite pretending to be a muslim' (Twitter, 22 February 2013). Four minutes later, she posts an image of a soul suffering anguish in hellfire, to which she authors a comment: 'May Allah guide the filthy shia creed or destroy them' (Twitter, 22 February 2013). Three minutes later, she posts another photoshopped image of Ayatollah Khamenei, this time with a bullet through his head and a blood-spattered wall behind him, an image which locates the viewer in the position from where the bullet originates (Figure 2.5).

Mahmood writes: 'how much sacred blood of Muslims has been killed due to stupid Ayatoilets ...' (Twitter, 22 February 2013). On the same day, she retweets an image together with text that purports to be a quote from Ayatollah Khomeini: 'A man can have sexual pleasure from a child as young as a baby. However, he should not penetrate' (Twitter, 22 February 2013). She tweets on the same theme later with the message 'sickness'. The following day, she posts images of the Ashura mud ritual that takes place in certain Iranian cities, where mourners enter a trance-like state and cover themselves with mud to commemorate the death of Husayn, grandson of Muhammad. As well as tweeting the image, she tweets an image of a pig in mud, writing, 'lol I'm sure this is what pigs do ... Fatwa tul Piggy' (23 February 2013).

Over a period of three months, Mahmood posts a constant stream of images that construct a powerful experience of disgust, experienced as fear of the collapse of borders and penetration. These focus on collapse of the sexual boundaries between humans and other animals, with a recurring suggestion of the possibility of eating animals that one has had sex with. She tweets images about homosexuality among Shia religious leaders, or the claim that Shia Muslims eat the faeces and drink the urine of their holy saints. One of her girlfriends responds to this post with 'EWWWWWWW oma'. Mahmood responds in turn: 'Disgusting' (Twitter, 28 April 2013).

These exchanges alert us to a critical dimension of the transformation Mahmood is both producing and experiencing: *disgust*. Sara Ahmed (2004) underlines the 'performativity' of disgust, that is, its capacity not simply to *describe* a sensation but to *constitute* it. She highlights the importance of fascination, of a powerful mixture of attraction and repulsion, something that is fundamental to understanding why Mahmood so frequently returns to this theme, which occupies more and more of the experiential world she constructs. Ahmed underlines the extent to which disgust is a 'speech act' that demands a witness – the claim 'that's disgusting!' implies something more than a person who has becomes disgusted or object of that disgust. Ahmed highlights the fascination, central to disgust, of being both attracted to and repulsed by the texture and qualities of what is felt to be disgusting. Disgust is thus fundamentally a *communicative affect*, one that 'generates a community of those bound together through the shared condemnation of a disgusting object or event' (2004: 85). We see this in the importance of responses to Mahmood's tweets, communicated in social media through 'EWWWWW'.

There is one further dimension of disgust, pointed out by Ahmed, which is fundamental to the pathway we encounter with Mahmood. As well as generating an object and a community, disgust also establishes a *truth*. The fact that I feel sick establishes that you have sickened me; my body tells me something experienced as an irrefutable truth: you are sickening. This is at the centre of the exchange about the Sufi celebration where Mahmood's friend asserts 'this video actually sickened me', and she in turn posts 'sickness'. The object of disgust, in that sense, contains 'the truth' of our response to it (Ahmed 2004: 85). Something is a sickness because I experience it as sickening. Just like racism, disgust serves to construct difference and borders, above all where these are unclear, where the 'other' is experienced as too close (Miller 1998: 9). This is the case for Mahmood, who posts to Tumblr about her difficulties with Shia Muslims visiting her family. The object of her disgust is part of her social world. In such cases, disgust becomes a substitute for a border, a means of protecting the subject from all that it is not.

Disgust is often associated with a response to things imagined or experienced as 'sticky', a visceral experience of contact between surfaces that are difficult to control, where things become 'out of place' (Douglas 1966) and transferred to where they should not be. This captures something of the *anxiety* associated with disgust, something that can be transformed into rage as a response to the danger of penetration or of ingesting what is experienced as disgusting. Such a fear of eating, swallowing or otherwise ingesting the disgusting is a central dimension to disgust (Tomkins 1991: 35), something that Mahmood returns to constantly with her tweets not only about Shia men having sexual relations with animals, but also concerning the eating of animals that they have had intercourse with or Shia Muslims eating and drinking the faeces and urine of holy saints. What is critical about disgust in the social world of Mahmood is the fundamental role of humour, where she combines disgust with the practice of *lol* and *ewwwww*, creating an aesthetic of the grotesque.

Cleanse this impure nation

In late January 2013, Mahmood reposts a declaration by Lashkar-e-Jhangvi, a group involved in the bombings and murders of Shia and other religious minorities in Pakistan, designated as a terrorist organization by the United Nations in 2003. The blog she reposts is entitled 'Shia Free Pakistan' and states: 'It is our religious duty to kill all Shias, and to cleanse Pakistan of this impure nation ... . It is our mission in Pakistan that every city, village and other place, every corner be cleansed of the Shia and the Shia Hazara.' The text, which claims responsibility for a killing that has taken place, goes on to state that the Hazaras had a chance to leave Pakistan in 2012; 'now God willing, LEJ in 2013 will not allow Shias to leave alive' (Tumblr, 23 January 2013).

In a remarkably short period of time, a cluster of completely new themes has entered Aqsa Mahmood's timeline. The affect shared here is not one of humour and amusement but disgust and revulsion, one that she nurtures in a constant series of blogs and tweets about what she believes to be Shia propensity for sex with animals or young children, or with men dressed as women, wearing make-up and women's jewellery. For Mahmood, all of these practices are filth, bringing with them the risk of contamination, a theme that we will see is fundamental to many experiences of radicalization. In her case, this is not a question of ideas but a sensory and sensual experience.

Purity versus impurity

Through the hundreds of images and comments she posts to Twitter and Tumblr, Mahmood constructs a sensory world organized around a series of binaries that reinforce each other. Her initial posts structured in terms of *good versus evil* in response to #Gaza progress to *innocence versus guilt*. Guilt is clearly linked to al-Assad and Khamenei, while innocence is reaffirmed by the harrowing images and interviews with child victims. At this point, she is within a paradigm of humanitarianism, one that underlines the needs and innocence of victims. But in a short period of time, this opposition mutates into something different, namely *purity versus impurity*, where the imaginary of helping the suffering becomes eclipsed by something quite different, an imaginary of *cleansing and purification*. This transformation is clearly evident in Mahmood's posts to both Tumblr and Twitter. In early 2013, these are full of images of suffering Syrians framed within a humanitarian imaginary. But, by late April, these images have become much less frequent as her preoccupation with responding to suffering gives way to a quite different imperative, namely responding to the threat to Islam posed by Shi'ism, which she frames in terms of the ease with which they may be killed: 'Unfortunately many Sunnis fail to see the nature of the shia, and keep defending them as if they are the oppressed. Love and Hate for the sake of Allaah (SWT). Their hatred for Ahiel Sunnah is deep and that is why they are so easy to kill them [*sic*] by the thousands in Iraq and Syria' (Twitter, 3 March 2013).

By March 2013, the transformation of Mahmood's social media profile into a platform for opposition to Shia Muslims had become evident to her family as well: 'My little sister has invited her friends over today and her closest friend is a Shiaa. And she has strictly warned me not to say anything … lol even my mum had told me to stay away from her friends. What am I gonna do? Dawah? Lolz possibly' (Twitter, 2 March 2013).

Trolling

Humour and the construction of social bonds through the pleasure of laughing at those judged different remains a constant part of Mahmood's Twitter feed, while it is much less present in her more austere Tumblr persona. Other traditions in Islam are mocked and ridiculed. She posts a screenshot of a Barelvi book involving spiritual guides and saints, commenting, '*LOL the shaik was a funny man.*' She posts an image of what is presented as a Shia devotional practice where a young woman places a Qu'ran on her head, followed by a series of tweets interacting with her friends:

Why is the Quran on her head? looooooooooool
No I can't take this. LOOOOOL
LOOOOOL OMG I laughed … do they use their shia Quran as an umbrella?? Idk.
Lazy shia movements
I asked her and she gave me some mad explanation as to why the do it.
cba cba x. (Twitter, 28 February 2013)

We can see the importance of play in this form of othering. Mahmood posts a picture of the Iraqi Shia leader, Muqtada al-Sadr, tweeting 'looking scarier than normal. Reminds me of @smellthedeen'. She tweets to another friend 'LOOOOOOOOOOL planet of the apes :')'. A few days later, we get a further insight when she tweets: 'It's so much fun trolling these Shias LOOOL :')' (5 March 2013). Someone has taken offence at Mahmood, something she takes evident pleasure in retweeting: 'I don't like this Axa girl being retweeted on my Tl tbh. And why is she insulting Shia boys' (Twitter, 5 March 2013).

Mahmood's response the next day is to return to a now familiar theme: 'When you say mutah I say Sistani. "… Every day is muharram, and every city is Karbala." Right okay. And every night is mutah' (Twitter, 6 March 2013). She completes the series of tweets with an image of Khomeni receiving a kiss from a child, quoting 'a man can have sexual pleasure with a child'. Above the image she posts again a single word: *sickness*. Such humorous exchanges continue with other friends as well, as we see in a text exchange with @smellthedeen:

> *Mahmood*: LOOOOOL ur a pig.
> *Smellthedeen*: LOOOOOOOOOL.
> *Smellthedeen*: Shias are pigs.
> *Smellthedeen*: I would happily kill one right now. (Twitter, 1 May 2013)

Mahmood tweets a screenshot of the exchange, adding as a commentary: 'liar'. Mahmood is proud that people follow her for the memes she creates. She circulates one of a Mullah smoking a joint, with a Bob Marley poster in the background (2 March 2013). She takes evident pleasure in trolling: 'Lol I've had a good day today, also I seen some beef tings kick of on the TL. Lol muzlim twitter is funny :')' (Twitter, 1 March 2013).

But, by May, there is less humour in her exchanges about Shia Muslims. On her Tumblr account, a follower says:

> *Comment*: sis, I don't think its even halal for ANYONE to speak in such a foul language whether its towards Shia or what not. Make Dua and leave the rest to Allah swt. May Allah forgive us all.
> *Mahmood*: Fear Allah, how could you even say that? Educate yourself upon that religion of theirs. And maybe then you'll realize the truth. Shias are going to answer to Allah (azzawajal) not YOU. Does that mean we don't speak out against them? We don't educate people on their wrongdoings? Why are you so persistent on me not to expose them?
> If you are still living in this Disneyland that we should have 'one Ummah' with Shias then I really do find you disgraceful. Saying that is like an insult to the 9,400 deaths of Ahlul Sunnah in Syria. And I'm not sorry if that offends any of youse, it's just reality. Take it or leave it.
> *Another response*: Some of the stuff on your page is really offensive, I hope that you meet a Shia and realize that behind the labels, we're all just *human beings who need to turn to Allah.*

Mahmood: May He guide you as I can tell you are a Shia,
                    really pity you I really do … Stop tarnishing
                    Islam with that filthy sect. (Tumblr, 15 May
                    2013)

We can see both continuity and transformation through these exchanges. Manhood and her friends set out to 'troll', that is, to provoke a reaction from others, where the reaction that is provoked reveals a truth which the person who is provoked may be hiding, or even unaware of (McDonald 2015). There are two kinds of humour involved in this activity: laughing *together* and laughing *at* the 'other' (who responds to provocation). Thus a type of community is formed by the pleasure of laughing together. This kind of dynamic is central to ritualized activities such as bullying, where the act of bullying involves not only excluding the 'other' but humiliating them and turning them into an object of humour. Laughing at a person being bullied is a mechanism of integrating a group, the whole process serving as a ritual through which group values are articulated and affirmed, while an 'other' is created and excluded. Through this, the bully makes a claim to construct a group – those who are laughing – and to speak on their behalf.

The two sides of humour as a relationship of inclusion and exclusion are at the heart of Mahmood's trolling. Trolling is a social activity, just as bullying; it is essential that those involved can laugh together at the reactions of their victims, and in so doing affirm their superiority and take pleasure in it. They may even ask their victims for the reasons behind their practice but, if the victim replies, it is important that they do not listen – that they demonstrate to each other that they *cba* (can't be arsed) because to listen to a response is to accord the speaker value and respect. But Mahmood sees herself doing more than simply laughing at or disrespecting Shia Muslims. Her last exchanges on Tumblr that I have quoted alert us to two key dimensions at stake when she uses the words 'expose' and 'filth'.

Filth

The language of 'filth' draws on the imaginary and viscerality that sustain racism and hate crimes. This imaginary was central to the Nazi regime and its presentation of the German-Jewish population as a 'cancer' and a 'national filth' (Appadurai 2006: 55). Racist abuse will always make recourse to images and metaphors of filth and dirt. The anthropologist Mary Douglas points to the sociological importance of 'dirt' as matter 'out of place'. But, in this case, dirt is experienced as filth, opening up a visceral or sensory domain experienced as the risk of contamination and impurity. For Douglas, the idea of purity is associated with 'categorical identity', in this case the purity or the homogeneity of the nation. The imaginary of purity and impurity is associated with the use of the word 'cleanse' to describe mass killings, either in the case of what came to be called 'ethnic cleansing', for example the Balkans in the 1980s or Rwanda in the 1990s. This is the word used to describe the 'purifying' of Pakistan that Mahmood blogs to her Tumblr feed, the imaginary of a Pakistan 'cleansed' of Hazari Muslims.

The anthropologist Arjun Appadurai highlights the way that this kind of imaginary focuses on the group that is perceived to be the closest, not the most distant. While the LEJ in Pakistan has undertaken killings of Christians and other minorities, its principal focus is the killing of Shias, a pattern also observed by the historian Faisal Devji (2005). Appadurai argues that it is the group that is closest that is perceived to be the most threatening because it is believed this group is in some way 'counterfeit'. He claims that racist hatred is often focused on relatively small population groups because it is these small numbers that threaten the completeness of what he terms the national 'ethnos', the fusion of unified people into a nation. Here, the presence of a small minority highlights the unrealized project of purity and the fearful condition of *incompleteness*. The theme of incompleteness is apparent in Mahmood's tweets when she takes great pains to emphasize that Islam is complete, and that any suggestion of incompleteness is to be opposed.

Mahmood constructs a sensory world through her social media posts, one that is organized around strong polarities. To begin with, her posts about Syria are about *good* and *bad* but progress quickly to themes of innocence and guilt by counterposing al-Assad and Khamenei with the innocence of terrorized and mutilated child victims. This transition is also reflected in the images of serenity and beauty in January and February, usually of males exhibiting mystery and romance, against a backdrop of idyllic streets, a world free of cars, pollution and crowds. The 'beauty' of the mujahideen continues to figure in her tweets of images of heavily armed young men taking the time to stroke or feed cats or kittens: 'Mujahideen of Syria and their compassion and mercy to even the animals' (6 March 2013). The mujahideen not only have smouldering eyes, they possess a childlike innocence, taking time to care for kittens even in the midst of terrible destruction.

The grotesque

The beauty and innocence of the mujahideen are contrasted with the grotesque photoshopped images of Shia Muslims that Mahmood posts to provoke a visceral reaction of rejection and disgust. Her blogs and posts, her trolling and memes, are deeply shaped by internet culture. Her slang is that of young people who spend their days communicating on social media. She not only circulates memes; she creates them. Memes are incongruous combinations of text and image, often generated by interactions between people, which often take the form of parody or satire.

In Mahmood's memes, humour plays a critical role, and this alerts us once again to the relationship between feeling and belief, the extent to which we have to be able to *feel* certain things in order to be able to *believe* them. We do not know if Mahmood 'believes' that Shia religious and political leaders have sexual relations with animals and children. Her claims are not based on evidence but on a mixture of humour and disgust, where humour allows the viewer to feel revulsion, humour being a medium for the viewer to feel connected to others who are feeling the same thing. In the case of bullying rituals, it is not sufficient that the victim be made to suffer. It needs to be demonstrated that the victim *deserves* to suffer, and this is achieved through their humiliation, a process where humour plays a critical role, involving laughing with and laughing at. It is through the embodied action of 'laughing at' that the community brought into being through the ritual *take part in* the humiliation of the victim. Laughing makes it possible to believe that the victim deserves what he or she is receiving. In a similar way, the grotesque memes that Mahmood circulates provoke humour precisely because they are *not realistic*. Those who receive and circulate these memes join in the laughter, sharing the feeling they communicate, a feeling that makes it possible to believe that the message embedded in them is true.

True Muslims, false Muslims

In January 2013, Mahmood posts two related images. The first consists of supporters of Syrian President Bashar al-Assad, crouched on their knees, touching the edge of an enormous portrait of their leader. This is juxtaposed with a second image: Free Syrian Army fighters, their guns placed before them, at prayer. Mahmood writes: 'Bashar al-Assad's supporters/Muslims (FSA)'. The juxtaposition of these two groups communicates the idea that one group worships Assad while the other is prepared to pray, while selflessly risking their lives. The juxtaposition defines the FSA fighters as Muslims, the others as idolaters. One is a group of true Muslims, the other is false.

Truth and falsehood become a binary superimposed on beauty and ugliness, purity and contamination. Such visceral themes extend beyond Mahmood's response to the war in Syria and become a medium through which her wider social world is apprehended, as we see in a series of tweets about groups she is not part of, each sent within minutes of the other:

> White girl twitter is so funny, they're so passionate over nothing. It's so cute.
> There is no room for homosexuality in Islam nor is that up for interpretation
> I'd hate to be a fat pig.
> Tuhin fan girls are so annoying.
> Hate when people that are literally fat as flip call themselves 'curvy' no, your a fat pig. (Twitter, 4 March 2013)

Distant suffering

In an increasingly mediated world, where the experience of the 'other' is more and more present in our lives, sociologists are increasingly concerned to understand the different ways that we experience and respond to what is called 'distant suffering' – suffering that we do not share but which confronts us with a demand for some kind of response. Luc Boltanski (1999) suggests three overarching frameworks of response to such distant suffering that we see in Mahmood's timeline. He calls the first of these 'denunciation', where we respond to suffering by focusing on the guilt of the person or the group causing suffering. In this case, the response to suffering is framed in terms of *indignation*, and a desire to make the person or group that is causing the suffering suffer in turn. The second is a response that he terms 'sentiment', one where the observer of suffering will focus less on the experience of the sufferers than on those who are helping them. This enables the observer to avoid being overwhelmed by the scale and horror of suffering; they can instead focus on the courage and humility of the person who is helping. This is one of the most common forms of response to disaster in many western countries, where a celebrity will go and visit the suffering, and accompanying media will focus not on the nameless suffering but on the selfless-ness of the celebrity who is visiting them. The observer does not feel the pain of suffering but, rather, gratitude towards the celebrity who is visiting sufferers. Rather than indignation, we experience what Boltanski refers to as 'tender-heartedness' (1999: 47).

Boltanski underlines the critiques of such sentimental responses to suffering. He discusses a famous image of a celebrity holding a criti-cally ill child, where we, as observers, feel gratitude to the celebrity as expressed in the eyes of a nurse who is watching. Modern-day exam-ples might include Angelina Jolie in her role as UN special envoy. Such images 'work' by constructing relationships between three people: the person suffering; the celebrity who feels their pain; and an observer who is either consoled by or expresses gratitude for the pres-ence of the celebrity. In such images, we do not feel the pain of the suffering child, say, but the sadness of the celebrity. In a sense, this becomes the means through which we not only learn about but also experience the world, as seen in the growth of travel shows following a celebrity as they discover a foreign country, sharing their amazement, joys and frustrations. One of the critiques of such sentimentality when encountering suffering is that we, the observers, take pleasure in these images, admiring the courage and emotional depth of the celebrity. When we share our reaction to these images, we do not talk about the terrible issues afflicting the victim but the generosity of the celebrity.

This structure of experience is important in the way that Mahmood experiences suffering in Syria. In March 2013, she retweets a widely circulated image which embodies the triangular relationship of the victim, the person expressing gratitude and the suffering helper whom we see in celebrity hospital visits (Figure 2.6). In this case, the victim of a recent explosion lies dead on the ground in the upper-left corner of the image. The fighter feels the pain of this horrific violence. A young boy looks at him, expressing not only gratitude but also tender-ness towards the fighter who is devoting his life to helping him and his family, despite the risk and loss this involves. This image captures the relational vulnerability of the fighter and the care and concern expressed by the child who squats next to him in order to comfort him.

For Mahmood, the victim of the violence is largely irrelevant, forming only the background. What is central is the suffering of the fighter and the gratitude and concern expressed by the young boy

Figure 2.6 Don't be sad. Twitter, 1 March 2013.

trying to comfort him. The two are powerfully linked as they transform their shared sadness into an experience that allows them to
access together the presence of God. When Mahmood retweets the
image, she adds the text: 'Don't be sad, Allah is with us.'

Sentimentality is often criticized for being staged, in particular
in relation to celebrity humanitarianism. In such cases, it is argued,
a celebrity comes into a hospital, is photographed with a suffering
person and then leaves. The gratitude that we feel as an observer, in
such cases, is doubly false: the expression of the suffering celebrity is
false; and the feeling of tenderness that we feel as observers is illegitimate, as the horror we should feel when confronted with suffering is
replaced instead by feelings of comfort and reassurance as we experience the compassion of the celebrity.

Celebrity encounters with suffering may not always be manufac-
tured but critics of such practices underline the potential for this.
However, the affective response solicited by the image circulated
by Mahmood relies upon a fabrication. In this case, two completely
unrelated images have been photoshopped to form one. One of the
original images is of a Free Syrian Army fighter in the immediate

aftermath of a bomb blast in Aleppo, and the other is a professional photographer's image of a boy, taken in Europe. The fact that Mahmood retweets this image demonstrates a complex emotional register. There is no evidence that she knows it is photoshopped. She did not produce it; it was circulating before her retweet. But it captures the complexity of her relationship with the fighting in Syria. For her, fighters are not killing machines. They feel the pain of those who suffer, as does the celebrity who visits the hospital. The affective relationship she has with them is not only one of admiration and gratitude, but also of tenderness. The fallaciousness of this image highlights the nature of contemporary propaganda, as does the earlier image that Mahmood circulated, purporting to be people at prayer amidst the bombardment of Gaza.

Boltanski goes on to explore a third type of response to suffering, which he calls 'aesthetic'. In this case, the observer does not experience indignation towards the evildoer, nor gratitude to the helper, but focuses on the suffering and the sufferer. Here, an observer experiences horror and a response that takes the form of what Boltanski calls the *sublime*; after an initial movement of fear, this become become reworked as 'delicious horror and painful enjoyment' (1999: 121). While we cannot directly 'apply' these categories, they offer a framework to help us think about the ways in which different radicalization pathways construct an experience of the response to suffering. In Mahmood's timeline, we read both indignation and sentimentality. Her response also involves an aesthetic dimension, increasingly evident as she displaces the horror of suffering with the grotesque horror of the 'other'. The 'agency' of those suffering disappears in the process. When she was commenting upon an image of people at prayer, believing this to be an image of Palestinians in Gaza, those who are suffering are exercising agency, praying under a rain of bombs. But within a very short time, such images of social struggle disappear from her timeline, as does any reference to Palestinians and their struggle for nationhood. The social struggle of Palestinians is replaced with a new category, Muslims, who are passive victims, defined uniquely by their gratitude for the action of jihadists.

Choons, eyebrows and hijabs

Thus far, we have highlighted the binary oppositions shaping the sensory world that Mahmood constructs through social media, and the extent to which the construction of these oppositions is a social activity, relying on the circulation of images and humour. However, during this period many of Mahmood's tweets and posts focus on herself; through them, she lives out intimate experience in public, from questions about what she should wear to whether to pluck her eyebrows. While personal, these activities of 'making the self' are also undertaken in relation to others; they are fundamentally communicative actions that address others: her parents, her siblings, other young Muslim men and women.

In one of her first posts to Tumblr, she blogs about wearing a hijab: 'Wearing a hijab is fardh *[a religious duty]*. However I absolutely hate to see sisters think just because THEY wear it and another sister doesn't it automatically gives them the right to judge them? And look down upon them? Of course not' (Tumblr, 22 January 2013). We also catch a glimpse of a kind of feminism, a reaction to pressure placed on young women by male friends and relatives:'I just want to start harassing muslim men about their hijab. Where is your beard akhi. Where is ur throbe akhi. I am just looking out for you brother. Ur a pearl, remember that plz' (Tumblr, 31 January 2013).

Here, Mahmood is naming a kind of pressure experienced as coming from 'brothers', but presented as an expression of care – 'ur a pearl'. It is significant that she identifies this as pressure not from her parents' generation, but from 'brothers'. Her use of the word 'harassing' suggests a kind of pressure experienced as illegitimate or inappropriate, even when wrapped up in a flattering message: 'Ur a pearl, remember that plz'.

Mahmood's interest in the hijab is not a rejection of fashion. In early February, she tweets an image from the cover of a fashion magazine showing a woman in a niqab, with kohled eyes, gold bracelet over gloves and massive jewelled ring. She comments: 'How swaggy is this ~' (Twitter, 12 February 2013). Later that month, she purchases an abaya, a loose over-garment or robe-like dress. While common in the Middle East and parts of North Africa, this kind of robe is rare in Pakistan, the country from which Mahmood's family originates. Purchasing this garment is a social process. Mahmood's friend @smellthedeen purchased a jilbaab a month earlier, posting to her Tumblr, 'Fell in love with this jilbaab and I had to buy it!' Mahmood 'liked' the post and a month later blogs about her own purchase:

:') just bought my first abaya – actual so excited. Lolz mums gonna freak once she finds out how much money I have spent on online shopping this week

LOOOOOOOL WHY DID I BUY AN XL ABAYA LOOOL MY
FRIENDS ARE LAUGHING AT ME FGS, I DIDN'T KNOW.
NEWBIE PLS. I WILL DROWN IN THIS ABAYA. ok rant over bye.
(Tumblr, 28 February 2013)

This purchase is located in a relationship to both her mother and her
friends. It is pushing the boundaries with her mother, who will 'freak'
at the amount spent. And acknowledging that she has purchased a
size that is too large affirms a status of belonging, albeit as a 'newbie'.
Despite its size, she tweets that she finds it liberating: 'My first abaya
came through today :') why the hell had I not started wearing one
already. They are so comfy. I'm not even kidding, I'm gonna wear my
pgyamas underneath my abaya and head to uni. Lol and apparently
WE'RE the oppressed ones [*emoji with tears of laughter*]' (Twitter,
4 March 2013).

The relationship with her mother remains central to what she
wears, as is the case with many teenage girls living with their parents.
In August, she purchases a niqab, a full-covering garment: 'yaaaay my
niqab has arrived today XD fndjsafcfdgvyhbsdcj its so pretty. I really
do not care what my parents opinion of this will be!' (7 August 2013).

But her relationship with her parents extends beyond what she
wears: 'My mum has seen all the PDFs on my laptop and flipped.
And my dad gets me in trouble for listening to Anwar al-Awlaki
loooool' (Tumblr, 3 March 2013). She returns to the same theme
the next month: 'I asked my dad to get me some books while he goes
to Pakistan next week. He got angry and said what "Al Qaeda" type
books' (Tumblr, 8 April 2013).

Like many young people, Mahmood uses social media to explore
the distance between who she is and who she once was. In April, she
posts four blogs to Tumblr on the same day. The first quotes lyrics
from Gary Jules's 2009 song 'Mad World', capturing a world where
everyone does what is expected of them, but find themselves trapped
as a result. This is the adult world but one where everyone does what is
expected of them and can be seen through as a result. Her second blog
evokes a childhood excitedly sharing the latest pop songs. The third
refers to her previous life on Twitter, what she has given up and what
she still misses, while the last focuses on a kind of experience of self:

All around me are familiar faces
Worn out places, worn out faces
Bright and early for their daily races
Going nowhere, going nowhere. (Tumblr, 19 April 2013)

Who remembers the CHOON 'sum next aunty'? I still know the lyrics.
I don't know if I should feel ashamed or ashamed (Tumblr, 19 April
2013)

I get more attention on twitter. I don't feel famous on this. But then I
complain that I don't like the attention?!? (Tumblr, 19 April 2013)

Sometimes loneliness makes you find your inner-self, perhaps the real
you. When you try to block out all those echoes and chaos (Tumblr, 19
April 2013)

Ten days later, she returns to the theme of distance from her previous
life: 'Loneliness adds beauty to life. It puts a special burn on sunsets
and makes night air smell better' (Tumblr, 29 April 2013).

These posts highlight the extent that becoming an individual
involves establishing distance from community, networks and
exchanges, establishing a relationship with a childhood self who is
now someone else, and even potentially disengaging from fame.
She sees the risk of growing up to be someone limited to a social
role or function, 'going nowhere'. Mahmood addresses the theme
of disorder, highlighting the need to block out 'echoes and chaos',
and she describes this in terms of greater sensory awareness of sight,
smell and beauty. In the middle of this series of posts about 'going
nowhere' and her childhood memories of favourite 'choons', she
posts an image of a young Palestinian woman, crouched on the
ground, picking up a stone to sling. This image appears as the only
alternative to a life 'going nowhere'.

In February, she begins to repost about rules to structure a Muslim
life. The first is 'Know your Mahrams', the list of people it is permis-
sible for males and females to socialize with. On the same day, she
retweets about #TeamHalalEyebrows writing, 'I'm surprised that
a lot of sisters don't know that those who pick their eyebrows, are
cursed by Allah and the angels' (Twitter, 25 February 2013). She has
come to believe a devout Muslim woman will not pluck or shape her
eyebrows and posts: 'reminder to the sisters. What's more important:
pleasing the creations or the creator?' She posts an image of a woman
plucking her eyebrows, with the message 'DON'T PLUCK', and a
quote from a Muslim scholar who asserts 'May Allah curse ... the
one who plucks eyebrows and the one who has her eyebrows plucked'
(Twitter, 28 April 2013). This is not an easy thing for her:

Not doing my eyebrows is one of the strongest fitnahs [*trial or strife*]
for me. In this day and age plucking your eyebrows is the norm and

many are not even aware how big a sin it is. Allah (SWT) curses those who pluck their eyebrows. In'shaa'Allaah may He give us sabr and the strength to stay dedicated to the Deen. #rant #eyebrows. (Tumblr, 29 April 2013)

In a later post, she describes 'the struggle when your mum and sister try and convince you to get your eyebrows done. This is my jihad for now ... Looool' (Tumblr, 7 August 2013).

I hate Shias

Mahmood is involved in constructing an 'us' through rejection of the 'other'. She tweets to a friend, advising her to 'follow xxx. He hates Shias' (Twitter, 26 April 2013). She watches a conspiracy video about the emergence of Shi'ism linked to this person's website; she then tweets to him '@xx thanks, I hate Shias too ;'). She is in the middle of a series of tweets about the need to hate Shias when she stops and tweets: 'What am I doing. I promised my mum I would do anymore shia Sufi ahmadi beef tings on twitter. D old me ded and gone [*hand holding up one finger*]' (Twitter, 24 April 2013).

A follower asks Mahmood and her new follower why they hate Shias. Mahmood replies 'Why not?' The person asks again: 'Why? :p I'm asking why do you hate them @_axaa because they are muslims? & Muhammad pbuh said not to hate on our brothers and sisters.' This prompts a reply from Mahmood, who posts her photoshopped image of a leering Khamenei complete with diamond ear-stud, adding as text a paternalistic: 'u do that bubs x.' Mahmood's interlocutor finishes the exchange by responding: '@_axaa ahahahahahahahahaha! Made my day. One shia is gonna represent all so now since you're a Sunni then all Sunnis are full of hate. Thank you x' (Twitter, 24 April 2013). Mahmood does not respond to this final reply.

Innocence? Makes me laugh

On 5 May 2013, Mahmood retweets a screenshot of a post defending Shia Muslims. The post states 'Shia cannot be considered infidels and therefore the rape of Shia women is not justified.' Mahmood places a question mark on the text as a whole, and circles 'May Allah have mercy upon the Shia of Syria and all those that died innocent deaths.' Along with the image, she tweets a comment: 'Still makes me

Figure 2.7   My input to the topic. Twitter, 1 May 2013.

laugh.' What is happening here? For Mahmood it is the suggestion of innocence in this 'defence of Shi'a' tweet, indeed its very possibility, which provokes laughter. In the social space of her timeline, there can be no innocent Shia because of its fundamental structuring that opposes purity and impurity, associated with either humour or sickness. The terms that recur constantly are 'filth' and 'disgust': 'What's even more disgusting are those who call for one Umma with them lot' (25 April 2013). Disgust is a constant. Visual material is central to the way Mahmood constructs disgust, while the humour associated with it serves three functions: integrating those who laugh together; confirming the radical otherness of those laughed at; and removing the need for any basis in fact for the claims made. This is embedded in very contemporary forms of idiom, one where humour is easily associated with images of killing, as we see in a meme that she has created, which she describes as her 'input to the topic' (Figure 2.7).

Over a period of six months, Mahmood through exchange with her friends, has constructed an experiential binary opposing purity and impurity, held together with an affective register of humour and disgust. It allows her and her friends to joke about killing, to articulate and share their disgust and, in her case, to contest the idea that rape of Shia women is not justified. This is the experiential register of both racism and hate crime, and it has evolved as the end point along the path that Mahmood has travelled: Good and Evil have become Innocence and Guilt, and this opposition has in turn mutated into the Pure and the Impure. The initial humanitarian concern with suffering seen in the context of #GazaMovement2012 has mutated. The concern with suffering has been replaced by a quite different preoccupation with cleansing and purifying, one where liquidating the Shia population of Syria is at the centre of her imaginary and draws on a digital culture of memes, humour and the grotesque rather than on any experience that we might consider religious.

The Khalifah: to save ourselves

The Khalifah is referenced in Mahmood's tweets in early March 2013. She quotes a 'haddith', or saying, attributed to the Prophet, that embraces the term 'Jahiliyyah' as it was reformulated by Sayyid Qutb in Egypt in the 1970s: 'He who dies without having pledged allegiance [*to the Khaleefah*] will die the death of a jahiliyyah [*i.e. in a state of being before Islam was revealed*]'. She follows this immediately with a message framed in terms of fear and urgency:

> Thus, in order to save ourselves from such a death, we much engage in working collectively to establish #Khalifah.
>
> Even raising awareness of #Khalifah can go a long way. Many muslims are not aware of the justice of the #Sharia Every little helps.
> Let us not forget to implement #Khalifah within ourselves before forcing it upon others. Strong reminder.

By July 2013, she is retweeting communications such as this appeal from @jamanwtf, Ifthekar Jaman's brother: 'You don't need to be a perfect Muslim to go and help the muhahideen, just keep your intentions pure and the rest is between you and Allah' (Twitter, 15 July 2013).

Mahmood leaves for Syria in mid-November 2013, her intention to depart becoming increasingly evident in a series of posts from mid-October: 'I don't belong here ☹ (Tumblr, 10 October 2013); Looking back, it will be all worth it. What I gained from gaining this knowledge cannot be counted' (Tumblr, 30 October).

In early November, she posts a link to a YouTube video of British fighters with al-Qaeda in Syria, followed up with a repost affirming that it is not possible to be a Salafi and 'abandon jihad'. She posts a declaration from Mohammad al-Adnani, spokesperson for ISIS, 'If a person who performs Hijrah for sake of Allah and left his family no one will slander him except the jaahil [*people living in a state of pre-Islamic ignorance*] and the intelligence services' (Tumblr, 14 November).

In the days immediately before her departure, she posts an image of a green bird, the jihadist symbol for a martyr, and quotes Ibn Taymiyyah: 'And whoever his sins are plenty, then his greatest remedy is jihad' (Tumblr, 14 November). On the same day, she posts an image of a plane taking off, expressing a sense of relief. The following day she posts a quote: 'Always leave loved ones with loving words. It may be the last time you see them.'

She departs the United Kingdom later that week.

Power

There remains one more transformation to understand – Mahmood's experience of power. This becomes increasingly evident in her rejection of diversity. While in October 2012 she was tweeting the Palestinian flag and creating memes with it as a background, by April 2013 she is tweeting against nationalisms, insisting on 'one flag, one war': 'Mayn I hate nationalism. Get rid of it plz' (Twitter, 2 March 2013). She starts to tweet about the need to establish a Khalifah to avoid a death in a state of jahiliyyah (March 2013), but at this time insists that it is not appropriate to force the Kalifah on others (3 March 2013), just as when affirming the importance of the hijab she insists that those who cover should not feel superior to those who don't. But, by November, just before her departure for Syria, Mahmood blogs: 'Brothers, prevent your women from unveiling.' She goes on to quote from a text on the obligation to veil: 'take hold of the hands of your women and prevent them from doing what Allaah has forbidden ... know that remaining silent with them (when they commit these evil deeds) is the same as participating with them in their sin and in receiving Allaah's anger and punishment' (Tumblr, 3 November 2013). The imagery here is that of the danger of a contagion of guilt and the need to use power to prevent this.

Mahmood's trajectory gives us an insight not only into how a concern with suffering, experienced in the categories of innocence and guilt, can mutate into categories of purity and impurity. This remains central during her time in Syria but becomes increasingly reframed in terms of the benefits accruing to those associated with the State, and a total destruction of any capacity for empathy with others. In September 2014, after less than a year with ISIS, she is posting about the benefits:

> Know that honestly there is something so pleasurable to know that what you have has been taken off from the Kuffar... . Some of the many things include kitchen appliances from fridges, cookers, ovens, microwaves, milkshake machines ... and most importantly a house with free electricity and water provided to you due to the Khilafah and no rent included (Tumblr, 14 September 2014).

By now, she is becoming an important figure in ISIS's attempts to broaden its support base internationally, and her Tumblr no longer focuses on sacrifices but on rewards: 'in these lands we are rewarded for our sacrifices involved in our Hijrah for example one is by receiving Ghanimah [booty]. And know that honestly there is something so pleasurable to know that what you have has been taken off from the Kuffar and handed to you personally by Allah SWT as a gift' (Tumblr, 14 September 2014).

Here the power of the state fuses with that of God and becomes sacralized. It is not simply the State that distributes booty to its supporters; it is God. And Mahmood herself merges into this new expanding totality as 'we'. Referring to the United Kingdom and the United States, she writes: 'We have conquered these lands once and we will do it again. This Islamic Empire shall be known and feared worldwide' (Tumblr, 10 September 2014).

After 18 months in Syria, Mahmood is justifying the sexual slavery of women captured by ISIS fighters: 'If Allah enables the Muslims who are striving and sacrificing their lives and wealth ... to make the word of Allaah over the kafirs, then He allows them to enslave the kufar when they capture them' (Tumblr, 19 July 2015). Mahmood tags her post under two headings: *mulk yameen* (female slaves) and *concubines*.

A transformation

It is clear from the extraordinary social media footprint that Mahmood has left that her experience cannot be understood within the categories shaping much of the debate about radicalization. She is neither poor nor excluded, and she never tweets about Islamophobia or the political or social disadvantage experienced by Muslims in the United Kingdom. She does not once tweet about UK foreign policy. She is not a victim of manipulation or grooming. She is active, and the radicalization process that she engages in is fundamentally a *social* one, constructed through affective communications that generate powerful transpersonal intensities such as humour and disgust.

When we first encountered her in 2012, she was identifying with different communities that she felt part of: she was a supporter of a local cricket team, describing their rivals as 'eww'. She described Gujjars as 'we are all amazing'; and she embraced her school's kilt, declaring 'I'm a true Scot.' This dimension of community is central to the radicalization pathway we see in Mahmood's case, where she comes to feel that the Sunni community faces an existential threat through the existence of Shia Muslims and when she takes on a specific commitment in Syria by encouraging young western women to join ISIS, marry and have children. She wants to build another community. But in this case it is one committed to the destruction, murder or enslavement of those who are not part of it.

This mutation has nothing to do with the culture of the communities she was part of in Scotland. It is a transformation lived through her experience of distant suffering, first of the Palestinians and then of that produced by the war in Syria. We can see this clearly in her social media engagement, where an opposition between good and evil is transformed firstly into innocence versus guilt (in the images of suffering children and al-Assad), later mutating into pure versus impure (the pure fighter and pervasive images of beauty juxtaposed with the sickness of Shia religious and political leaders, framed as rupturing boundaries: sex with children, sex between men, sex with animals). This mutation is made possible by Mahmood's use of humour as a medium of inclusion/exclusion and of the grotesque that enables a radical dehumanizing of the 'other'. This is not a transformation driven by ideas but by a sensory regime of humour, excitement and pleasure, combined with a disgusted fear of contamination: an opposition that forms the experiential basis of racism and hate crimes. Other themes are present here, such as the search for hidden knowledge and conspiracies, but Mahmood's path is not fundamentally shaped by a response to conspiracy. It is a development of her response to suffering, first of the Palestinians, then that produced by the war in Syria. At the beginning of this process, suffering was a major theme in Mahmood's posts to social media. But, as 2013 proceeds, these images become eclipsed by images of purity and beauty juxtaposed with various manifestations of impurity and

the grotesque. By the time of her departure, there are no more suffering children on her timeline: a pathway that began with the shock
of discovery of suffering ends with a celebration of the potency of the
Islamic State, with a 23-year-old woman rejoicing in not only the
dispossession of whole communities but the sexual enslavement of
women captured in war.

3

DIY Religion: Hidden Worlds, from Fear to Bliss

The answer to every question

At that point I knew that I had no control over what was happening. The only control that I had was would I admit it or not ... I knew the answer to every question would be there.

Ahmed, Movement Against Crusaders, interview (London, 2012)

Ahmed and his companion are members of al-Muhajiroun and, like a great many people who have become radicalized, are converts to Islam. The story Ahmed (a pseudonym) tells is replicated by hundreds of others; it is a story of being born again. He describes his life as a university student:

I could see there was a lot wrong with the world, I wanted to change it through music – I was a musician. But I didn't know how to. I got pretty much depressed, seeing how selfish people were. And [I] ended up drinking, a lot. I'd easily spend £200 a night on alcohol, I'd drink and just get drunk. All the time. This was when I was in university. Then I met a friend, in university, he was another revert [*term for convert*], he'd just become Muslim.

Ahmed goes on to describe the effect his new friendship had: 'the more he told me, the more I agreed with it. You're not allowed to drink, instead of fornicating you should get married. Even though I was an alcoholic, it was not something I wanted to be doing. You could feel the negative effect it was having.' It seems Ahmed knows that he should be able to find a way to disengage from the cycle he is in, but he cannot. One event destabilizes him further:

I had been with a girl for about three years, and I wanted to marry her. But she left me to go to university on her own selfish little expedition, for no reason. So when the idea of marriage ... it hadn't really hit home, it didn't really hit home until that point, until having that pain, that loss. But really, I was clutching onto the girl, to make myself happy, so even that was selfish really.

He began to read books and material found on the internet:

I read about the scientific miracles of the Qur'an, the embryology was something that really got me, my mum had had two girls ... and I had studied child development, so I knew quite a bit about that process. So the embryology in the Qur'an was fascinating for me, it was precise, it was completely precise, you can't fault it in any way. And then other scientific miracles. I read a book, *130 Evident Miracles in the Qur'an*, and it's just irrefutable, the Quran is the word of the creator, and therefore the path that I should follow.

Ahmed has discovered a hidden truth, scientific knowledge in the Qur'an that cannot be explained in any other way than as a miracle. As he talks about his discovery, he begins to speak faster, the memory of the shock and exhilaration of discovery still lingers. He then describes the day that his friend was to get married, and he had been invited to participate:

My friend was getting married ... I walked into the mosque, and I had already dreamt about it, about this mosque. I'd never been there in my life, but it was the same as in my dream. And the people in there were the same as in my dream. And the questions they were asking me were the same as in my dream. And the answers I was giving were the same as in my dream. At that point I knew that I had no control over what was happening. The only control I had was whether I was going to actually admit that or not?

Ahmed had foreseen his future in a dream. The event destabilized him; it gave him no other choice. The next day he made his shahada, his declaration of Muslim faith.

The path Ahmed maps out is one that occurs widely in accounts of religious conversion: a shift from a life of disorder to one of coherence. In his case, this is associated with a discovery of knowledge that is hidden in plain sight from all who care to look. Before he 'reverts', his world is one of chaos: drinking, violence, adultery, cannabis abuse. It is experienced as lacking any pole or principle of order: 'you have intercourse at sixteen – that's the world I was brought up in.'

Now he has found security, an escape from chaos. But danger still lurks:

> you know the truth, get on the path, and walk it. Shatan is whispering to you, 'have that spliff'. You have to attack it, walk the path ... when I became Muslim, even before I read it, I knew that it [*the Qur'an*] was the truth, and I knew that it would have the solution for everything ... I knew we needed to have Islamic law.

Ahmed describes how he spoke to a local imam (Muslim teacher) about this, who advised him that such change was more complex. But Ahmed disagrees: 'Allah is telling me to cut the hand of the thief. But I can't do it, it's something I can't do. So it is up to every Muslim to make the situation arise where you are implementing sharia. Giving people their rights to clothes and shelter, and cutting the hand off the thief.'

Ahmed's friend participating in the interview, and also a convert, amplifies this theme. He contrasts what he believes to be a lack of crime during the Turkish Caliphate, while in the West, 'there's no discipline, no authority'. In the months that followed this interview, these two young men joined a 'sharia patrol' attempting to police the streets in a British urban neighbourhood. They filmed themselves intimidating people into emptying bottles of alcohol or stopping holding hands in the street. In one case, a man that the group believed to be homosexual was forced to declare in a YouTube video that he was dirty and filthy. In another case, the two were part of a group that attacked men drinking in the street, filming themselves as they declared that they were there to 'enforce Shar'ia law in Allah's land', and 'Kill the non-believers'. In 2013, both received prison sentences following convictions for assault.

The interview with these two young men lasted only 90 minutes and, like all interviews, it offers us only a partial account of a complex transformation. Nonetheless, we can identify an experience lived as a transformation from a world of disorder to one of order, a transformation made possible by discovery of powerful hidden knowledge. The transformation was so profound that Ahmed knew that the Qur'an would offer answers to every question, even before reading it. But, while controlled, the threat of disorder remains pervasive – in Shaytan's whisper about the pleasures of a spliff. Danger is still present and will remain so until sharia can be imposed. These two young men set about imposing aspects of what they believed to be sharia in urban Britain through violent intimidation, which they filmed and uploaded to the internet. Several people involved in this group later travelled to Syria.

19 HH

What attracted me to it? Quite frankly, for me it was the videos produced by Omar Omesen and Mourad, like *Al-Mahdi and the second Caliphate*. They really captivated me.

Karim, phone interview from prison to French journalist David Thomson (Thomson 2018: 196)

The principal pathway to jihad from France in the years 2011–2013 was through the work of a Franco-Senegalese street preacher from the city of Nice, Omar Diaby – who took the moniker Omar Omsen, combining Omar and Senegal. Diaby migrated to France from Senegal at the age of five, growing up in Nice. During his time in the city, he was involved in different gangs and criminal enterprises, leading to several convictions and periods in prison, including a conviction in 1995 and five years' imprisonment for killing a man in a car collision, which the court believed was an act of gang warfare, and, in 2002 and 2003, when he was convicted for the armed robberies of two jewellers in Monaco. After one such period, Diaby joined a small group known as Forsane Alizza (Knights of Pride). He is believed to have attempted to travel to Afghanistan in 2011 and succeeded in leaving France in 2013, eventually establishing himself in Aleppo, where he set about inspiring a *katiba* (brigade) of French-speaking fighters linked to al-Qaeda's al-Nusra Front. Diaby was interviewed by a French journalist, David Thomson, in 2013. He explained that on leaving prison he had received a revelation in a vision in which he was visited by both God and the angel Gabriel. According to his story, at the time of this vision Omsen looked to the heavens and saw a cloud formation of the number 19, together with another in the shape of HH. These would become the marker of the videos he would produce: HH for a new account of 'the History of Humanity', and the number 19 referring to the number of participants in the attacks of 11 September 2001.

Karim, quoted above, is in prison after having returned from Syria to France. He refers to the impact of Diaby's videos, in particular *Al-Mahdi and the Second Khilafah*, a film consisting of a mash-up of video from television news reports, accompanied by Diaby's narration. In it, Diaby tells the story of 'the Mahdi', a successor to the Prophet Muhammad who will be discovered at a time of great crisis and suffering, and who will lead the Muslims to victory over their opponents. A key sign of this development will be an army 'rising up' in Syria and Iraq, with Diaby affirming that 'each person claiming to be Muslim must join this army'. Diaby's voice-over comments on the deeper meanings hidden in events that are widely known, featuring in television news clips: the death of the king of Saudi Arabia; a plot to stop the establishment of an Islamic state in Syria. The Mahdi will not be recognized by all Muslims, only by a courageous minority. He will create his army, but a Dajjal (false messiah) will arise in the desert, a deceiver who will take human form and attempt to seduce the Muslims and who will create an army largely consisting of Jews in an attempt to defeat him. The sections of television news are interspersed with film cut from Hollywood and French B movies, ranging from Saladin's armies entering Jerusalem, trolls and fighting elephants from *The Lord of the Rings* to video footage of jihadist groups in Syria, all pasted together into one narrative.

These videos follow the style of a Hollywood epic, combining mash-ups of images and sounds, with stories of secret knowledge and immense power released by its discovery. The musical soundtrack is intense and full of foreboding, the colour palette is dark. The aesthetic is one where there is hidden danger but also frisson and intensity, risk but also power to be accessed via this hidden knowledge about the history of humanity. Diaby's videos were linked to a website, www.19hh.net (now taken down, but material can be found in the internet archive). To give an idea of its impact, a discussion forum linked to the site had more than 50,000 distinct users, and each film was also linked to a Facebook discussion forum. The comments on these pages focus above all on the personal experience of those who view the films:

> over recent months I have been very disturbed by what I have discovered. We are in a year called the 'year of truth', and everything that we see around us confirms that reality... . Your video about the Mahdi forces me to tell you of a dream that I had... . (http://web.archive.org/web/20131006224104/http://www.19hh.net/)

Or another:

> It is so good to be able to discover the truth and to discover the things that are hidden. Above all it offers a concrete response to this unease (*mal-être*). It also pushes me to be critical of myself. These shocking videos are full of vitally important information; they provoke thinking and heartfelt transformation for the sincere Muslim.

The videos are so good, but the background is so stressful. They would have been better without the sound effects.

Brother Omar, in relation to all your works and the intention that you put into them and get from them, do you receive directly signs from God? (http://web.archive.org/web/20131006224104/http://www.19hh.net/)

The hundreds of such responses to these videos underline themes of shock and stress, the enormity of the hidden truths they reveal being so powerful as to destabilize everyday life, which suddenly becomes both trivial and vulnerable when faced with the significance of the revelations. The reliance upon an aesthetic of *The Matrix* and *The Lord of the Rings*, together with material cut and pasted from daily television news broadcasts, means that the observer is not simply swept up by an epic message, but also into a fundamentally *familiar* universe. The observer already has the codes necessary to understand what is happening. The world that Diaby reveals functions as *The Matrix*, a conspiracy to hide the truth. Just as Neo (who features in the videos) has the choice of taking a tablet that will let him see the truth, so too does the observer of the video. The references to *The Lord of the Rings* are equally pervasive: *The Return of the King* is the return of the Mahdi who will set in motion the final days; the band of faithful is al-Qaeda, while *The Two Towers* implies the twin towers, temples of adoration of money, destroyed by the 9/11 attacks. An aesthetic of *Assassins Creed* evokes the idea of assassins who cleanse the world of evil. Diaby's videos do not work at the level of intellectual propositions. Instead, they create a mood of foreboding and increasing tension, one where the observers discover themselves trapped in a pervasive conspiracy of false reality. What counts in these videos is their sensory structure, based on the tension between anxiety and release, with discovery serving to link the two.

Collective identity?

One of the key themes in the more sociological literature on the emergence of jihadist movements suggests that these can be analysed in terms of *collective identity*. This term played an important role in the North American sociology of social movements, with American scholars arguing that, as people became integrated into a new community, they began to develop a sense of 'we', such that the

'I' becomes fused with the 'we', with sociologists employing terms such as 'we-ness'. It is striking that in these videos we do not find a language of 'we', despite the recourse to the term *ummah*. In the material produced by Omar Diaby, actual people and their lives are absent. These are mythical stories, closer to the structure of computer games, using a perspective that locates the observer 'above' the action, creating a sense of power (Rose 2016). In Diaby's main film, a *History of Humanity*, viewers are reminded of their location as audience right from the beginning, with the introductory credits simulating as far as possible the 'sensory surround' of a modern cinema. As Thomson (2018) observes, the structure of the video demonstrates extraordinary narcissism – the history of humanity begins with the arrest and detention of Diaby, an event which takes up the first third of the film, after which an innocent child starts to speak of a world 'out of control' – beginning with the proposition that humans are descended from apes, and from there embracing the totality of the chaos of modern society, from consumerism, gay marriage, gay adoption, self-destructive drug use and the likely legalization of incest. These are all themes we noted in the experience of Ahmed above. The narrative here is not one of collective identity. Instead, the narrator of the film, speaking as a child, declares that he had 'no answers to his questions', again evoking Ahmed. The sense of being lost in something vast and disorienting is conveyed to the audience by the sound of a rapid heartbeat, of a person lost in the vastness: 'I had no answers to my questions. It was all too difficult, so I preferred to live a tranquil life' (19 HH History of Humanity, https://ia801600.us.archive.org/8/items/19HHRETOURAUXORIG INES/152214744.mp4, 30.24 mins).

These films generate a kind of sensory overload, held together with sound and image. In them, 'the Muslims' are referred to as a global category, defined by their experience of a global form of oppression that takes the form of twenty-first-century capitalism, above all the corruption and disorder it both creates and lives off. The solution to this oppression, captured in images of blown-up children, lies in jihad. The video presents a Muslim world arranged in two groups: the quietist Salafis, who say that the response to suffering and oppression is prayer, and then what Diaby refers to as 'our group' – those who practise jihad, against the governments of Muslim countries who have betrayed the *ummah*. These powerful traitors, governments and scholars, 'hide the truth'; they 'put the faithful to sleep in order to maintain the present system'. Here is the life-and-death struggle to reveal what is hidden in plain view – hence the importance of television images that we are all familiar with which, once they are put into a new format, reveal to us a truth hidden in plain sight. The relationship that the audience develops with these videos is described by Karim above as being 'hooked' ('they really got me'), caught in a relationship of *fascination*. Farhad Khosrokhavar (2017) points to the increasing incidence of this kind of fascination in experiences of radicalization, one that is particularly evident in prisons, where a significant 'number of psychologically fragile – even psychopathic and unstable – individuals are fascinated by radicalization' (2017: 129).

Diaby's videos can be seen as a jihadization of western and Islamic themes of apocalypse. Themes of apocalypse have played a role in all Abrahamic religions, as well as in different movements that are at times considered religious. In Japan in the 1990s, the Aum Shinrikyo sect believed that the end of the world was approaching, and it was the role of the sect to accelerate this by setting off a nuclear explosion (McDonald 2013). Different apocalyptic movements in the United States have sought to spark race wars that they believe will ignite the end of the world. As Filiu (2012) argues, currents within both Christian and Jewish movements today increasingly focus on the Middle East as a land of apocalyptic events, themes we find at the centre of Anwar al-Awlaki's videos. To the extent that we believe the world is coming to an end, other systems of value become fractured and disorganized, the day-to-day disappears or becomes insignificant.

If you love someone, you're going to say it

I was really impressed when I saw how handsome this guy was. When I saw his picture for the first time, I was jealous. This guy looks like what the prophet would have looked like. That inspired me and I wanted to copy him.

@BrotherOzzy, A tribute to my brother, Audioboom,
December 2013

On 16 December 2012, Ifthekar Jaman, a call-centre worker living in Portsmouth, England, streamed a video to his social media followers. It was not about politics nor religion but a tutorial about how to wear a turban, something he had been asked for several times in ask.fm. On 15 December 2013, a day short of a year later, he was killed in a firefight at Ghazwat-al-Khair in Syria. He had been in the country for seven months; for most of the time he had been, in the words of a close friend who accompanied him, an 'emir of the kitchen' (a cook). The day he was killed was the first time he had taken part in fighting. But at the time of his death he had thousands of social media followers, had appeared on BBC television and was described by the American magazine *Newsweek* as an 'icon to a generation of European Islamists' (Perry 2015). Many of his followers on Twitter publicly shared their grief at his death. One posted the audio tribute quoted above.

In his video, Jaman does more than show his followers how to wear a turban. He plays with his cat, he offers advice about how to apply kohl eyeliner or how to plait a beard, and shares the secrets of coconut oil (for the maintenance of long hair) and blackseed oil for his beard. He shows his audience his crossbow and later his sword, and, dressed in his turban, he looks like a character from *Prince of Persia* (http://www.ustream.tv/recorded/27779491). Throughout this demonstration, he calls on his audience to give him feedback, constantly checking his Twitter feed for audience reaction. Much of the time he spends giggling. He shifts the discussion to talk about his beard and how he shaves it:

> I used to shave it here a lot, to that to give it a shape. I heard it was ok to give it a shave here. But anyway, ah, I saw Osama bin-Laden, and he had loads of hair here too, so I kind of … I really like Osama bin-Laden I'll be honest. I mean, he looks like a nice guy. When you see pictures of him, he actually looks like a really nice guy. I don't know if you guys feel the same, but I think he looks like a genuine, like decent cool guy. So yeah, I um saw he kept the beard here [*points to upper cheek area*], he didn't shave it around here, nice turban style … I'm not saying anything bad about it, but I just prefer not to shave it here. It's a natural kind of flow, 'cos I saw Osama bin-Laden had it.

A woman sends him a direct message on Twitter. He responds by telling her that his advice will be useful for her husband. He is not of the strict Salafi view that he should refuse all contact with women who are not family members. Someone tweets: 'You can't just say you like Osama bin-Laden.' Ithefkar responds: 'Why? If you love someone, you're going to say it, innit? Don't worry it's cool man, Incahallah, we'll meet in Jannah, because I really believe he's there. Don't hate me, don't hate me.'

He then turns to ways of wearing a scarf: 'If you want to look like a ninja, just in case.' He wraps it around his head, so only his kohled eyes are visible, and the effect is of a woman wearing a hijab: 'I look like a hijabi [*laughing*]! Mate, I want to take a picture, make a new profile! Guys, guys, guys! I'm a guy, ok! Just … for fitna's sake, guys, I'm a guy.'

The phone rings, he takes the call:

Are you watching me? Do I, oh … do I look like a woman? Don't get attracted, right. [*Listening*] Did I tempt you, because … I am a male. I'm a male, yes, I'm sorry man, you can't, you can't … I don't have no sisters available either. [*Laughing*] Yeah, don't worry, you won't be getting sinful looking at me because I'm a male. [Laughing and addressing someone off camera]. That's so funny! [*Returns to camera*]. Yeah, don't worry, you won't be doing sin, you're all right man!'

Voice caller [*now on speaker phone*]:	'Show everyone your biceps!'
Ithfekar:	Huh?
Caller:	Show everyone your biceps!
Ithfekar:	Say it again?
Caller:	Show everyone your biceps!
Ithfekar:	I haven't got none.
Person off-camera:	You don't want to associate with guys like that.
Ithfekar to camera:	Is my hair cool? Do you guys like my hair?

This video, made four months before Jaman left Portsmouth to travel to Syria, offers an insight into the kind of sociability he shared with other young men. This is not a hyper-masculine world of fighters or violence; Jaman is making a video tutorial about how to wear a turban and apply eyeliner. He takes evident pleasure when he discovers himself looking like a woman, something that provokes one member of his audience to go beyond scoring him on Twitter to ringing him and confessing to being attracted to him. Jaman's reaction is not one of anger. He laughs; but a friend in the room warns him of the danger. This exchange points to a kind of sociability on the edges of homoeroticism, and a world constructed through social media where the intimate is central: how to plait one's hair, how to wear eyeliner, how to wear a turban. There are obvious similarities between this video and the video blogs of young women who share advice about fashion, hair and make-up. Jaman is having fun, laughing and giggling. When warned of the risks, his response is to ask his audience, 'Do you guys like my hair?'

In the months before he departed for Syria, Jaman posted short audio blogs. One highlights the extent to which his religiosity is embedded in a modern, indeed North American, paradigm, evident in his embrace of key themes of 'design', where he sets out to demonstrate 'how obvious it is that we have a creator'. He first begins by arguing that a mobile phone could not be simply created by accident. He goes on to argue:

> In the same manner, no one can say that the universe does not have a creator... . If you were to put all the galaxies together and you zoom out, you will see another design. Were all these designs made by accident, by a big bang and then everything went into place? That would be like saying a mobile phone [exists] by accident. If you admit that there is a creator for a mobile phone, you must also admit that there is a creator of the universe. Even more of a reason to believe that there is a creator of the universe, because it is much more detailed. (https://audioboom.com/posts/1090383-an-obvious-creator-god?playlist_direction=forward&t=0)

On 4 December, Jaman posts a link to a video of Anwar al-Awlaki on his Twitter feed. In it, al-Awlaki argues that a battle in the Arabian Peninsula is coming. It will be of momentous proportions: 'The great jihad of the Arabian Peninsula will begin, the base from which the greatest army of Islam will march forth.' Echoes once again of *Lord of the Rings* and Omar Diaby, but this time posted by a young man who explores who he is with eyeliner and who 'loves' bin Laden.

It takes my breath away

I discussed a shared imaginary at work in Ahmed's discovery of secret knowledge, in the visual grammar of Omar Diaby's videos and in Jaman's preoccupation with intelligent design and the scale of the universe. We get a sense of how this 'works' in two tweets that Jaman makes in January 2013. He posts an image of galaxies, one that emphasizes the scale of the universe, with the observer looking up into the infinite vastness of the heavens. He writes, 'If this takes my breath away, what will seeing Allah do to us??! I really want this so bad, I really want to please Allah.' He follows this with another tweet on the same day, this time with an image of huge mountains. He writes: 'Our Lord created high mountains & many stars, what are we? Nothing, we are nothing. Yet we can please him, Subhanallah' (Twitter, 4 January 2013).

These images convey the enormity, power and majesty of the universe, with the viewer positioned looking up into the vastness in a way that takes one's breath away. There is a sense of vertigo here, of standing on the edge of something massive, of being swallowed up. What we have here is the theme of 'the sublime', a theme that emerges in the European Romantic movement, when poets and artists developed a new sensibility and alertness to the power, majesty and also terror of nature, closely linked to the search for self within European culture. In all these images of extraordinary power, there is danger. These images are about a sensory reaction rather than an attempt to represent reality.

The Romantic Movement was in part a reaction to the rationalism of the Enlightenment, but it was also a movement exploring sources of selfhood, in particular through encounters with nature which came to be experienced in new ways (Taylor 1989). Murray Roston, whose work centres on the search for selfhood in modern literature, notes that Romantic poets set out to experience power, creativity and awe in nature, often understood as divine creativity, from where they suggested that such creativity could also be located within the self. For the Romantics, extending the ways we can experience nature extended the ways we can experience ourselves. This new Romantic sensibility is also pointed to by the literary theorist Thomas Weiskel, who explores the transformation of the word 'vast': while remaining a descriptor of size and scale, this increasingly became understood as a 'metaphor for the imaginative capabilities of the viewer himself who, absorbing, as it were, the infinitude of the natural scene, expands his own creative facilities to share their limitlessness' (quoted in Roston 1996: 378).

The concept of 'the sublime' that arose from this cultural movement may help us understand certain dimensions of the culture of the contemporary jihad. The term 'sublime' was first used by the Anglo-Irish philosopher Edmund Burke who, like many of his contemporaries, was interested in understanding passions and emotions. He understood the sublime as a response to powerful ideas of pain or threat in cases where one is not in actual danger as such – the sublime thus operating in a way 'analogous to terror ... productive of the strongest emotions which the mind is capable of feeling' (Burke 2008 [1757]: 36). Anne Mellor summarizes Burke's argument, pointing to the way he suggests that the experience of the sublime leads to an experience of the Deity:

> Confronted with such overwhelming objects as the Alps, huge dark caves, a blinding sunset, or a towering gloomy ruin, the human mind first experiences terror or fear, then – as our instinct of self-preservation is gradually relaxed – astonishment, admiration, reverence and respect

... from the aesthetic contemplation of a sublime landscape, one is led to a sensible impression of the Deity by whose power such magnificent scenes are created. (Mellor 1993: 86)

For Burke, the sublime is attached to categories of landscape, where awe and terror are followed by reverence and awareness of the infinite that they inspire, all themes we see in Jaman's tweets above. For the Romantic authors, the sublime becomes a 'mode of "seeing and feeling"' (Mellor 1996). For Wordsworth, the sublime involves a feeling of 'intense unity' with nature, where 'the self-conscious mind can be overwhelmed by the power of the sublime [and] effectively loses self-awareness [as it is] led to an experience of participation in awesome, immeasurable and enduring power' (Mellor 1996: 229–30). This Romantic tradition emphasizes that looking at something is not simply taking in visual information and processing it but is a *mode of embodied engagement*. The Enlightenment philosopher Emmanuel Kant agreed with the Romantics that the sublime is a mode of feeling and experience, not a characteristic of landscape or the natural world. But where the Romantics pointed to the presence of images of might and awe, proposing a fusion of self and the infinite, Kant argued that the experience of the sublime is associated with the *inability* to produce meaning when confronted with such images or experiences. Instead of this anxiety being reconciled within theories of 'oneness', as in the Romantic tradition, Kant points to an experience where powerful and opposed emotions are experienced at the same time: where we experience the 'inadequacy of our imagination' (Ginsbourg 2014), where the encounter with something so great and overwhelming constitutes an 'outrage on the imagination', where in the absence of 'anything leading to particular objective principles' we find instead 'chaos' and the 'wildest and most irregular disorder and desolation' (Kant 2007 [1914]: 63).

From this perspective, the sublime involves not a fusion into the infinite, but a quite different type of experience, 'the mind's confrontation with an idea too large for expression, too self-consuming to be contained in any adequate form of representation', where what we find instead is 'the desire to present that which is unpresentable' (Mishra 1994: 20). The literary theorist Vijay Mishra suggests that this desire is at the centre of the movement of gothic literature of the Romantic imagination in stories of vampires and ghosts, dark castles, ruins, graveyards and desolation, all involving 'an unamenable dread', a source of fascination that brings with it the threat of a symbolic blockage, one that 'threatens subjectivity itself' (Mishra

1994: 19–20) – something that Jaman hints at when he writes 'we are nothing'. Such dread and fascination are at the centre of the video world constructed by Diaby. Thomas Weiskel (1976) suggests that the sublime experience is one where conventional systems of meaning break down, an experience so intense as to produce an experience of 'temporary aphasia', where speech fails. As Jaman describes it, the awe of the universe leaves him breathless. But his encounter with the majesty of the universe does not lead him to think of himself as all powerful, but to ask 'what will seeing Allah' feel like? For Jaman, this cannot happen in life, only in death.

A month before his turban tutorial, Jaman reposts another image to Twitter. This is a screenshot of text on martyrdom, entitled the *Burial of the Martyrs*. It reads 'Allah's Messenger supervised the martyrs' burial and said: "I bear witness that anyone who is wounded in the way of Allah. Allah will resurrect him on the Day of Resurrection with his wound bleeding a liquid which is blood-like in colour and musk-like in scent."' The screenshot was circulated with the message, 'If ever on the battlefield, do dua that you get shot by many bullets as possible ☺.' Jaman retweets, adding 'I do!' (Twitter, 8 November 2012).

Shirk, power and fear

These themes of vastness and disorientation, and the potential for loss of self, offer us ways of thinking about the place of death within the jihadist imaginary. There are, however, few discussions of the place that *fear* might occupy within experiences of radicalization. In one case that led to the killing of a man in the British city of Rochdale in 2016, fear appears to have played a critical role.

Jalal Uddin was a 71-year-old imam in the British city of Rochdale. On a late February evening in 2016, he was making his way home from evening prayers at his local mosque. As he was crossing a park, he was attacked by two men, one wielding hammer blows to the head, face and mouth. The assailant's accomplice was 21-year-old Mohammed Hussain Syeedy, previously an engineering student at a local university. The victim was originally from Bangladesh, locally known as a 'spiritual healer' who practised taweez, or Ruqyah in Arabic, a South Asian practice involving wearing amulets or small lockets containing written prayers or quotations from the Qur'an to ward off ill health and to offer protection from evil spirits. Syeedy was later arrested and convicted, while his accomplice fled to Turkey and is believed to have travelled to Syria. At his trial, evidence tendered indicated that Syeedy was part of a group who had been keeping Uddin under surveillance for several months and discussing him at length in WhatsApp chats, referring to him as 'Voldemort' and 'the magician'. They believed that the practice of using amulets to ward off evil spirits was an example of 'shirk' (black magic). This belief is the product of a social process, constructed through a series of shared activities. Syeedy and his friends would spend days following the imam, and photographing themselves and circulating the images as they did so. Those featuring Seedy included him wearing a military-style kevlar vest outside the mosque; in another he holds a black ISIS-style flag outside the mosque, in another he is holding the flag over a street sign that has been altered to read 'war zone'. He and his friends are constructing a kind of imaginary world where they are fighters undertaking 'raids', tracking a sorcerer. In June 2015, the WhatsApp group was discussing taweez, one asking 'is that Taweez', another member replying 'Yh, disgusting', alerting us once again to the social construction of disgust. By August, the group was focusing on Mr Uddin, one of its members sending Syeedy a message, 'just currently doing a Taweez raid with xxx'. This 'raid' involved theft of a book Mr Uddin used that was kept at the mosque. A second message was sent to Seedey, 'found [the] stash', to which he responded, 'Burn it'. The person who had the material sent a further WhatsApp message to Syeedy: 'destroying it'. Syeedy's reply was 'Allahu Akbar'. The stolen book proved difficult to burn so it was stored under water, before it was thrown into a stream. In his testimony, Seedy describes the book in the following way:

> In my view, the images in that book were inappropriate according to the teachings of Islam, so these can be quite dangerous. When people are involved in Taweez, they are involved in the supernatural. So it's easy to cause harm in these situations.
> By ripping it up and putting it in water and throwing it away, it would destroy the spirits and that kind of thing. (Court transcript, quoted in *Manchester Evening News*, 5 September 2016, available at http://www.manchestereveningnews.co.uk/news/greater-manchester-news/jalal-uddin-murder-trial-live-11842450)

In Syria, ISIS engaged in destroying what it considered to be 'shirk', or accessing forbidden forms of supernatural power – pulverizing ancient cities such as Palmyra, smashing museums (while also plundering them for sale on the black market). Much effort was directed to destroying popular forms of religiosity, such as praying at the graves of saints buried in mosques. This destruction played an important role in the activities of many Europeans who joined ISIS, who would post videos and accounts of the destruction of graves to social media. The public execution of 'sorcerers' was part of this. In July 2014, Reyad Kahn, a young man from Cardiff who had joined ISIS, was tweeting about executions he claimed to be involved in. On 17 July, he tweeted: 'We killed the JN amir in deir whilst dressed as a woman trying to escape. You die the way you live and this guys dress had sequins.' Later that same day, he tweeted an image of artefacts with the attached text: 'Some of the sihr we found in the JN emirs house' (pic.twitter.com/wtcLnGnAoC). This tweet would be found the following year on Seedey's phone in Rochdale. Evidence presented in court showed that Seedey had also downloaded material on Jinn, including the details of a seminar on the 'World of Jinn'.

Like others chronicled in this book, Seedey constructs a narrative of himself through making and sharing images. The affective grammar of these communications is pleasure and risk, excitement, fear and the frisson of danger. Almost every stage of this process was undertaken through social media, allowing a close reconstruction. Surveillance, 'following', circulated images, selfies at different stages, photographs with ISIS images – including ISIS arm patches, ISIS flags, the single-finger salute practised by jihadists, the references to 'taweez raid', a street sign amended from 'traffic zone' to 'war zone', all documented in mobile phone images – suggest an experience somewhere between that of a football supporter and an aspiring jihadist. As in Diaby's videos, the familiar becomes unfamiliar, strange and threatening, so much so that a former engineering student will transport a book in a bucket of water to ensure that the power of the spirits present in it cannot cause harm.

Mediated memories

On 17 February 2015, three girls, aged 15 and 16, boarded a plane at London's Gatwick Airport to travel first to Turkey and then to Syria where they planned to live in 'the Islamic State'. Within two months, the three were married to foreign fighters who had also travelled to Syria. Like most 15-year-olds in Europe, their world is fundamentally made up of friends, one in which social media are best understood not as a transmitter but as a habitat (Mitchell 2005: 208). For these young girls, as for Seedey and his friends, circulating images among friends is central to their experience. Joanne Garde-Hansen explores such practices, arguing that in contemporary societies the mobile phone is less and less a technology to 'be in constant contact', and more one through which young people in particular construct a *way of being*. The circulation of images plays a key role in this process. These do not constitute a closed photo album with its linear narrative but increasingly form the basis for what Garde-Hansen, drawing on Ashuri, calls 'joint memory' – memory that is shared and accessible to 'members of a community who were absent from the occurrences in time, in space, or both' (Ashuri 2011: 106). The relationship between the personal and the public is increasingly produced through what the media theorist José van Dijck calls 'mediated memories', or the 'activities and objects we produce and appropriate by means of media technologies, for creating and re-creating a sense of *past, present and future of ourselves* in relation to others' (van Dijck 2007: 21; in Garde-Hansen 2013: 90, emphasis added).

Social media and associated producing and circulating images have become a means through which we construct 'shared stories of being and becoming' (Garde-Hansen 2013: 90). Today's circulation of images immerses us 'in a default archive or montage of embodied, fragmentary and episodic lives' that Garde-Hansen refers to as 'networked memory' (Garde-Hansen 2013: 91). This means our relationship to memory, and to the boundaries that constitute *my experience*, are both becoming more fluid. The American historian Alison Landsberg points to a transformation in the social production of memory, arguing that during the twentieth century memory became 'prosthetic', increasingly being produced 'at the interface between a person and a historical narrative about the past'. Memory, she argues, is no longer fundamentally transmitted through family and generations; instead, it emerges at what she calls 'experiential sites', such as cinemas or museums. This, she argues, is what happens:

> In this moment of contact, an experience occurs through which the person sutures himself or herself into a larger history ... the person does not simply apprehend a historical narrative, but takes on a more personal, deeply felt memory of a past event through which he or she did not live. The resulting prosthetic memory has the ability to shape that person's subjectivity and politics. (Landsberg 2004: 2)

We can see this transformation at work in social media, where what Landsberg calls 'experiential sites' are giving way to new types of networked experience. What Landsberg calls prosthetic memories are increasingly experienced *through the body* as a result of engagement with cultural technologies. She writes:

> Prosthetic memories become part of one's personal archive of experience, informing one's subjectivity as well as one's relationship to the present and future tenses. Made possible by advanced capitalism and an emergent commodified mass culture capable of widely disseminating images and narratives about the past, these memories are not 'natural' or 'authentic' and yet they organise and energise the bodies and subjectivities that take them on. (2004: 26)

Landsberg captures a significant transformation that occurred during the twentieth century, where the creation and circulation of memory has shifted from community rituals and generation relations to new cultural technologies able to generate powerful embodied experiences. Understanding this at work today is fundamental to any attempt to understand contemporary radicalization, as we see in the experience of these three girls.

Sisters

For the three girls who left London for Syria in 2015, sharing images is a way of sharing feelings and, through responses, experiencing something together. In December, one of them visits a well-known chain store that sells waffles and ice cream; she tweets a picture of her plate of waffle, two ice creams and cream, with the text 'They do the best chocolate waffles,' together with emojis of faces with hearts. She posts an image of the food she is about to eat, sharing the pleasure of anticipation. She frequently tweets about trainers. She asks her followers if she should buy a pair of Vans. She tweets a photo of her feet wearing a pair of Nikes, adding 'Bun [*forget*] huaraches, it's all about air forces.' She is part of contemporary culture where who we are is shaped by our consumer preferences, where we are the sum of our 'likes'. Her language is that of young people. She tweets an image of the Premier League football table, complete with fist-pump emojis and hearts when her team reaches the top of the table. She posts a selfie showing off her brightly painted nails. She's confident, connected and expressive; she is part of western youth culture.

This girl also explores other themes in her posts, and in the process constructs other 'ways of feeling'. A month before departing, she posts an image of a book written by the medieval scholar Ibn

Taymiyyah, *The Friends of Allah and the Friends of Shaytan*, together with an emoticon of open-mouthed amazement. Ibn Taymiyyah's writings appear regularly in jihadist posts, not as a source of discussion but as an authority to be heard. The book argues that humanity is polarized into two groups, those close to God and those close to Satan, and that those close to God will necessarily embrace jihad. A few days earlier, she had been tweeting about 'the hypocrites', people who are all alike, bidding vice and forbidding virtue. Her tweets make no secret of the fact that she is concerned about a deeply polarized world, but they do more than describe the world in these terms. They are part of *shaping her experience of the world*. But unlike Aqsa Mahmood, she is not tweeting about impure Shia as a source of danger and contamination. She is focused on sincerity, or Ikhlas. It is the *sincere* who are opposed to the *hypocrites*: 'Ikhlas is so so so important. The prophet (PBUH) said "a group of my UMMAH will continue to prevail and they will never be harmed by those who forsake them, until the hour begins"' (9 February 2015).

The pure, according to her, are destined to prevail despite the attempts by others to harm them. But how does she identify with this group? Not through revulsion at the grotesque. This young girl constructs a sensory world of images in which *beauty* becomes a way to experience innocence and purity, posting an image on 17 January, a month before her departure, of African girls in white hijabs, alongside the caption: 'Never seen this much beauty in picture [*hearts emoji*] ALLAHUMABARIK.' She contrasts such images with others detailing suffering as the violation of innocence. Another image she posts is taken from the World Exposition held in Belgium in 1958, where different countries established exhibitions to illustrate their way of life. In this case, the image is from an 'African village', the tweet entitled 'human zoo'. It is clearly racist, showing an African girl seemingly in an enclosure, watched by a crowd of white people. A woman in the watching crowd is offering the child something to eat, which the text attached to the tweet describes as a banana. She tweets: 'I feel so sick, the cruelty is in believable [*sic*]. Look at the date not even that long ago' (Twitter, 15 February 2015). Memory of an event in which she did not participate has become her own, in this case established through a 'truth of the body' – 'I feel so sick'. Her response to both these images is one of tenderness. It is important to note that the images she posts are of young girls who are still children. She herself is fifteen, no longer a child but also not yet an adult, and it is significant that she is constructing an emotional register in relation to childhood innocence. This is captured in particular by the 'African village' image, where the child photographed clearly does not recognize the oppressive situation she is part of: she is too young and innocent.

The girl does not discuss these images beyond her brief tweets. But together with others they contribute to a 'structure of feeling' that highlights and associates innocence, beauty and purity, serving to create a world of feelings in which she can explore who she is. We can see this in two types of images that she tweets. The first is the love of sisters, a theme that becomes increasingly important as she approaches her departure. The images are of the girls together in a London park, in one image standing together on a bench, in another sitting together. Under the first image, she comments 'we thought we were prestige so we stood on the bench,' following this with a fist-pump emoji. She entitles the second 'Akhwaat' (sisters), followed by love hearts to celebrate an adolescent fusion into a peer group, in this case an Islamic sisterhood or *Akhwaat*. She receives a response from a follower who offers more love hearts, together with the affirmation *Maa Sha Allah* (what Allah wants) and 'Adorable'. She responds 'thanks', together with two emojis: a V for victory, together with 'crying because it's too beautiful'.

These images and emoji evoke an experience that is important to understand. Psychologists and psychiatrists of adolescence point out that the transition from childhood not only involves separation from parents but new types of fusion with the peer group. Philippe Gutton underlines the importance of a culture of 'peace and love' in an adolescent experience that largely remains emotional, without necessarily being translated into action. But he also points to the potential role of a kind of religious experience in such fusions, one evoking the origins of the word in the Latin *religare*, which means 'to bind together' or 'link'. Where a fusional dynamic is associated with religious experience, Gutton (2015: 17) suggests, adolescent co-identity can be lived as a kind of intimate relationship with a shared partner who is both present and absent. An experience of fusion with the group is combined with an implicit reference to a 'great Other, common to you and me', where that great shared 'other', God, comes to symbolize love, lived as a kind of mystical experience, one that does not find words but also one that does not threaten to destabilize the group through jealousy.

This young girl doesn't tweet about the grotesque or fearful events. She tweets about beauty but where the experience of beauty is vulnerable, under threat in a world divided between the *sincere* and the *hypocrites*. A month before leaving, she tweets a verse from the Qur'an about hypocrites: 'The hypocrites, males and females, are all alike. They bid vice and forbid virtue ... they forgot Allah, so He forgot them. Surely, the hypocrites are the sinners' (Twitter, 16 January 2015). In the week before she leaves, she tweets in succession: 'I feel I don't belong in this era' and 'Imagine living at the time of the prophet sub han Allah: Ibn Taymiyyah said: 'The distinctive attribute between the believer and the hypocrite is: Sincerity' (Twitter, 8 February 2015).

The tweets about *belonging* to the group of sisters are mirrored by *not-belonging* to 'this era'. Belonging/not-belonging is one of the matrixes around which youth experience is constructed in western society. It is central to social transitions to adulthood. She overlays these with the categories of *hypocrisy* and *sincerity*: the sincere do not belong to this era. Tweets about Muslim oppression certainly figure in her timeline. In January, she retweets an image of a mosque fire in Houston in the United States, a result of arson, together with a list of attacks against Muslims in the United States and Canada. But this theme is by no means central, just as Syria is not central. The focus is much more about her and her experience of belonging/not-belonging.

There is, however, a further crucial element in 'not-belonging', one we see in an image that this young girl tweets a month before she went to Syria (Figure 3.1). It is an image of herself, focused on her beloved trainer shoes. At first it seems there is nothing else but her and the surface she is standing on. But she adds the word 'Waiting ['Waiting..']' to the image. Through this, anticipation is created and shared. It becomes an experience of pleasure, one where 'not-belonging' is lived as desire, socially constituted through the shared action of waiting.

Another dimension to her experience is revealed in a series of tweets a week before her departure, where she is reacting to a discussion with someone, possibly about her decision to move to Syria.

Ugrh jahils [*stop emoji*]
Quick to make conclusions without knowledge all of a sudden think you are qualified ... Kk.
Sometimes staying quite [*sic*] is better than debating with a fool.
(Twitter, 10 February 2015)

The term 'jahils' refers to someone who is living in the state of ignorance that characterized the world before the advent of the Qur'an. The term's closest English-language equivalent would be 'heathen' or 'unholy ignorance'. The tweet 'Ugrh jahils', combined with the hand facing outwards, affirms that she does not need to listen to something

Figure 3.1 Waiting .. Twitter, 18 January 2015.

that she finds disgusting. She is part of a world of privileged knowledge, and those who do not have access to this knowledge are jahils;
they are fools living in a state of unholy ignorance. She not only turns
her back on them, she is confident of her superiority. The next day
she makes clear her intention to depart, tweeting a formulaic declaration widely used among jihadists: 'MAKE DUA FOR ME, REALLY
NEED IT. PRAY ALLAH GRANTS ME THE HIGHTEST
RANKS IN JANNAH, MAKES ME SINCERE IN MY WORSHIP
AND KEEPS ME STEADFAST' (Twitter, 11 February 2015).

This young girl has constructed a sensory world, one that is notably
different from that of Aqsa Mahmood, for whom disgust at the grotesque allows the construction of a world divided between purity
and impurity. It is also different from that of Ahmed and his search
for order in a world of disorder. Rather than focus on what she per-
ceives as ugliness, this young girl links beauty, vulnerable innocence
and truth – in each case, around images of young girls who are still
children – the innocent beauty of schoolgirls and that of a girl trapped
in a 'human zoo'. It may be significant that in both these cases, the
innocence of these girls is linked to a kind of beauty that does not

aim to please men. This is echoed by her followers who send her love hearts and comments such as 'adorable' on her images of 'sisters'.

On the day before she leaves, she retweets a story about the vulnerability and protection of women. Given that it took seven tweets to tell the story, on the day before her departure for Syria, this merits an exploration:

The story of Mu'tasim and the black and white horses

1. A Muslim woman is captured and put in prison & a Roman kafir slaps her. She shouts and cries 'O Mu'tasim [*Caliph*] where are you?'
2. When she says this, the kafir laughs and says 'yes, indeed your man Mu'tasim is coming. He's coming in a black and white horse to save you.
3. When this news reached Mu'tasim, he purchased seventeen thousand black & white horses. Mu'tasim dispatches the army (commander is Mu'tasim).
4. And they go towards the kuffars land, where the kuffars army is defeated and crushed. The Muslim woman and the kafir are brought to Mu'tasim.
5. Mu'tasim says to the woman, 'Tell this kafir that Mu'tasim has come on a black and white horse to save you.' (Twitter, 14 February 2015)

This story circulates widely on different internet sites but it clearly means a lot for her to tweet it on the day before her departure. It evokes the theme of the vulnerable woman in need of a protector, just as the image of the girl imprisoned in the human zoo. And in this case it is the benevolent power of the ruler who will spend enormous sums to protect a woman at risk. The story she evokes focuses on the power of the Caliph, but this then translates into a decision to move to Syria to marry a fighter who occupies the same protector role within this imaginary. This is why there is never any question that she is travelling to Syria to marry a Syrian and create a new society there. She is going to marry a fighter, someone who has dedicated his life to the protection of the vulnerable, just as did the Caliph.

After completing the story, she tweets a final quotation from Ibn Taymiyyah: '"Whoever desires everlasting bliss, let him adhere firmly to the threshold of servitude." Ibn Taymiyah. SO BEAUTIFUL AND ACCURATE.' This is one of her last tweets before leaving the United Kingdom and, once again, she links beauty and truth.

She does not define herself as a freedom fighter but as someone who 'desires everlasting bliss', the path to which is through unconditionally serving something or someone infinitely more powerful. For this young girl, purity is a quality of the vulnerable single girl, one that locates her in a relationship of dependence upon a masculine power. There are the two poles that recur in the images she creates: fusion into the group of sisters; and the vulnerable purity of the single girl. This tension appears reconcilable only through the potency and power of the Caliph, whose love and protection can be shared while maintaining the sisterhood. Here, we see a radicalization pathway not constructed around awe and fear, nor order and disorder, but around imagined bliss in relation to a shared and powerful other.

Between the uncanny and bliss

The paths we see in this chapter vary, but certain tensions and themes recur. While present in different ways, none of these paths appear to be a response to the suffering of Muslim communities, or what we might call 'Islamophobia'. What does recur, however, are themes of order and disorder, configured in different ways. Ahmed highlights personal disorder – drinking, disorientation after being left by his girlfriend – combined with what he sees as a moral disorder resulting from a collapse of social order: fornication at the age of sixteen, no respect for parents, crime and violence. He describes the shock of discovery of a hidden reality, first revealed through scientific proofs in the Qur'an, then reaffirmed through dreams that allow him to predict events. But despite the order he has been able to embrace, Shaytan remains ever present in the form of the attraction of a spliff, an attraction that promises to send him back into the world he has left. The only option is the implementation of sharia to silence the chaos once and for all.

The theme of disorder is equally central to the world constructed by Diaby, but this time on an epic scale. The world is populated by spirits and devils; threat is ever present. The familiar images of television news hide within them portentous meanings. Here is a theme that recurs throughout this book: *the familiar is shown to conceal a hidden meaning, one that puts into question the previous certainties that structure our lives.* There is no 'argument' built up by evidence in Diaby's videos, while their use of television news images means that observers experience the events they report as 'true'. But the relationship that the audience develops with them is one of becoming 'trapped', caught in a relationship of 'fascination'. Similar themes are evoked in the way that Ifthekar Jaman communicates his encounter with the sublime – something so vast and so awesome that it is beyond comprehension and produces aphasia, an inability to speak when confronted with something so terrible – 'this takes my breath away.'

Anthropologists, more than sociologists or political scientists, have focused on attempting to understand the sublime as a form of social practice. James Siegel explores the wave of witch killings that occurred in Indonesia in the months following the collapse of the Suharto regime in 1998, exploring the mixture of rage and fear involved when mobs invaded the houses of 'sorcerers' and brutally killed them. Siegel argues that the collapse of the state centre created a deep uncertainty, leaving people at the mercy of 'undefined power'. 'Amid this confusion, "naming the witch" seemed to offer some sort of foothold', affirming one's own identity as 'not witch' (2005: 160, 189). In Kant's classical discussion, the sublime involves an experience of nature that produces a sense of awe that is so overwhelming that the person lacks words to express it, as illustrated by Jaman. But this experience can be an important, positive dimension of the *construction* of subjectivity: 'a person's confrontations with the sublime and the subsequent struggle to define the limits of one's powers of cognition are vital to the crystallization of self-consciousness' (Geschiere 2013: 174).

Such experiences of the limits of our cognitive powers can strengthen subjectivity: 'our powers of cognition help us also realise their limits; an experience that seems to be borderless is contained and ordered' (Geschiere 2013: 174). For Kant and the Romantic Movement, while the sublime was certainly dangerous, it was also containable. But in cases of sudden social collapse, as with the Suharto regime in Indonesia, or more chronic forms of social crisis, such as the 'collapse of the future' evident in parts of Africa today (Piot 2010), the danger remains present. In such cases, argues Geschiere, 'when people are not capable of bringing closure to the experience of the awesome, the sublime turns into the *uncanny*' (Geschiere 2013: 174, emphasis added). And here he turns to Freud, for whom 'the uncanny is closely linked to the familiar: *what is so frightening is the familiar turned weird*' (2013: 177, emphasis added).

What we have seen in this chapter are not experiences of religious conversion, but social logics of fear, discovery and embodied imagination. Personal transformations are central. These are associated with a kind of experience lived as the discovery of a reality that is both disturbing and threatening, but also one that opens out a new world. In some cases, there is significant evidence suggesting a kind of fear, evident in Seedey's fear of the power of spirits in a stolen book. Ifthekar Jaman captures an experience close to the western model of the sublime, of awe that takes the breath away, linked to an experience of desire that we will explore later. Omar Diaby creates a world peopled by supernatural beings such as Jinn, but the door to that world is one where the mundane becomes an experience that unsettles, a door opening out to an extraordinary battle. On walking through that door, one's life takes on a new significance. Most of these accounts underline transformation when confronted by a vast reality.

The anthropologist Talal Asad argues that to understand contemporary religious experience, we need what he calls 'ethnographies of the human body'. By this, he means the body's 'attitude to pain, physical damage, decay and death, as well as to bodily integrity, growth and enjoyment, to the conditions that isolate persons and things or connect them strongly with others'. He goes on to ask 'What architecture of the senses – hearing, seeing, smelling, touching, tasting – do particular attitudes and sensibilities depend on? How (whether through projects or fortuitous developments) do new sensory perceptions take shape and make older ways of engaging with the world (older experiences) and older political forms *irrelevant*?' (Asad 2012: 51).

If the experiential grammar of Diaby, Seedey, Amhed and Jaman is constructed around disturbing events, hidden meanings and vastness, the fragments of experience we can construct in relation to the girls who travelled to Syria in 2015 also points to a fusion, not into an epic drama but into a world of friends who share the love of a powerful other. The girls are not watching alarming videos or musing about awe and death, but the tweets we have explored suggest a kind of memory experience, where the beauty and suffering of innocents become theirs and, in the process, so too does the urgency of protection in a world where sincerity means not belonging. This is an experience that is formed around the intimate rather than the epic, beauty rather than the grotesque, innocence rather than guilt, bliss rather than fear. But it is no less powerful.

In this chapter, we have met embodied imaginaries and the fundamentally social and communicative nature of their construction. Asad reminds us that our experience of the world is partly 'sensuous-emotional' and partly 'intellectual'. We sense the world, he argues, before we turn to interpreting it. Much of the discussion of counter-narrative in the field of radicalization has focused on ideas and ideologies, leading observers like Gilles Kepel (2015) to claim that the global reach of theorists of jihad is the key to understanding radicalization. This chapter suggests a quite different logic at work. Rather than lengthy tracts and lectures, we find experiences that expand, but also fundamentally disturb, what is sensed and how it is sensed. These experiences range from fascination, anxiety, awe, vertigo and dread to a promise of bliss that will allow individual love within a fusion experience. To borrow from Asad, in this chapter we saw sensory perceptions and memories that make previous ways of engaging with the world irrelevant or so dangerous that they threaten life itself.

4

Mediating Violence: Filming the Self

If you're watching this, I'm probably dead, or I'm probably like a legend or something.

> Aseel Muthana, self-recorded video, 2014, two months before travelling from Cardiff to Syria

Being in the world

We saw in chapter 1 that much popular discussion of the relationship between social media and radicalization is framed in terms of ideas such as 'recruitment', 'indoctrination' or 'grooming'. This draws on older theories of media, understood in terms of a sender–receiver relationship, where a sender generates and communicates ideas or images, which are then received by an audience (Castells 2013). This approach is organized in terms of a dichotomy of 'active' and 'passive' and sets out to understand the 'impact' of the media. This approach to media and society evolved in the middle of the twentieth century as social scientists began to grapple with what they saw as the impact of emerging 'mass media'. At the time, one of the key questions explored was the role of the media in Nazi Germany, where it was argued that the Nazi use of radio was key to Hitler's rise to power (Adorno 1991). In the experiences we have begun to explore, a model based on a sender–receiver paradigm does not work. The types of communication seen here point instead to *forms of sociality* (Couldry 2012; McDonald 2015).

The Spanish sociologist Amparo Lasén points to a key dimension of this change by highlighting the importance of images and the visual to contemporary social life. She does so through considering the different nature of images that people circulate today. She begins with an analysis of domestic photography undertaken by Guy Stricherz in his beautiful book of images, *Americans in Kodachrome, 1945–65* (2002). Stricherz examines two decades of American domestic photography from 500 American families. Here, we see a significant pattern. Among the 100,000 pictures of domestic and personal life he examined, fewer than a hundred were self-portraits (Lasén and Gómez-Cruz 2009: 209). These photographs taken between 1945 and 1965 were fundamentally shaped by the *roles* that people occupied, the great majority being images of domestic life capturing images of parent and child. This book demonstrates the visual imagination of the American post-war institutional family, evident in the way the overwhelming majority of the photos are 'posed' for the camera as people set out to represent themselves in terms of the social roles they occupy.

Today's 'visual grammar' is radically different. Where Stricherz finds fewer than one in a thousand photos is a self-portrait, today's digital photography has a massive proportion of such photos, a social phenomenon recognized by the *Oxford English Dictionary* making 'selfie' the 'word of the year' in 2013. In 2009, Lasén found more than 12,000 groups dedicated to different forms of self-portrait on the photo-sharing site Flickr, a development signalling the extraordinary expansion of self-filming, from You Tube to video diaries, as well as the explosion of websites and platforms associated with an increasing upload culture, from activism (McDonald 2006) to pornography or what has been called 'cyber-exhibitionism' (Lasén and Gómez-Cruz 2009). On such sites, it is not unusual for a person to upload hundreds or even thousands of self-portraits. These are not simply visual representations 'reporting' a news event. Rather, taking, uploading and curating photos of oneself has become a form of agency epitomizing what sociologists call *individuation*: this practice of making oneself visible is one element in a process of self-construction, increasingly part of social practices to generate recognition, which Lasén and Gómez-Cruz suggest are a 'guarantee of the subject's being' (2009: 214). Such photos and the visual practices associated with them represent a new type of relationship between public and private, most evident in the increasing proportion of photos taken in intimate locations, in particular bathrooms and bedrooms.

Such communication increasingly creates a form of 'intimate visual co-presence' (Ito 2005), enabling new practices of 'being' with others. When a person takes and shares a picture of an everyday experience, such as what they are about to eat for lunch, they are not seeking to transmit the 'meaning' of that experience; they are constituting a 'sensation' through the action of sharing it with others. Taking a photo of a plate of food and sharing it, for example, turns an otherwise solitary act of eating into the social act of a meal (Kaufmann 2010). By sharing images of food, we are involving others in the construction of *our* experience of eating. These practices highlight contemporary ways of 'being-in-the-world' and the decisive role played by sensation, a development captured by the French philosopher Gilles Deleuze when he argues 'we become in the sensation and something happens through the sensation' (Deleuze 1981: 31).

Taking photos and circulating images is central to contemporary radicalization, but dominant approaches to radicalization offer little insight into this practice. It is very hard to suggest that problems within Islam can explain the extraordinary importance of social media in experiences of radicalization. Equally, accounts constructed in terms of western foreign policy, marginalization or Islamophobia offer us little insight. We need instead to construct tools to begin to understand the social media practices that have become central to jihadist cultures.

Ecstatic violence

The killings undertaken by 23-year-old Mohamed Merah in the French cities of Toulouse and Montauban in 2012 illustrate the same visual imaginary. Merah killed three off-duty soldiers at a cash machine outside a military barracks, and several days later shot a teacher and three children leaving a Jewish school, the youngest three years old. Before these killings, he purchased a wearable HD video camera. He filmed the killings, collating them into a video, and attempted to upload them to social media. When this failed because of the file size, he transferred the images to a memory stick, mailing it to a television station. Merah was killed at the end of a 32-hour siege. During this time, negotiations between Merah and the police took place. These were recorded and are available for analysis (*Libération* 2012). Merah, like many jihadists, came from a background of low-level criminality. His father had been imprisoned for cannabis trafficking, while his brother had also been imprisoned for drug trafficking as well as violence. Merah himself had a history of violence. He had been placed in care from six years of age, and as he grew up was involved in a series of violent incidents, including reportedly punching a social worker in the face when told he could not spend a weekend with his family. His judicial background included cases of violent aggression towards young girls and teachers, and his mother also brought charges against him. When he reached the age of 18, he had 14 convictions, having been arrested for offences including purse snatching, burglary and aggravated robbery, which had led to two periods in prison. In 2007, he was part of a group who carried out a 'home-jacking' using a stolen 4x4 car – escaping by driving at more 180 km per hour. People who knew him described how proud he was of this exploit, as the police chase had been filmed and appeared on television (Khosrokhavar 2017). The following year, 2008, Merah applied to join the French army but was rejected because of his criminal convictions. Following that, he applied to join France's Foreign Legion but discontinued the process. It would later transpire that Merah received psychiatric support following an attempted suicide by hanging in December 2008.

Khosrokhavar suggests Merah highlights three dimensions of violence: a real dimension, where Merah takes what he wants and imposes himself, both as criminal and jihadist, without the least regret. Then there is a mediated dimension, which Merah relives through playing video games, watching *Faster* and war films that fascinate him. Finally, there is what Khosrokhavar calls an 'ecstatic' dimension, one that removes any fear of death and any guilty conscience. This ecstatic dimension is reinforced, argues Khosrokhavar, by the act of filming himself (2017: 86). Khosrokhavar notes this trajectory is also shared by other French jihadists, such as Zacarias Moussaoui (convicted of involvement in the September 11 attacks of 2001), who also came from a chaotic and violent family where personal experience is lived as a kind of injustice, combined with a double negation of identity – neither French nor Arab. In such cases, jihadist radicalization permits two things: overcoming the indignity of poverty and a life in chaos, while at the same time locating oneself within 'the sacred'. This allows 'the legitimation of absolute violence against others on the basis of victimization (I am the victim of a society that has totally excluded me, which authorizes me to be completely immoral towards it)' (Khosrokhavar 2017: 87).

Khosrokhavar draws on the work of the French philosopher Georges Bataille, especially his concept of 'ecstatic violence', to explore Merah's action. Such violence seeks *all-encompassing destruction*, one that will unify destruction of *the 'other'* with the destruction of *the self*. Such violence is characterized by its *excess*, by a total absence of limits, leading to an experience of dissolution of the self followed by fusion into something larger (Bataille 1986). It involves a collapse of time into the moment, something we see when Merah says: 'I knew that I was not going to last long. I knew that I would be able to make some, some attacks, and I knew that I was going to be arrested or killed quickly.'

While there is a complete absence of empathy for the victims of his killings (one is a three-year-old child whom he shoots in the head), Merah is visibly concerned with what we might call fame. Several times during the negotiation, he sets out to clarify that he is dealing with the national counter-terrorist police, not simply the local police. A kind of narcissism is central: his killings and his death will set in motion a profound transformation: 'My goal is to do my duty, and also to wake up the Muslim community and bring it to life, so that they wake up and in turn attack, so that there is no peace in France' (http://www.liberation.fr/societe/2012/07/17/transcription-des-con versations-entre-mohamed-merah-et-les-negociateurs_833784)

I die like Jesus Christ

A similar imaginary is shared by school shooters. School shootings are not random, senseless events that can only be understood in terms of mental illness or psychosis. School shooters believe themselves currently, or previously, at the bottom of a hierarchy that they experience as humiliating and destructive of their individuality. They see themselves as freedom fighters, prepared to kill and die on behalf of people that they believe to have been oppressed by the culture of a school hierarchy. And they create video messages, as French sociologist Nathalie Paton (2015) argues, to encourage others to follow them:

> I didn't have to do this. I could have left. I could have fled. But no. I will no longer run. It's not for me. For my children, for my brothers, and sisters that you fucked. I did it for them … When the time came, I did it. I had to. Thanks to you, I die like Jesus Christ, to inspire generations of the weak and defenceless people. (Seung-Hui Cho, YouTube, 2007, recorded while killing 32 people and wounding 27 others at Virginia Polytechnic)

> The struggle for which many brothers died in the past, and for which I will die, is not solely because of what is known as 'bullying'. Our fight is against cruel people, cowards, who take advantage of the kindness, the weakness of people unable to defend themselves … I died to inspire you, brothers, to defend and strengthen yourselves. My wish is to establish a

union between you so that the stronger and more courageous brothers support and protect brothers who are weak. Together you will be much stronger. I want you to fight for justice. (Wellington Oliviera, 7 April 2011, video message recorded before killing 12 children at his former primary school in Rio de Janeiro, Brazil)

Merah wants to believe his killings and death will wake up the Muslim community. Seung-Hui Cho sees himself dying as Christ. Wellington Oliviera declares that killing 12 children at his former primary school will make those who are bullied stronger, more able to fight for justice. Such killing is completely dissociated from indoctrination or narratives. Just as Merah pauses in his killings to assemble a video montage, Seung-Hui Cho, having killed two people, sent NBC television a multimedia package including an 1,800-word manifesto, 43 photographs and 25 minutes of videotape (Johnson 2007). He then proceeded to continue with his killing. Seung-Hui Cho and Wellington Oliviera both massacred as many people as they could before they in turn were killed. Seung-Hui Cho compared himself to Jesus, taking a photo of himself in a pose replicating the crucifixion; Oliviera takes a photo of himself in the same pose and posts it to the internet. Despite these explicit references to Christianity, no one has suggested that the problems in the Christian religion in some way caused the violence that these two engaged in.

Violence reveals a truth

Cho and Oliviera believed that their act of killing would be a transformative event, demonstrating that they were heroes and Christ-like. What they do will be so immense that a rupture will occur, the oppressed will rise up and the power of the oppressor will be broken. Cho kills not only to save but also to punish. Those he kills are guilty, and their guilt will be revealed by the action he is undertaking: 'You have never felt a single ounce of pain your whole life, thus, by destroying you, by giving you pain, we attempt to show you responsibilities and meanings of other people's lives.' Cho believes these acts of extreme violence will reveal a reality that is otherwise not seen. Framed in this way, these killers seek to demonstrate that their action is not that of an isolated and deranged person. This is the purpose of all the images and texts accompanying these actions – they set out to *reveal a truth*.

The intention to make visible a hidden reality is also central to the mass killing undertaken by Pekka-Eric Auvinen in November

2007 in the town of Tuusula, Finland, when he killed seven students and the female principal of the school he attended. As other school shooters, Auvinen believed he had been bullied and that he was regarded as having little value, but that the killings would reveal how wrong people were to have this opinion of him. On the day before the killing, he posted a text and video to the internet, in which he described himself as an 'unemployed philosopher', declaring that 'the people are living in the world of delusion' (http://misc.nybergh.net/pub/jokela/sturmgeist89-youtube.txt). He constructs a dichotomy between himself, as a 'godlike' individual, and the 'de-individualized' others, undifferentiated members of conforming, unthinking groups: 'Collective de-individualization is a phenomenon where the individual will be trained as part of the mindless herd controlled by state, corporation, church or some other organization, group, ideology, religion or mass delusion system ... It is just done so that people will think they are free and don't realize they are being enslaved.' Compared to these slaves, Auvinen considers himself free:

> [The] Majority of people in society are weak-minded and ignorant retards, masses that act like programmed robots and accept voluntary slavery. But not me! I am self-aware and realize what is going on in society! I have a free mind! And I choose to be free rather than live like a robot or slave. You can say I have a 'god complex', sure ... then you have a 'group complex'! Compared to you retarded masses, I am actually godlike. (Auvinen 2007)

For Auvinen, his act of killing will make the reality that is hidden clear to all: his 'godlike' status compared to the 'retarded masses'. His fellow students are not only worthless, they are ignorant. The reality that up to now has not been recognized, his superiority, will become clear through the scale of his action. Auvinen's killing is not primarily instrumental, nor expressive; once again, it is *revelatory* – it seeks to *reveal a truth*. In this case, the truth is not only the mindless conformism of others, but the fact that he is not a *nobody* (Paton 2015).

These mass killings possess an intelligibility. The perpetrators see themselves as the humiliated victims of a system of power and status in their school. In many cases, the killings take place in smaller towns, where the pattern of status and humiliation that exists in school is replicated in the community at large, so that time out of school does not offer any escape from a system of relationships experienced as demeaning. These killings, however, are aimed at much more than turning the tables on the powerful in the school. They are about *becoming someone* and achieving fame in a culture of celebrity that is evident in television reality shows and the quest for thousands of friends or followers on social media. To become famous, these killers and their killings need to be visible, to be 'mediated' (Serazio 2010). In the process, they become an *individual*, as famous as the celebrity who needs no family name to be identified, someone who is uniquely recognizable (Ehrenberg 1991). This singularity is achieved by becoming visible, by posting images of oneself and the act of killing on the internet. Nothing in this quest for fame can be left to chance, hence the importance of documenting and recording one's actions and the preparations leading up to them.

Film directors will be fighting over this story

In the months leading up to the Columbine High School massacre of April 1999, Eric Harris and Dylan Klebold, the two schoolboys who murdered 12 students and one teacher, made videos of themselves prior to the event, as well as recording hours of taped conversation about what the event meant. In one film, *Hitmen for Hire*, they play the role of two armed protectors, dressed in black trench coats, who defend students who are being bullied at school. In this narrative, a boy being bullied hires a 'hitman' for protection:

Dylan: We've got to save this retarded boy.
Student: I'll pay anything!
Eric: All right. It's twenty dollars a day in school. You know we can't have any weapons on school grounds.
Student: Th-that's fine! I'll ... I'll get 'em off the property!
Eric: All right. We'll protect you on school. Take away any bullies that are pickin' on you. Whatever. And off school grounds we could relocate this person. That'd be a thousand dollars.
Student: Thank you SO much!

Klebold and Harris imagine themselves protecting the weak at school and killing ('relocating') the bullies outside school grounds. They visualize themselves as powerful, thanks to their ability to access and use weapons. They spend many hours videoing themselves rehearsing the April attack and making audiotapes explaining the meaning of their actions. Their original plan involved explosives, not only to be used to kill people at the school but also to be detonated in order to kill emergency personnel who respond to the incident. In the 'basement tapes' where they record their conversations about the proposed killings, Harris describes always 'being at the bottom of the ladder' as a result of his family constantly moving house, and people making fun of him: 'my face, my hair, my shirts'. Klebold talks about the hard treatment he receives from 'the stuck up kids'. 'I'm going to kill you all. You've been giving us shit for years' (Gibbs and Roche 1999).

The imaginary of the two boys is nourished by video games: 'It's going to be like fucking *Doom*. Tick, tick, tick, tick ... Haa! That fucking shotgun is straight out of *Doom*!' The tapes are not just for themselves. They continually predict the reaction of the audience when it sees the video recordings. However, the killings are not simply revenge upon those students who have mocked them. They take great pleasure imagining the scale of the killings, discussing and laughing about where the bombs will be placed, declaring that they want to kill 250 people before they die. The imaginary of the event is completely different to a simple revenge killing: '[film] directors will be fighting over this story', says Klebold, as he and Harris discuss which director could be trusted to make the best movie about them, 'Steven Spielberg or Quentin Tarantino'. Klebold and Harris are living the mass killing they will undertake as a 'story' in which they are the lead characters.

Klebold and Harris are determined to underline the originality of what they are planning: 'Don't think we are trying to copy anyone', says Harris to camera, referring to earlier school shootings in Oregon and Kentucky. He asserts that he and Klebold had the idea long 'before the first one ever happened'. What they are planning to do is superior, 'not like those f***s in Kentucky with camouflage and .22s. Those kids were only trying to be accepted by others' (video quoted in Gibbs and Roche 1999). The scale of the killings that Klebold and Harris have such pleasure imagining does two things: it demonstrates their originality – it will be of such scale that they cannot possibly be compared to 'kids only trying to be accepted'. And it will establish their fame to be championed in film by Tarantino or Spielberg.

A decade later, Auvinen's killing reflects these themes. However, with the advent of the internet, he doesn't have to make videotapes and leave them to be found in his basement; he can upload video to YouTube. His video begins with a photo of his school, which disappears in an explosion of blood, out of which materializes a photo of himself, pointing a gun at the camera – the images held together by a soundtrack of 'Stray Bullet' by the German industrial rock band

KMFCM (https://www.youtube.com/watch?v=S0FWpz6gn54). Just as Harris warns, 'Don't think we are trying to copy anyone,' Auvinen is equally determined that his own agency will be recognized through the killings he will undertake. In the text accompanying his video, he declares: 'Remember that this is my war, my ideas and my plans. Don't blame anyone else for my actions than myself. Don't blame my parents or my friends ... Don't blame the movies I see, the music I hear, the games I play or the book I read.' He goes to great lengths to create a series of videos around images of himself, murder and music. This is not simply premeditation or planning, but, as Serazio suggests, he is engaged in *pre-mediation* – he wants to shape the meaning of his violence. He is producing a media account of his action, just as a decade earlier Harris and Klebold imagined film directors turning their exploits into a movie. But despite his claims for singularity and uniqueness, as Serazio observes, Auvinen's video consists of derivative and repetitive use of material widely available on the internet. He is incapable of articulating a statement that is more than a 'hodge-podge of texts whose fame predates, and will succeed, him' (Serazio 2010: 22).

Key to all these killings is an imaginary of *scale*. These killers want to do far more than inflict revenge upon particular individuals who have bullied them; victims are chosen at random. It is the scale of killing that makes these events unthinkable. These killers want more than fame. They want to inflict violence on such a scale that *reality itself fractures, that the unthinkable becomes real,* with themselves at the centre of this action.

Scale and its mediatization define contemporary mass killing. During the Second World War, the Nazis attempted to keep their death camps secret. And during the Bosnian war of the 1990s, mass executioners went to great lengths to limit knowledge of the massacres. But for today's killers, mass murder is a means to reveal. This is central to the 2011 massacre of 77 people undertaken by Anders Breivik in Norway. He commenced killing at one site through an explosion, then proceeded to another, intent upon killing as many people as possible. At one level, these murders served as a platform to promote his message, in this case a tract of 1,500-plus pages, together with a video he posted to the internet which calls on conservatives to 'embrace martyrdom' in a civilizational war against 'cultural Marxism' and the 'Islamization of Europe'. But at the end of his video, two photos of Breivik appear. In the first, he is aiming a semi-automatic rifle; in the second, he is wearing an imaginary dress uniform of the Knights Templar, his chest proudly bearing imitation

Figure 4.1 Abdul Sanchez Hammer. Facebook, 14 February 2014.

Figure 4.2 Seung-Hui Co. Video sent to NBC News, 6 April 2007.

military medals for awards that he had never received. He too has become someone, just as Auvinen did.

There are significant convergences between the violence and cultures shared by school shooters and jihadists. Above all is the theme of individuation and transformation. As Nathalie Paton argues, this is central to the digital world created by the school shooter, who depicts a transformation from being 'nobody' (ignored, made to suffer, etc.) to being defined by the exercise of power, even as a 'living God'. The gun is central to this. It is associated with superhuman power; it becomes the instrument of transformation. It becomes the voice, the means through which others will experience the potency of the shooter. This is represented visually when the gun is directed at the camera (Figures 4.1 and 4.2), or is photographed as an object of fascination, a pattern repeated widely among jihadists.

Fan cultures

The mass killings undertaken by school shooters have given rise to 'fan cultures' in the form of internet-based networks of people exchanging stories and images of shooters who have died (Paton 2015). Participants in these fan cultures or 'interpretive communities' write poems, share stories and circulate images celebrating the deaths of people whom they refer to as 'martyrs'. School shooters are seen by their fans as having sacrificed their lives in a moral fight against school bullies. Currently, such communities are completely outside the field of radicalization studies but understanding them may offer insights into different forms of internet-based communities that have developed around the ideal of giving one's life for jihad.

These fan cultures are not simply examples of individuals fascinated by violence or by the horror of killings. They display a cluster of sensations and emotions, ranging across disgust and desire, repulsion and attraction. Social relationships are constituted around the visual experience that fans share. In such cases, the act of *gazing* at visual representations 'activates certain possibilities of meaning, certain forms of experience, and, most importantly, certain *relations* among participants of the visual event' (Sumiala and Tikka 2011: 149, emphasis in original). The term 'gaze' carries the active sense of 'look', as opposed to the more passive sense of 'see'. The action of looking at violent events is a shared practice among people who come to embrace jihadism, just as it is central to the fan cultures around school shootings. In the case of jihadism, however, a too easy reliance upon narratives of propaganda has meant an absence of analysis of the *act* of gazing, the way this activates possibilities of meaning and, through them, constructs shared experience and relationships.

Fan cultures and desire: #Freejahar

In the days after the arrest of Dzhokhar Tsarnaev following the bombing of the Boston Marathon in April 2013, a social media campaign called for his release. As we saw in chapter 2, Aqsa Mahmood posted links to this campaign on her Tumblr, including images of Tsarnaev and claims of a conspiracy to hide the truth about the bombing. Among the images that Mahmood posted was a leaked photograph of the body of Tsarnaev's brother laid out on a medical examiner's table, purporting to show that the pattern of gunshot wounds proved that police accounts of his arrest were not truthful. The campaign for Dzhokhar Tsarnaev was built around #*Freejahar* as a hashtag, 'Jahar' being Tsarnaev's childhood nickname.

Max Read (2013) suggests that this campaign illustrates a collision between conspiracy theories with the world of boy band One Direction's teen fans. This reflects how much the campaign was embraced by young girls who had no previous engagement with political campaigns, and that a significant proportion of the 'infrastructure' for the campaign involved sites that had either previously been used by their owners as fan sites for pop idols or, if newly created, drew heavily on the aesthetic of those sites. One such site, with its original name 'One Direction Infection' still visible, has been overwritten with material about Tsarnaev. Its colour palette is bright pink, not what we usually expect on pro-jihadist websites (an archived version of the site is here: http://web.archive.org/web/20130425194729/http://free-jahar.tumblr.com). Here, we see claims that the bombing attacks were staged by the FBI; a picture of Tsarnaev with his girlfriend (but with her face scratched out); and a GIF of the bomber dancing, while previous photos of pop idols are replaced by images of Tsarnaev. These sites overlap with the campaign on Twitter, complete with images of wounded people and arguments that the lack of blood suggests fake injuries and a staged government conspiracy. This repurposing of the fan site captures something at work in contemporary culture, evident in the way other mass killings undertaken by attractive young men provoke similar responses (see, for example, the social media activity of 'Holmies', a fan culture that revolved around James Holmes, convicted for the murder of 12 people and injury of 70 others at a midnight cinema screening of a *Batman* movie in the American city of Aurora, Colorado, in July 2012).

Alone against the enemy

While not framed in the language of One Direction fans, we find similar responses to Mohamed Merah on pro-jihad social forums in the days following his death. Overwhelmingly, one theme predominates: in taking the path he did, Merah demonstrates that he is not defined by the crowd but is a true individual, one defined by his relationship to the sacred:

> He was alone.

> Today you faced the enemy alone, but not really alone. God helped you even if no one else did, and by your hands, a new page has been turned.

> He established a relationship with Allah, not with his creatures. (http://ansar-alhaqq.net/forums, 22 March 2012)

Farhad Khosrokhavar (2017) explores the social logic involved in such individualization through death. This pattern, he argues, is particularly present among young men who grow up in stigmatized and excluded neighbourhoods where other paths to success, based on individualization, are blocked. It is difficult to find a job once a potential employer knows you come from a stigmatized neighbourhood, and success at school is very difficult, not only as a result of poor-quality facilities but also at times because of a student culture that rejects learning as middle class. Here, the only options appear to be theft or low-level drug dealing. Khosrokhavar suggests that, for certain groups of young people, there is a kind of inevitability about a pathway into low-level crime. Social failure, argues Khosrokhavar, 'collectivizes'. Embracing a radicalized form of Islam allows a rupture with this world of crime. It is a rupture with 'destiny' or *mektou'*, lived as an expression of *individuality*. In the discussion forums dedicated to Merah in the weeks following his death, it is this image of the noble individual that recurs, with Merah as a tragic figure, a figure that owes much to western culture, captured in roles portrayed by the likes of James Dean.

Fan cultures and disgust: Ewwwwwww your brave to hold it!

At some point in late 2015, three British fighters in North Syria were involved in an execution. The three were members of a *katiba*, or 'battalion', of British fighters who called themselves Rayat al-Tawheed, and who were part of a group transporting a bag of heads to load onto a pick-up truck. As they walk, one of the British fighters is filming and focuses his camera in a close-up shot of the heads exposed in the bag. Once they reach the pick-up, they begin unloading. A man with a London accent picks up a head that has already been placed on the vehicle, points it directly to camera to frame a close-up image and shakes his head, saying, 'Kaffir! Disgusting'. The person filming responds: 'Allah Akhbar'. A second man with a London accent picks up a different head, points it to camera, saying, 'Shia Kaff!' (archived video).

In this video, we encounter the proximity of life and death. Death is not hidden, as in Nazi camps, but made visible. In this case, the victims are decapitated, mutilated in such a way that the bodily integrity that made them human has been taken from them. They are carried in a large bag, filmed in close-up, no longer recognizable as people that once lived, loved and were loved. They have been reduced to something horrific and abominable, resembling practices of mutilation seen in conflict zones in other countries such as in Mexico's drug wars today or in Colombia in the 1990s (Uribe 2004). The killers have taken not simply the life but the humanity of their victims. The deliberately voyeuristic filming emphasizes the power of the living who can turn the dead into objects of horror and disgust, something that is underscored by the two British men who each display a head to camera, their tone and words expressing disgust.

One of these young men posts a 30-second clip to his social media account. Once uploaded, it provokes a reaction:

Female 1:   Ewwwwwww your brave to hold it!
Participant 2: This is @xxx kinda things loooooo im in tears eeewwww.
Participant 3: Loooool, would have been better if it was FSA heads.
Participant 2: Looool why FSA same thing they're all kuffars anyways lmao [*laughing my arse off*].
Male 1:   Lol that's abit deep to call em ALL kuffar.
Participant 2: Ok ok not all of them lmao at least murtard lol. (Roussinos 2014)

Who are the people in this chat, and what are they doing? One participant uses a female avatar, another a male one, so we might reasonably presume the gender of these two. The avatars of the other two are unclear. However, the language used by Participant 2, a combination of tears of laughter and '*eeewwww*', suggests a female (studies of gender and language use on Twitter reveal that female users are more likely to use pronouns, computer-mediated communication words (*lol, omg, lmao*), and expressive lengthening (*coooool*) (Bamman, Eisenstein and Schnoebelen 2014). Of the four participants in this chat, it is likely that three are female.

The chat interaction is brief, but visceral, as it fundamentally consists of sharing emotion or affect. The participants' voyeurism means that they can share in the power of the executioners. The first female admires the bravery of fighters who are able to break the taboo that separates the living and the dead by picking up and holding a bloodied head. Mutilation removes the humanity of the victim, who becomes an object. The disgust of those handling the heads is shared by those who observe through a shrieked 'ewwwwwww' at the thought of touching 'it'. The victims are completely exposed to the gaze of those who film and those who watch the film. They no longer have any space defined as private or intimate that they can control; the manner of their death has rendered them completely open to the regard of the other.

Those responding to the video share a heightened state of emotion, communicated in elongated words and the fundamental role of humour. As we have seen, humour is central to rituals of humiliation. The act of laughing together not only forges a bond between those who observe the act of humiliation; through their laughter, they cease being observers and become actors; they share in the act of humiliating the victim. We saw earlier that, in a ritual of exclusion, an audience is fundamental to the process of bullying, where the act of laughing turns observers into participants. In this case, laughing declarations of disgust mean that observers can share in the affect, and thus the agency, of those committing this act, even though they are thousands of miles away.

The *lol* culture of participants in this conversation suggests that they are young and most likely British. They are living in a country where there is a strong separation of the domains of the living and the dead, where dead bodies are almost never shown on television or in other media. This practice finds its origins in respect for the dead, evident in practices such as covering the dead at the site of an accident or in hospital. The video these young people have watched tears this prohibition apart, making the dead the object of scrutiny and disgust. The four young people in this chat group are fascinated and repulsed by the mutilated bodies. They construct and share disgust, the social activity we saw to be central to the mediated world produced by Aqsa Mahmood.

Mutilation of the body does more than create an occasion for shared disgust. The work of Primo Levi offers us an insight into what is happening here. Levi was a holocaust survivor who attempted to understand what would otherwise appear to be the senseless violence and extreme cruelty of the Nazi camps. If the people imprisoned there were to be killed anyway, Levi asks, why devote resources and effort to humiliating and undermining them before their deaths? Levi argues that such cruelty was an essential dimension of the Nazi camps: 'Before dying, the victim must be degraded, so that the murderer will be less burdened by guilt' (Levi 2017 [1986]: 111). As Wieviorka observes, cruelty allows the murderer to turn the victim into an object, to strip the victim of humanity. It turns the victim into a non-human, to be destroyed just as an object so that 'the negation of the subjectivity of the other serves the affirmation of oneself' (Wieviorka 2004: 266). Such cruelty effaces the idea of a common humanity. We see this process at work in this social media conversation, in its focus on whether those killed were *kuffars* (infidels) or *murtads* (apostates), and whether it would have been better to see the heads of Free Syrian Army fighters, former allies turned enemies and thus traitors. Each post is accompanied by a *lol* (laughing out loud), and two add an *lmao* (laughing my arse off). In this case, the act of gazing has rendered those killed impure and disgusting, radically other.

The fake jihad life

Filming the self and uploading it to social media can raise uncertainty about what constitutes reality because life itself becomes a kind of reality show. We can see this in a video posted to social media by 17-year-old Aseel Muthana two months before he departed for Syria to join his older brother to fight with ISIS. The video is filmed with a friend as the two are walking up a hill overlooking the Welsh capital of Cardiff:

Muthana: [*camera points at ground*]: Journey up to, what's the hill called? Asda Hill, isn't it. You can't see, it's kinda dark. It's like, diaries of shaheeds [*martyrs*]. I got killed. If you're watching this, I'm probably dead, or I'm probably like a legend or something by now. [*Camera lifts, friend points replica gun at camera*]

[*points camera at face*]: Show my face!
[*points camera at city below*]: Oh, Look how beautiful it looks. Cardiff! Cardiff! We're in Cardiff [*gun is filmed again*]. Let's keep moving. Allah ul akbar. Do you know some nasheeds [*religious chants*]?

Friend: Huh?

Muthana: Let's sing some nasheeds!

Friend: Listen to us sing?

Muthana: Let's sing some nasheeds!

Friend: Go on, you go first.

Muthana: OK. I shall start with …

Friend: One that we both know!

Muthana: [*laughs*] Mate, what do you know?

Friend: [*unintelligible*]

Muthana: No, I'm thinking jihad nasheeds man! [*continues walking*] Hey, what's that song from Rocky? [*starts to hum theme tune to Rocky*].
[*Camera images of gun being pointed*]

Muthana: Are you depressed, are you stressed? Do you have no friends? Then come join us at Cardiff Hill, aka Asda Hill. This is the fake jihad life.
[*Turns to friend*] Hey, show the gun, show the gun!
[*Friend holds gun to camera*]

Muthana: Glock 16! Ja, ja, ja ! 16 or 19. Show the gun, show the gun, man!! [*shouting*]. The gun, akhi [*brother*], what the heck, what're you doin?!
[*Friend holds gun to camera, 'gangsta' style*]

Muthana: Allah u akbar! This is by the factory! Let's go up by the factory! There's smoke coming out of it! Let's pretend it's, like, an operation. We just blew up like a, a check point or something. Allah u akbar! I think you can see it if you look carefully! You can see it! Look, there's smoke coming out! Can you see it! Allah u akbar! Allah u akbar! [*imitates jihadists celebrating blowing up a target*]
(*Guardian*, 10 February 2016)

Muthana and his companion are not capable of singing any nasheed together; they have to be content with humming the theme tune of the Sylvester Stallone film *Rocky*. But through the act of filming, they are able to turn an imitation gun into a gangsta weapon, and the smoke coming from a nearby factory into an 'operation' that they can celebrate, imitating the videos that they have seen of ISIS fighters shouting with joy as an explosion detonates. They are able to produce, as Muthana himself says, 'the fake jihad life'. But even at this point, if his video reaches an audience, 17-year-old Muthana, just like the school shooter, will probably be either be dead or a legend. He too will be *someone*, living his life in the first person: 'I got killed or I'm probably like a legend.'

Shit man!

In 2015, Mohammed Rehman and Sana Ahmed Khan were convicted of planning an attack to coincide with the tenth anniversary of the 7 July 2005 bombings in London. Their internet history demonstrated repeatedly accessing online film about those events. Their experience also invites questions about the nature of what is real. Rehmam created a Twitter handle, @InService2God, with the 'avi' being a screenshot of 'Jihadi John' holding a knife. The name he has given himself is 'Silent Bomber'. He tweets: 'Westfield shopping centre or London underground? Any advice would be appreciated greatly' (Twitter, 12 May 2015). In other tweets, he makes similar statements: 'I'm preparing for an Istishaadi [*martyrdom*] operation'; 'Now I just make explosives in preparations for kuffars lol & when I've made the required amount I'll be wearing them on my chest.' On 11 May 2015, he tweets photographs of an explosion taking place on the edge of a lake or river, adding as text 'Test detonation of my keys to paradise ☺ 35 pounds of HME'. He creates a second Twitter account, @InService2Godd, with a background of the flag of the Islamic State and an avi of a British jihadist fighting with ISIS. He writes in his bio: 'Learn how to make powerful explosives from the comfort of one's bedroom #LoneWolves. Join the ranks of the defiant #IslamicState.'

Rehman also uploaded a video of a small explosion that appeared to be filmed in the garden of his house. There is no musical soundtrack to the explosion; all we hear is the hushed noises of excitement and anticipation as the person filming repeats 'God is great' in Arabic, and what seems to be another person moaning in anticipation. Just before the explosion, a young woman is heard exclaiming, 'Shit man!' in response to increasing tension. As the explosion takes place, the man filming whispers 'Fucking hell!'. Rehman later uploads a photograph of an improvised explosive device after it has exploded. He attaches a message to the image: 'Not bad for an amateur LOL a martyrs [*sic*] nutrition.' Later, he tweets: 'I've rigged my house to blow at the push of a button at my bedside if the popo try to raid man. NOBODY gets in the way of my Jihad!'

Not surprisingly, this activity led to a police raid in late May 2015. Evidence tendered to the Court indicated that this was not a pure fabrication, and included photos of 10 kg of urea nitrate stored in Rehman's house, together with a notebook that included instructions for making improvised explosive devices.

It is impossible to imagine this experience without the mediation that accompanied it. The tweets, uploaded images and video all allow those involved to create increasing tension and anticipation, leading up to the test explosion in the garden. A relationship is created with followers through *LOL*, called upon to *join in the project* through laughter. Laughter is a way of participating in the 'build up'. It allows followers to share in the amazement when a successful explosion is detonated. What is striking is the extent to which these images from this 'LOL jihad' accompany a stream of images focused on violence in Syria – dead babies and blown-up hospitals. Despite the constant tweeting of these images, there is no evidence of any relationship between this couple and a broader movement of solidarity with people caught up in the Syrian war.

It is clear that this project allows a kind of intensification of the couple relationship – it provides a shared project, it connects the pair with momentous events and allows Rehman to construct a persona for himself as the 'silent bomber'. Evidence tendered in court established that he was a heavy drug user throughout this period, and while the couple were in fact married, this was a relationship unknown to their families, both continuing to live with their respective parents. This alerts us to the extent that a project of radicalization can offer something that a couple may share and build on, where what is shared is loyalty to something bigger, something created as reality through the affective experience generated through social media.

Fusion and unreality

Other examples highlight the role of mediation in the intensification of couple experiences. One of the most striking took place in France in September 2016, where a car loaded with gas bottles was left to explode near Notre Dame Cathedral in Paris. One of those involved was 29-year-old Ornella Gilligmann, a mother of three children. She declared in documents submitted in court that she had met a man, Abou Omar, through the social media channel Periscope a year earlier. She described falling in love with him, leading to her divorcing her husband and, one month later in August 2016, religiously marrying Abou Omar by telephone, although they had never met. It was Abou Omar, who claimed to be linked to ISIS, who directed her involvement in securing the gas bottles and car.

Many of their exchanges consist of the eroticization of a power relationship. Abou Omar does not address Gilligmann by name, but calls her Woman (*femme*). Gilligmann refers to him as Man (*homme*). It would later transpire that Abou Omar was in fact a 19-year-old woman, Ines Madani, who may also have had other masculine names, and in the space of a year held different identities on Twitter, Facebook, Snapchat, WhatsApp, Periscope, Skype and Viber. Soren Seelow (2016b), the journalist who has explored this case, suggests that the relationship between the two in the period leading up to planting the car bomb was 'fusional' – with more than four thousand contacts between the two in the month before the attack.

We see similar fantasies of killing overlapping with sexual frisson and played out through social media in the case of Madihah Taheer and her husband Ummariyat Mirza, convicted of terrorism offences in the British city of Birmingham in 2017. In late 2013, Taheer was using Facebook as a platform to support Mirza's fundraising efforts on behalf of Syria (Facebook, 22 December 2013). But in the year that followed, their relationship appears to have turned inwards, evident in traces they have left on social media. In December 2014, Mirza replaced his 'avi' with an image of a smiling dead jihadist, while in May of that year Taheer began posting to Facebook about the impending establishment of the Khilafah (27 May 2014). A year after this, they are competing to establish who is more radical, who was the first to recognize the promise of the Islamic State:

Taheer: I saw a pic of our khalifa before u did therefor I am more radical.

Mirza: I'm more radical than you, I took u in. I introduced u to dawla [*the state*] and Twitter and jihad. Ur my student. (12 March 2015)

In September, Taheer got into an argument with another couple on Facebook, after which they discuss this with each other. In this case, Taheer tells her husband-to-be that they can marry, provided that he kills for her:

Mirza: I would end up killing everyone. Imagine if we were married man.

Taheer: Can we get married already ffs I want u to kill ppl for me, I have a list.

Mirza: The day of nikka [*wedding*], I'll kill them all. Give me the list, the only thing that stops me is we are not married. I will defo, I'm not joking.

Taheer: Lool, u can't have it til u put a ring on it. (Facebook, 5 September 2015)

A year earlier, Taheer had posted to her Facebook account an image purporting to be of a 'Syrian bride-to-be', asking her fiancé for 15 decapitated heads of pro-Assad fighters as a dowry (Facebook, 12 June 2014), and her demand to her fiancé appears to mirror this. A week later, the couple discuss the same person again and what they would like to do to him:

Mirza: I legit want to stab him 27 times, like really fast ones, like brutal an fast. Trust me.

Taheer: Sounds so satisfying

Mirza: It's my dream, the method.

Taheer: OMG mine too. Not stab 27 times but to hurt/kill him in some way.

Mirza: Stabbing kuffar [*non-believers*]/munafiq [*hypocrites*] fastly and brutally is my dream. I have a knife I want u to buy me.

Several months later, Taheer purchased a hunting knife, together with a dummy for Mirza to practise with. The dummy was made of a hard plastic that he did not like because it hurt his hand when he hit it:

Mirza: I'm telling you wallah [*I swear to God*], I know I won't use this one as much as the other. I know the difference in feeling. Same way I like hitting u. It's fun, it's nice to hit skin, to feel flesh contort under the force.

In these exchanges, all mediated through Facebook, Mirza shares with his wife-to-be the pleasure he feels in hitting her, a pleasure he needs to feel when hitting a dummy serving as an imaginary victim. Here, there is an eroticization of power relationships, where the promise of violence sustains a dynamic of anticipation and release, and the pleasure of violence is the basis of a claustrophobic relationship, while also the only pathway connecting them to a world beyond each other.

Mediation, individuation

Academic and policy literature is well aware of the importance of social media to radicalization. However, very often this is framed in terms of concepts such as 'indoctrination' or 'grooming', with radicalization understood in terms of a sender–receiver relationship. In this chapter, we have explored the *agency* involved in uses of social media, in particular the fundamental importance of *individuation*, or constructing selfhood. Once we approach radicalization from this perspective, we immediately see parallels with the mediated ecstatic violence of school shooters, who in their attempts to reveal what they consider to be a hidden truth embrace excess and a murderous desire to fracture reality. This also helps us understand the fan cultures that admire not only school shooters, but jihadist violence, evident in the *lols* and *lmaos* of a group of British young people responding to a display of mutilated bodies. We also find 'mediation' in friend and couple relationships, where filming the self creates the 'fake jihad life', and where tweets, texts and posts make possible transformations that sustain a world of intensity, secrecy and urgency, where social actors adopt multiple identities, and where a fascination with death and violence can merge into a kind of virtual love, combining what Seelow describes as 'reality fatigue combined with deadly delusion' (2016b). Here, we encounter a fascination with the forbidden and the frisson of danger, mediated games of power and submission, where sexual desire appears central yet disconnected from the limits that make up human experience.

5

From Drug Dealer to Jihadist

In every prison I've gone to, one minute I was at the top, loads of money, drugs, people kissing my bum ... Then the next thing I know, I'm getting stabbed, or I've stabbed someone ... After five years of that, you realise you're going nowhere ... The people in my jammah, the older ones are like uncles to me, the younger ones, they look up to me.
Jamal, Movement Against Crusaders, 2012

Next stop Damascus – plenty of banks to rob there!
Unnamed companion of Abdelhamid Abaaoud, leader of November 2015 Paris attacks, self-recorded video, Northern Syria, 2015

It's not as easy as pulling out your 9mm on the back roads of the streets of London and blasting a guy with it, as he's not going to blast you back. It's not as easy as putting your feet up on the couch after a hard day's work on the corner [*dealing drugs*].
British fighter, Rayat al-Tawheed recorded video, Northern Syria 2014

Back in the day, it was no different from being in a war.
Jamal, Movement Against Crusaders

It is clear that many authors of jihadist violence have criminal backgrounds, as evidenced by the horrific attacks in Paris in 2015 and Brussels and Nice in 2016. The increasing incidence of criminal pathways into violence underlines the importance of prison experience in the trajectories of those involved, with many describing experiences of personal transformation and conversion occurring in prison. The growing inclusion of people with criminal backgrounds in jihadist networks illustrates the need to move beyond older paradigms and debates. In particular, we need to understand the ways in which the passage from crime to jihadism entails transformation, and to what extent it requires continuity.

You realize you're going nowhere

When we interviewed Jamal (pseudonym), he was 30 years old. His mother is British, his father from the Caribbean. He had recently been released from prison following a long sentence for offences that included firing a shotgun at police during an arrest. At the time, he had previous convictions for assault, burglary, robbery and violent disorder. He began by speaking about his father, who also possessed a long criminal history: 'by the time I was 14 or 15, I was basically doing the same thing as my father; going on road [street term for involvement in crime].' He described his experiences in prison. He had already served three prison sentences that together made up more than half his life: 'to be honest, you get used to it.' Jamal is physically big and able to assert himself while in prison, but this last time he became aware that his life was 'just going around in circles'. He describes a world where being at the top involves the exercise of violence, but with this comes the danger of either being a victim of a stabbing or being involved in stabbing someone else. The violence can swallow you up, trapping you in a cycle you are unable to control. Its onset is unpredictable, instigated either by someone else or oneself (McDonald 1999).

At the time, many of his friends were of Turkish origin: 'There were a lot of Turkish brothers I used to hang around with. They had a family unit, they had brothers, they still had a mum and dad, brothers used to come and stay in their houses. You'd see that, and you'd see your own house ...' His description of a close-knit Turkish community contrasts strongly with his description of the estate where he grew up: 'there was a lot of violence. We did things together, we'd fight together. As we got older it got worse, knife fights and then shootings.'

Jamal's description of his prison experience is constructed as one of disconnection from others: 'Prison is not a nice place; locked in your room from 7.00 every night; locked in a 12-foot room; no family contact; most of the time they move you to a prison so far away that no one can come and see you; the screws are racist.' The first two times he is released from prison, the people he describes as Turkish brothers urge him to make a change: 'I came out, and I'd see these brothers, who would say, "Do you really want to spend your whole life in prison? Stop this, there is something here for you".' But, he says, 'I never used to hear it.' There are no close friends in his story; family and neighbourhood appear only to be sources of violence. He describes what sociologists call 'anomie' (Durkheim 1951 [1897]), a social world where community and its socialization are weak or absent. He describes a world of violence and competition for the control of territory: 'back in the day, it was no different from being in a war.' Thanks to his size and strength, Jamal is often at the top of this world.

The transformation Jamal describes is very different from those associated with the internet. It is much closer to classical accounts of religious conversion, which involve becoming part of a new community and in the process taking on a new identity:

> But as the years went on by ... I met certain other brothers in prison, and little bit by little bit, you are [pause] living like a Muslim ... Like Allah says, innit, you are who you hang around with. I met some other brothers, and they basically taught me everything I needed to know.

Becoming part of a new community is fundamental to Jamal, and central to this is embracing new rules for life:

> Gradually you learn more. You can only implement stuff in your life the moment you learn it, brother. Other brothers know more, they can say you are doing this wrong, you have to wear your trousers above your ankle, you can't wear that tee-shirt because it's haram. For me, it was a gradual process of learning, having the right people around you.

He describes becoming part of al-Muhajiroun as not so much joining an organization but as becoming part of a new family of brothers:

> When I first came to Islam, the brothers I was hanging around with [in prison], they didn't have great deen, innit. If I'm kuffar, their deen's coming down to my level. They're doing drugs, they're hanging around with a girlfriend. Then you meet other brothers, who tell you this is not Islam brother, and in a couple of years you will be hanging around with them brothers. You know, that's exactly how it happened. I met more brothers who were more in tune with the Deen of Allah.

This is not a transformation that occurs in a single day but a process that takes place over many months. There is no contact with a mosque or formal religious leader. Jamal has been taught by 'the brothers' that he is 'hanging around with'. But at the same time, he undergoes a change. He is no longer a receiver of religious instruction or *dawah*. He becomes a giver. And the type of questions he is concerned with have also changed:

> The brothers from before, the main difference is that I'm teaching them now. When I see them, I give them dawah. Before they would give me a lot of dawah. And it was not even real dawah, it was more or less 'you got to be Muslim'; 'we have a better way of life'; 'our women are trustworthy'; 'I can go to prison for ten years and know that my wife won't be cheating on me'. That's the sort of dawah that some brothers give, innit. You know, 'look at us, we live better than you'. That is very enticing when you come from nowhere … Now, the dawah that I give them is completely different, it has nothing to do with that. It's more based on what I've learnt about Islam … I give them books and things like that, CDs. The ones that are in prison, I send them talks to let them know 'you're halfway there, just keep going bro'. The true deen's out there, do you get me?

Jamal's initial interest is provoked because Islam appears to explain the community cohesion he experiences with the 'Turkish brothers' – one which offers 'a better way of life', captured by the confident assertion that 'I can go to prison for ten years and know that my wife won't be cheating on me.' But then he describes a shift. It is not simply he who is 'giving *dawah*', but the *dawah* he is giving is 'completely different' from practices that sustain community life. Now Jamal's *dawah* is based on what he has learnt from his new brothers. And this involves learning about the 'true deen' from the books and CDs that he promotes, in particular to brothers in prison. This is 'decontextualized' *dawah* (Roy 2014), not linked to concerns about community but consisting of rules for behaviour and an account of Muslims' domination by the kaffirs.

Many young people grow up with experiences like Jamal's, and many become part of more or less structured groups, often called gangs or crews. In its classical form, a gang is an attempt to create social organization as a way to impose order on a social world experienced as disordered, and to produce security and safety in a world shaped by risk and danger (McDonald 1999). It does so by creating group cohesion and identity where a group will unite in opposition to another. Loyalty to the group is generated though competition with similar groups for limited resources, in particular access to locality and respect. For example, in London, to demonstrate its power and to humiliate its opponent, one group will enter the territory of another and members then film themselves in some way disrespecting the neighbourhood of the other, posting video to social media. The external competition for limited resources, in particular the resource of 'respect', is matched by internal group structures of loyalty. Gangs involve structures of hierarchy (McDonald 1999), where becoming part of a gang will entail some kind of initiation ritual, in which an old identity is shed and a new one constructed by the group. A gang is a territorial form of social organization, one that combines internal hierarchy with external relationships of competition. In so doing, a gang does more than sell drugs or steal cars, generating income for its members. A gang produces order and security in environments of disorder and insecurity. It creates 'respect' (Bourgois 1996; McDonald 2003).

The 'brothers' of al-Muhajiroun that Jamal describes are not a gang; they are not seeking to defend territory against another gang. But it is a community constructed against the society it is part of and so, like a gang, it is able to develop strong dynamics of inclusion and exclusion, a strong opposition between 'us' and 'them'. And just like a gang, al-Muhajiroun possesses a strong internal structure, based on giving or receiving respect:

> The people in my jammah, I have respect for every single one of them. I got a load of love for them as well. The older ones are like uncles to me, the younger ones are like, they look up to me... . It's much more than a friendship... . There's limitations for what you would do for a friend, but there's no limitations to what I would do for my brothers, in Islam. It's not a surrogate family, it is a family, innit! Every brother in it is a family member, we have the same mentality, we have the same goals, we want to implement the same things.

Here, however, authority is no longer based on the ability to exercise violence. It is founded on access to knowledge. Receiving this knowledge is fundamentally what Jamal has experienced as a transformation. He describes what his new friends have given him: 'The knowledge that they give me... . First of all, they brung me out of jahilya, they brung me from a "so-called" Muslim to a "true" Muslim, as I understand it.' The leaders are articulate and charismatic. The only account that Jamal offers of what he might become in the future is shaped by power and status in al-Muhajiroun:

> If I need anything, any form of knowledge – you know, you know, they are so intelligent, you know the talks are, you know, very inspiring! You hear people talk, and you know, you say 'yeah man, that's how I wanna live, I wanna learn this knowledge, I need to learn this knowledge so

that I can give talks, so that I can do this'. And at the end of the day, you're not going to get that from people who don't know it basically, and that's what entices me, that's what keeps me loyal to my friends.

There is almost something mystical in this. Those who have power and status in al-Muhajiroun derive it because of their access to esoteric knowledge, events and Hadiths from the past, which function today through the power of allegory, knowledge that opens up hidden meaning about today's world. Jamal stopped attending school by the age of 14, but he is fascinated by those with the power to unveil hidden meanings about both today's world and himself. At the moment, his role is some distance from that of the leaders:

Obviously there's more knowledgeable brothers than others, that's why they are elevated, you get knowledge from them innit. I'm a newcomer, I haven't been there that long. The Emir sets out who does what, innit … [At demonstrations] I am on security. I go to the gym, I have a bit of size. I'm used in that capacity innit. As a newcomer I don't really have a position, that people know me.

Even though he is a newcomer, Jamal has a role in the group's activities: 'We do street dawah … Basically, Friday night, Saturday night, it's peak time for brothers to go off the rails, you get a lot of jahilya. Brothers go off the rails, imitate the kuffar. So we walk around, stop, just pull them over and ask them what they are doing.' This is the Muslim patrol that Ahmed described in chapter 3.

At the time of this interview, Jamal was insisting that his life had been transformed through his relationship with 'the brothers'. But in many ways his new world mirrors the world he was trying to leave. It is based on a strong hierarchy, as is the world of the gang. And just as a gang generates internal loyalty through external conflict expressed in metaphors of 'war', al-Muhajiroun embraces a similar imaginary:

Back in the days, it was no different from [pause] being in war basically, yeah, innit! I would have been in it, punching people, beating up people all the time. Now I'm like, we fight when we have to, for the sake of Allah. If I was to get locked up for the sake of Allah, I don't have a problem with that.

In the years following this interview, Jamal would be convicted three times. The first time was for harassing a young woman who was speaking to a group of men. He called her a whore and them kaffirs, language suggesting the imaginary of 'clean' and 'unclean' that we

Figure 5.1   Abdelhamid Abaaoud in Syria, wearing HD video camera, February 2014.

have met many times in this book. His second conviction was for possession of false documents while attempting to leave the United Kingdom, showing a determination to widen his violent career from the streets of his home town on a Saturday night to the streets of Syria. His later conviction involved hospitalizing a schoolboy he found kissing a girl in public, suggesting that the imaginary of war, so important on the estate, remained just as central to Jamal's life after his introduction to the brothers of al-Muhajiroun.

The tourist terrorist

On a mild Friday evening in November 2015, nine young men wearing suicide vests launched a series of attacks on bars, cafés, sporting events and a concert in Paris. They killed 130 people, injuring a further 350. Of those killed, 89 were massacred at the Bataclan Theatre during a concert by a touring American band. The attacks were coordinated by 28-year-old Abdelhamid Abaaoud. Originally from Belgium, Abaaoud travelled to Syria in 2013. During his time there, he wore an HD video camera to record his exploits, often filming his friends while they filmed him (Figure 5.1). He was a prolific user of social media, posting a constant stream of photos and videos. In one, he poses in an action shot, huddled down in a large tyre, taking aim at the enemy. In another, he and a friend are smiling as they take a selfie, with Abaaoud laughing as he brandishes his gun. He posts the image to Twitter with the message 'the tourist terrorists' (Twitter, 13 June 2014).

He is proud to announce to his followers in Belgium that he is living the 'five-star jihad'. In another video, Abaaoud films two friends driving a powerful car in the town of Hraytan, North Syria, in February 2014:

Abaaoud [*laughing*]:	My brothers, can I ask what you are doing with a car like this in the Land of Sham?
Response [*laughing*]:	As you can see, we've left behind the world of luxury!
Abaaoud [*laughing*]:	God willing!
Response [*laughing*]:	We're off to Damascus for some robberies, with God's help!
Abaaoud [*louder laughing*]:	God willing!

In a later sequence, Abaaoud is being filmed. He is driving a trailer, towing the bodies of some seven people killed in a massacre that took place in Hraytan on 12 February 2014. Once again, he is smiling as he addresses the camera:

Abaaoud:	Before we used to tow jet-skis, quad bikes, motocross. Big trailers full of baggage, full of gifts when we would go away on holidays. Now you can film my new load!
Friend with camera:	God is great! [*shouts*] [*Directs video to dead bodies tied together behind trailer*]. Look at these apostates! Look at these apostates! God in heaven! Drag them! Drag them! Drag these infidels my brother! Look at that one with the head of a Smurf! Oh, doesn't it stink, my brothers! Oh, it stinks!

Abaaoud drives the car, dragging the bodies towards a mass grave in the middle of a field. The ropes break just before reaching it, much to the amusement of the group. Abaaoud gets out and takes a selfie, together with the fighter holding his phone, making sure that the dead bodies are in the background. He is still wearing his video camera around his chest. He had earlier posted images of himself playing football with a decapitated head.

Filming does not simply record these events. Filming them transforms their meaning. This is central to the 'five-star' jihad posts that European and North American jihadists took great pleasure in sharing on social media, photographing and filming themselves swimming in the pools of houses confiscated by ISIS. Use of the camera in this way 'reformats' their experience, not only as tourists enjoying themselves but also as a band of brothers drawn together by their comradeship and the excitement of their mission. In the excerpts above, two themes are apparent. The first is continuity, evident in the pleasure of driving a car taken from someone else and in the promise of travelling to Damascus to undertake robberies. In the second, the disrespect accorded to the dead is part of their dehumanization. Film is central to this.

Abaaoud died several days after the Paris attack, killed during a gun battle with police in Paris. He had a string of criminal offences, including a failed robbery attempt in 2011. He had attended an elite private school outside the neighbourhood he grew up in but had dropped out, securing work as a sales assistant in the family clothing business. Following the failed robbery in 2011, his family sent him to Egypt to 'settle him down' and for him to 'study theology'. He returned in 2012, presenting himself as the master of a new knowledge of the classical Arabic of the Qur'an, together with verses and Hadiths. Acquaintances report that he never attended a mosque, nor demonstrated any kind of religious piety. However, his knowledge of religious texts and quotes meant he had an answer for every question. He had become an authority. In 2012, he became involved with Sharia4Belgium, a group formed in 2011, modelled on and supported by the UK-based al-Muhajiroun. His knowledge gave him the ability to identify the meaning behind otherwise banal events. On the first day of Ramadan, publicity for a new brand of women's underwear had appeared in the neighbourhood. An acquaintance recalls him seeing in it more than simple advertising: 'An accident? You're joking, my friend! It's against the Muslims!' (Vincent 2015).

In January 2013, Abaaoud departed for Syria from where he generated a constant stream of photos and videos to social media. He constantly posed for selfies, and his habit of wearing a video camera imparts an experience that is close to a reality TV show. He had left behind his life as a shop assistant; he was now the leader of a battalion. In Syria, Abaaoud was a new person and had taken a new name, Abu Omar al-Baljiki. He filmed his exploits, regularly sending video files back to 'the brothers' in Belgium. As leader of his brigade, he promised that he would 'personally' support those who answered his calls to join him, a combination of personal authority and patron-age similar to the culture of 'caids', the benevolent authoritarianism of the leaders of criminal groups. The spirit of adventure was the impetus for his departure, life in Belgium being, 'Too calm. I'm not going to spend all my life selling suits for 20 Euros' (Aubenas 2016). There are constant references to holidays in his communications: 'the tourist terrorist'. He is keen to celebrate the fact that, in Syria, 'Here we have everything, above all since we've got Nutella from Turkey' (Aubenas 2016). He takes great pleasure in insisting on his superi-ority in the face of the bumbling police efforts to capture him. He boasts of returning to Europe, even when there was an international warrant for his arrest (Dabiq 2015). To demonstrate his power, he did return in February 2014, where he met his 13-year-old brother after school, and returned to Syria with him, posting a triumphant picture to social media: 'The youngest jihadist in the world.'

Brothers

Four months after the Paris attacks, two brothers, Ibrahim and Khalid El Bakraoui, aged 30 and 27 years old, blew themselves up in attacks on Brussels airport and metro system. Both had significant criminal histories. The theme of brothers recurs across contemporary jihadism. Dzhokhar and Tamerlan Tsarnaev planted the pressure-cooker bombs at the Boston Marathon in April 2013. Said and Cherif Kouchai stormed the satirical newspaper *Charlie Hebdo* in January 2015. Salah and Brahim Abdeslam were both involved in the Paris attacks, Brahim blowing himself up in a café, Salah fleeing back to Belgium. Abdelhamid Abaaoud took his 13-year-old brother to Syria, posting images of him on Twitter. Brothers Karim (25) and Foued (23) Mohamed-Aggad travelled together to Syria from Strasbourg during the winter of 2013. Karim returned to France in 2014, while Foued returned in 2015 to participate in the murder of 90 people at the Bataclan Theatre in Paris.

In a significant number of these cases, the family background had been disrupted by either the death or the absence of a parent, leading to the involvement of social services. At one level, the brother rela-tionship can be understood as reconstructing a family unity that had previously fragmented (Khosrokhavar 2017). However, the brother relationship takes on a particular importance in a world of crime shaped by the potential for unpredictable violence and shifting loyal-ties. Here, a relationship with a brother can be a source of security, continuity and confidence. Not only do brother relationships figure prominently in jihadist violence, they are over-represented in crime generally (Beijers et al. 2017; Kendler et al. 2014). The brother relationship can take on special significance in a dangerous world.

Soldiers

Part of the transition from armed criminality to jihadism is the shared imaginary of being a 'soldier'. While contemporary gangs lack the integrated hierachy of those depicted in classical sociological accounts, they are nonetheless forms of collaboration involving vertical relationships of authority and loyalty, with authority associated with 'elders' who lead 'crews' of 'youngers', often referred to as 'foot soldiers', with fields of conflict and action frequently described as the 'front line' (Windle and Briggs 2015). This image is captured by Jamal when he describes life on the housing estate in which he grew up: 'Back in the day, it was no different from being in a war.'

If the imaginary of war plays an important role in armed criminal cultures, in jihadism this is amplified and 'Islamicized'. We can see this in a video posted by one of the leaders of the British group of fighters active in Syria in 2014 and 2015, Rayat al-Tawheed (Banner of God):

> It is not easy to stand in front of a tank while it launches at you. It is not easy to raise this simple piece of metal and pull the trigger.... It's not as easy as pulling out your 9mm on the back streets of London and blasting a guy with it, as he's not going to blast you back with it. It's not as easy as putting up your feet on the couch after a hard day's work on the corner [*selling drugs*]. This is practically the Muslim man's job and career – to fight for the sake of Allah.... I ask Allah to bless me with the status, the status, of a Mujahid. But even the status of a Mujahid is heavy ... You don't just come here and put on a tactical vest, grab a kalishnikov, short throb, big beard, short trousers, and that's it, you've become some kind of Emir kattab [*leader of a militia*]. So brothers, please, it's not like on road [*British street slang for criminal life*]. (Masked fighter with London accent, Rayat al-Tawheed, self-recorded video, North Syria, 2014)

The core of Rayat al-Tawheed was made up of young men from London. Their imaginary of jihad was fundamentally shaped by that of Hollywood, deeply indebted to images evoking Bruce Willis and 'real men'. In these, we see a recurring focus on the self rather than being drawn into the surrounding chaos.

Figure 5.2 Looking forwards. Tumblr, 2014.

At the same time, the images produced by this group evoke the opportunity offered by jihad to make a new life, a new start that wipes away the past. We saw purity play a central role in the transformation as illustrated by Aqsa Mahmood, who creates a pure experience through opposing guilt and innocence, beauty and the grotesque, the purity of the House of Sunnah against the grotesque impurity of Shia Muslims. In the case of the young men making up Rayat al-Tawheed, this takes a different form. Here, the focus is on purification of the *self*, turning one's back on one's past (a theme completely absent in the case of Mahmood and her friends). Themes that we find in Ifthekar Jaman's engagement with the majesty of the natural world recur constantly in images widely posted to social media, almost always by young men. In these, the young man is alone, no longer surrounded by the chaos of violence but answering the call of destiny. The image above (Figure 5.2) may have little to do with jihadism but has been widely reproduced by the social media feeds of young jihadists in Syria: what counts here is turning one's back on the past, simply looking forward. Or at least this is the discourse that is embraced.

One younger member of Rayat al-Tawheed, a former college student, tweets under the handle @9MMillimeter. He posts an image of three men, all blindfolded, kneeling on the floor: 'Got these criminals today. Insha'Allah will be killed tomorrow. Cant wait for that feeling when you just killed some1.' Five minutes earlier, he posted an image of his locker: 'This is how my locker looks now, I wish it looked like that back at college' (Twitter, 24 December 2013). What is striking here is the close proximity of two types of image: one showing the banality of life evident in a tidy locker; the other the power and pleasure involved in anticipating killing. This too can be shared, constituted through posts to social media.

Another young fighter with Rayat al-Tawheed posts a picture of himself to social media. We cannot see his face, just his body. The image focuses on his hand. It is not cut nor is he suffering any injury, but his hand is covered in blood. Blood has also stained his trousers. He posts a message with the image: 'My first time.' This prompts the following exchange:

Participant One:	First time slaughtering a goat mate lol.
Poster:	Nah I don't think it was a goat.
Participant One:	Sheep?
Poster:	Of course you know.
Participant Two:	Killed a kaffir?!
Participant One:	looooooooooool /\/\ gorom times.
Poster:	Where you at?
Participant Three:	I thought you were injured in battle looool … I was like sins *are gone IN SHA ALLAH.*
Participant Four:	First of many, ak!!! [*bro*] (Roussinos 2014)

There is a different kind of affect here from the 'ewwwww disgusting' to that we saw in the previous chapter. This time what we find is the pleasure and frisson of taking a life. This exchange is not about shared disgust; instead, it is a rite of passage, a transformation. A different kind of community is formed around this act, not based on disgust and humour but on a kind of celebratory practice. The focus is now on the transformation of the killer, something that was absent in the earlier video. He has broken through a barrier. He is now on a path – 'the first of many'. Here, humour is a means to participate in the pleasure of this rite of passage, rather than simply noting or observing it: guessing at what was killed (Participant One); surprise and delight (Participant Two); offering an alternative interpretation (Participant Three); and expressing confidence that this will continue (Participant Four). The early posts in this discussion play an important role – establishing the equivalence of the victim to that of a goat or sheep, something reaffirmed by each post involving a *lol*.

There are multiple dimensions at stake in the experiences described in this chapter. The trajectory from delinquency allows a continuation of the same action in the celebration of the power of the gun, the pleasure in fighting and humiliating victims, the imaginary of the soldier and war and the pleasure in taking booty. Criminal activity is overlaid with a kind of religious discourse, the pleasure of war against society accorded religious themes. This is stabilized in a way similar to a gang experience, the new grouping offering status, respect and honour. Now the jihadist is the anti-hero, his war against society has become sacralized (Khosrokhavar 2017). Despite the rhetoric about having left the gangster life behind, what we see above all is its continuity.

6

The Gamification of Jihad: the Cyber Caliphate

For us to be here, it's freedom. Totally freedom! I can walk around with a Kalashnikov if I want to, with an RPG [*rocket-propelled grenade*] if I want to... . It's actually quite fun, better than, what's that game called, Call of Duty? It's like that, but really, you know, 3D. You can see everything's happening in front of you, you know it's real, you know what I mean? It's really good.

Abu Sumayyah Al-Britani, https://eaworldview.com/2014/06/syria-interview-islamic-state-of-iraq-abu-sumayyah-al-britani-conflict-caliphate/

You can sit at home and play call of duty or you can come and respond to the real call of duty ... the choice is yours ...

Tweet by Birmingham-born Junaid Hussain, Northern Syria, 2014

Gamification

In this book, I have attempted to explore the agency involved in radicalization experiences. Rather than approach people who embrace jihadism as vulnerable victims or evil monsters, forms of agency and self-making are considered. This means taking seriously the social world of relationships and imagination out of which social actors construct radicalization pathways. One of the most pervasive themes we find among jihadists who travelled to Syria is that of fun and laughter. Sometimes, this is linked to experiences of camaraderie and fellowship. At others, laughter is associated with inflicting horrific suffering on the 'other', including massacre or torture. Behind many of these experiences are references to online games: Junaid Hussain challenges his Twitter followers not to 'sit at home and play *Call of Duty*', but to 'respond to the real call of duty'. The pervasive nature of these references among jihadists alerts us to the importance of gaming to jihadist young men, and possibly to the role of 'simulated experience' as we saw with Aseel Muthana, who two months before departing for Syria cries out 'let's pretend we're on an operation!' while filming himself against smoke rising from a factory.

What sociologists, media researchers and business analysts call 'gamification' is one of the most important forms of social change at work in culture and economy today. Games are increasingly integrated into learning experiences and programmes. Early games sought to reward players through badges and icons, but increasingly games set out to *create worlds* that open out new kinds of immersive experiences. These are organized around what Nigel Thrift calls 'infrastructures of feeling' (2011), emotion structures, in particular structures of tension and release (Collins 2008) which are also associated with addictive experience (McDonald 1999). One of the key structures of globally successful games is the principle of 'glory'. Thrift (2011) points out that increasingly games seek to 'produce an experience of immersion which both limits (through selective engagement of attention) and expands what can be sensed'. The influence of gaming as a paradigm of action is extending beyond the better-known areas of education and marketing and becoming increasingly significant in the blurred lines linking military training and entertainment, so much so that observers such as Thrift argue that we are witnessing the development of a 'military–entertainment' complex. In 2014, the so-called Islamic State created a promotional video game entitled *Grand Theft Auto: Salil al-Sawarem* (sound of swords clashing), a first-person shooter game in which an American sets about murdering more than a hundred law enforcement officers in the United States, set to a soundtrack of a thumping heartbeat and nasheeds. In the United States, *Call of Duty: Black Ops 2* features a cameo by a former CIA director.

Games and religion

Social scientists are increasingly attempting to understand the relationship between games and religion. Playing games is fundamentally a social activity, as is religion. Games, as Jane McGonical (2011) argues, offer those who play them a sense of purpose where they become 'fully alive, focused, and engaged in every moment', encountering 'power, heroic purpose, and commitment'. For her, games offer meaning, purpose and community to many who may not experience these in other areas of their lives. Rachel Wagner explores not only the way in which games today are coming to occupy the social role once occupied by religion. She also sets out to explore the way in which religion and religious experience are transforming as a result of the impact of games on culture more generally. Evangelical Christians, she notes, describe the Bible as an 'owner's manual', a reliable handbook of rules we need to follow to achieve success. More directly linked to the questions we are exploring, she considers the development of what she calls 'first-person shooter religion' (2012).

Gaming is an immersive world structured by rules, and first-person shooter games are a particular form: 'First Person Shooters rely on a unique mode of perspective. They allow entry into a typically strictly coded, scripted environment in the form of a subjective, personal inhabitation of an entity that engages in violent destruction of enemies' (Wagner 2012: 188). This is a specific model that combines 'alienation, detachment, fear, or violence' within an immersive experience that emphasizes empowerment, lived as motion and action, even while the path the player travels is actually pre-designed (Galloway, in Wagner 2012: 189). Wagner points to its ritual nature, as 'the player moves through a pre-scripted experience with an intense feeling of agency and performance. This kind of control is very fulfilling, especially for those people who might feel powerless in their everyday lives' (Wagner 2012: 189). A structuring dimension of this process is the fundamental need for winners and losers, friends and enemies. This, argues Wagner, is a kind of 'metaphysical sorting ... a desire for the belief that there is good and evil' (2012: 190).

There is a kind of transformation at work here. Games researcher Sun-ha Hong describes two dimensions. First, the ritual structure of the game allows the player to develop new skills and exercise new powers. Secondly, such changes are not only evident in the development of the player, but they can bring about transformations in the game itself. Hong argues that the world of the game does not seek accuracy but is a 'pragmatic pillaging of historical, mythical and ritual elements' (2015: 36) – Norse legends, themes from *The Lord of the Rings*, the Crusades, the Black Death – all these find themselves mashed up in contemporary games, just as we find most of them in the videos of Omar Diaby. There is an important question here of the stance the player takes in relation the imaginary world they find themselves at first confronting, later inhabiting. Hong argues that the player is not asked to believe what they are playing is *real*, but rather that 'this could have been real' (Hong 2015: 37). This, argues Hong, amounts to what he calls a 'mode of engagement'. The player finds himself suspended in the time and space of the game, in a world that he in fact knows to be fantasy. There is a specific experience here that is not 'total immersion' but rather 'awareness and its suspension': the player is never required to believe, but only to act 'as if they believe enough' (2015: 43).

All of this highlights an issue recognized by Hong and other researchers working on games. In order to 'work', players find themselves located in periods of myth and epic. The player knows the game is not real but takes part as if it is. Cultural theorists attempting to make sense of these patterns suggest that, while we know that the game is not real, the experience of playing is so transformative and empowering that we come to a point where 'we require the image and spectacle to connect to a felt sense of the real'. In that sense, the kind of engagement generated in the game can lead to actors connecting to a past and a real 'beyond game content', dreaming of and desiring a 'collectively imagined tapestry of "mythic time"'. Hong argues that this represents not mere youthful escapism but a more significant cultural transformation associated with new media technologies, leading to a 'radical aestheticization and stylization of the real as myth' (2015: 50).

The processes at work here are not simply relationships of cause and effect. Instead, social and cultural transformations reshape the very category of experience linked to an aestheticization of the real as myth. This is manifest in the action of mass killers such as Anders Breivik, who presented himself as a stylized Knight Templar, complete with imagined uniform and imitation military awards. Video games played an important part in Breivik's trajectory. Evidence presented during his trial indicated that for most of 2006–7 he spent his time playing *World of Warcraft*, an online multiplayer fantasy game. In this, his avatar (the character he inhabited) was known as Justicar Andersnordic. In the manifesto that he posted to the internet at the time of the massacre he carried out, Breivik claimed to be part of the Knights Templar National and Pan-European Patriotic Resistance Movement, occupying the role of 'Knight Justicar', the character he had created for himself in *World of Warcraft*. The real as myth plays a central role within emerging extreme-right movements in Europe and North America, as shown in their references to Odinism (Bjorgo 2014: 60). But gaming and an associated aestheticization of the real as myth are also important in jihadist pathways. At one level, this appears obvious in the constant references to games, such as *Call of Duty*, and for the figure of the anti-hero associated with this. But, at a deeper level in this development, we are confronted by the issue of what is 'real' and the relationship that different actors establish with what they construct as real.

Several people who knew him, for example, note how important playing *Call of Duty* was for the 17-year-old Aseel Muthana in the months before he travelled to Syria. Perhaps more important, though harder to make sense of, is his suggestion of 'let's pretend we're on an operation' when filming himself and a friend outside Cardiff, where the act of filming allows a stylization of the real as myth. In this case, the act of filming allows Muthana to transform smoke coming from a factory into that from the destruction of 'an operation'. He and his companion are unable to sing any Muslim nasheeds, having to content themselves with the theme tune to *Rocky*. But smoke coming from a factory, combined with the action of self-filming, allows him to experience, if only briefly, the intensity of an operation, sharing the emotion of those in Syria who undergo intensity and release as they film suicide bombers driving towards a target before obliterating themselves.

One of the most hated hackers on this game

These themes are central to the radicalization pathway experienced by Junaid Hussain. Originally from Birmingham in the United Kingdom, Hussain was killed by a drone strike in Syria in August 2015. He had been in territory controlled by ISIS for just over two years, where he had travelled with his wife Sally Jones and one of her children. During this period, Hussain had been linked to a number of actual and attempted attacks in both the United States and Britain, and in the period leading up to his death he had circulated a list of the contact details of US government employees on social media, calling for them to be killed. While in Syria, he had gone under the name of Abu Hussain al-Britani and played a central role in creating what IS called its 'Cyber Caliphate', involved in hacking websites and social media accounts. He maintained a prolific presence on social media, his accounts regularly being suspended and recreated. He had been in direct contact via social media with several people involved in attacks in the United States, most notably one on an anti-Muslim art event in Garland, Texas, in May 2015, in which a guard was wounded and the two attackers killed. But Hussain's experience as a 'hacker' did not begin with his arrival in Syria.

In an interview with a gamer website before he left the United Kingdom, he stated that he 'started hacking' at the age of eleven. His initial efforts focused on gaming, during a period when he used the screen name TriCk:

> I used to play an online game and there was someone going around in this game hacking random people's accounts via cookie/session stealing. I randomly got hacked by this kid, I wanted revenge so I started googling around on how to hack.
>
> I joined a few online hacking forums, read tutorials, started with basic social engineering and worked my way up. I didn't get my revenge, but I became one of the most hated hackers on this game. When I got to the age of 13, I stopped playing this game, found it childish, and went back to them hacking forums where I started learning my basic stuff. (Kovacs 2012)

The game he is referring to is a first-person shooter game *Soldier Front*. It involves a digital world where success is achieved by overcoming challenges and finding hidden assets, whether these be weapons, ammunition, health, and so on. Finding these allows the gamer to proceed to higher levels, increasing his power and defeating opponents on the way. The game is a world experienced in terms of layers, one where greater knowledge and skill allows the player to progress through layers and gain *respect* or *reputation*. When he describes himself as becoming 'one of the most hated hackers on this game', Hussain is referring to his reputation. His first successful 'hack' involved taking control of a website and sending out a message about himself, presenting this as sent from another person's address. What is the content of his message? It is about himself: 'The website ... was hacked by TRICK AKA SAYWHAT?, I didn't think he was capable of hacking the site but he was, and I admit he is a good hacker' (26 August 2009). Earlier in 2009, Hussain claimed to have taken control of another site, prompting a more senior member of the game to respond:

> This Kid Apparently thought he Hacked dxt not too long ago, you might remember seeing as how he posted a couple screenshots ... He is an epic fail in the making. To dxt he is simply a pest, and that is all, Hes like a small bug that we flick from time to time to get a small laugh. And he delivers on time every time with his fail hacking attempts. (http://www.gamerzplanet.net/threads/a-message-to-all-about-trick-aka-saywhat.320441/)

Success and failure, respect and disrespect are the currency of this world. For Hussain, the path to respect involves taking control of accounts through phishing, a form of deception where a person fraudulently gains access to information by impersonating a trustworthy entity. Once he has taken control of the account belonging to someone else, he sends messages celebrating his abilities. This is a practice not all admire, however, some treating him as a 'pest'.

Beyond the game

In the account that Hussain constructs of his own development, he describes discovering a world much bigger than anything that he had ever found hidden or embedded in a game: 'When I was 15, I became political – it started from watching videos of children getting killed in countries like Kashmir & Palestine. I wanted to know why this was happening and who was doing it, there was loads of questions in my head' (Kovacs 2012). Like many people we meet in this book, Hussain discovers 'distant suffering' (Boltanski 1999). For some, it is a sign of a world in a process of decomposition. For others, it epitomizes the opposition between good and evil that mutates into pure and impure. Hussain's response to suffering goes in a different direction: 'I browsed the net, read books, watched documentaries, etc. I was getting more and more into politics, I started researching deeper into stuff like the Free Masons, Illuminati, The Committee of 300, etc.' (Kovacs 2012).

In the layered reality of the game, all is not what it seems, and it appears that Hussain 'activates' this experience in response to distant suffering, asserting that such a reality can only be explained by hidden forces that have created it. He uses an identical phrase to that used by Mohamed Merah: 'I started researching.' Merah travelled to Afghanistan. Hussain sets out to get 'deeper into stuff' and in the process discovers a 'truth' that is shaping the world.

Conspiracy, trust and distinction

The violence and suffering that Hussain 'sees' point to a structure of responsibility, one where three groups exercise hidden power: the Freemasons, a fraternal organization with its origins in crafts associated with working stone in Europe; the Illuminati, alleged to have been founded in Bavaria in the 1770s, which in the centuries since have grown into a secret society controlling the world through a new world order; and the Committee of 300, an alleged group of 300 people, largely based in British-Jewish aristocracy, also seeking to control the world, responsible both for the Second World War and the financial crash of 2008. The reputation of these hidden groups extends beyond that found in airport fiction and has become a significant part of contemporary popular culture, associated in particular with the internet. Given the extent of the power believed to be exercised by these groups, it would at first appear difficult to accept that they could all exist together – surely there is only room for one group to secretly control the world. However, in a culture of conspiracy, logic is largely irrelevant.

We can understand conspiracy theory on several levels. Veronique Campion-Vincent (2005) highlights the ways it parallels other systems of knowledge based on a hidden realities, such as astrology or spiritualism, where the ability to access hidden meanings can open up new forms of knowledge. The faceless groups that Hussain identifies are not only in the shadows; they have been in existence for at least a century, if not longer. Conspiracy theory brings with it the power to cast a light on these hidden 'realities', and in so doing offers the prospect of control in a world that otherwise appears unintelligible. Conspiracy theory does not work principally at the level of idea, but is sustained by *affect* or shared emotion – in this case, the exhilaration of breathless discovery, one that provokes uncanny experiences of déjà vu, of movement in the shadows just out of sight, of hidden forces not so much seen as sensed (Stewart 2007). The rise of conspiracy theories as a way of experiencing the world captures significant social and political change, ranging from a decline of trust in media and science to a more general suspicion of government. This decline of trust is not limited to less-educated sections of the population, as evident in the decline in support for vaccination against preventable disease, and increasing incidence of these diseases in Europe (in France, for example, 'distrust' of vaccination among the population has risen to 40 per cent) (Taïeb 2016). The range of conspiracies is wide, from the proposal that the United States government or Israel were behind the attacks of 11 September 2001 to the belief that condensation traces left by jet airlines are in fact 'chemical trails', secret efforts to control climate, defined as 'geoengineering'.

Conspiracy theories are a response to a world experienced as unintelligible in as far as they offer explanations for complex problems. But as well as offering explanations, as the French political scientist Emmanuel Taïeb argues, conspiracy theories displace *responsibility*, particularly in response to extreme events that otherwise appear unthinkable. Here, conspiracy theory combines with rumour to amplify and extend the reach of ideas that are otherwise unbeliev-able. The Israeli intelligence organization Mossad, it is argued, was responsible for the September 11 attacks, the 'proof' being that four thousand Jewish employees failed to turn up for work at the World Trade Centre on the day of the attacks. This example underlines the extent to which political actors integrate rumour into commu-nications strategies – the source of the rumour that Jewish workers failed to turn up to work was a false news report first broadcast by Al-Manar, Hezbollah's radio station in Lebanon (Taïeb 2016). This shifts responsibility away from the actual authors of the attack, even after they admit that they undertook it. The response in jihadist-supporting forums to the killing of Mohamed Merah took a similar form, with discussion focusing on the nature of his wounds, whether it was he who was actually killed, and so on. Conspiracy theories were also central to jihadist-supporting forums discussing the execution of the *Charlie Hebdo* journalists. In various images of these events in the news, the wing mirrors on the doors of the car used by the killers appear to be different colours. This was because they were reflec-tive chrome – but it was widely seen as proof that several cars were involved, suggesting that the murders were in fact the responsibility of security services. One prominent French political commentator declared that the killers were already on their way back to Tel Aviv, while Jean-Marie Le Pen, former leader of the Front National and presidential candidate in 2002, declared in the national press that the executions bore the hallmark of France's secret services (Taïeb 2016).

If the increasing importance of conspiracy theory points to a decline in trust of national media, it is also a mechanism of 'distinc-tion' through which a person can claim to see through falsehood to discover truth. The person who embraces conspiracy theory is confi-dent of their superiority over others who are not capable of seeing the truth where it is hidden.

Hacktivism, script kiddies and elephant worshippers

In Hussain's account of his personal transformation, discovering such a hidden system of power is a deeply affecting event: 'It made me angry, it changed the way I lived my life and the way I saw the world. I then started using hacking as my form of medium by defac-ing sites to raise awareness of issues around the world and to "bully" corrupt organizations and embarrass them via leaks etc., which is how I got into activism' (Kovacs 2012).

There are several dimensions to what Hussain describes as 'hacktivism'. During this period, he was part of several hacking 'crews', the last being TeaMp0isoN. These hacked into address lists on relatively unsecured servers to make data thus obtained public – a type of action known as 'doxing'. One of the first examples of this action, in December 2010, accessed and published online the list of customers who had purchased clothes from the English Defence League (EDL), uploading some 350 names to the internet.

Throughout this period, while insisting his life has changed, Hussain is continuing to take control of poorly secured websites to use them as a vehicle for messages. What is striking is his insistence, repeated many times, that the United States government was behind the September 11 attacks as part of a more generalized attack on Muslims. This raises the question of the 'real' that we discussed above. Hussain defaces websites such as that belonging to an EDL clothes supplier with the same pleasure with which he defaced websites while playing *Soldier Front*. Does he believe that the United States government was behind the killing of some three thousand of its citizens, despite the information about those involved and the later explicit acceptance of responsibility by Osama bin Laden? To play this game, Hussain does not have to believe his post. He just has to believe that it is possible. In the process, the real becomes reconfigured as myth.

Most of the 'hacking' that Hussain was involved in up until 2010 involved defacing low-security websites. He was prolific – some 1,456 images of TeaMp0isoN-defaced websites are archived online (http://www.zone-h.org/archive/notifier=TeaMp0isoN/page=50). The earliest are similar to graffiti tags – 'TriCk aka Saywhat? WaS HeRe!' (18 October 2009). By 2010, the defacements have widened focus. He takes the themes he has developed to demonstrate his superiority, directing these at pro-India hacker groups such as the Indian Cyber Army.

Message to Indian Cyber Army (Indian script kiddies)

Making fake pictures and claiming to do something you didn't do is lame.
We hacked your site and you didn't fuck all back as you couldn't, stop going around acting like your something big, let me break it to you kids – you can't hack, ur a bunch of kids who go around doing SQLis on Pakistani websites.

> Stepping up to our level and challenging us was not a good idea, kids like you are not welcome in the hacking scene go back to worshiping elephants and kissing ur dad's feet, im surprised u have internet in your country bet is dial up? – TeaMp0isoN. P.S. FUCK INDIA – FUCK HINDUS – FUCK ICA.
>
> http://www.zone-h.org/mirror/id/10678791

In 2010, Hussain derides 'dirty elephant worshippers' in hundreds of defacements of low-security sites in India (http://www.zone-h.org/mirror/id/10780112). These posts, with their constant references to dirt and filth, alert us once again to the experiential structure of racism. Across these hacks, Hussain continues to assert his power and skill, referring to opponents, whether pro-India or Anonymous-linked as 'script kiddies' (a derogatory term for people who use off-the-shelf techniques to access others' websites). He presents himself as a defender of the 'hacking scene' and appears to be setting out to reverse the rejection he first experienced on *Soldier Front*, where he now treats his opponents as 'kids'. From late 2010, Hussain begins to deface UK-based websites (ticket sales, toy sales, etc.). During this period, there is no explicit political message. He falls back on themes from gamer culture: his superiority as a hacker; and the idea that in 'owning' others' websites, he is living a higher or epic life – achieving 'destiny'. His description of his own life as 'achieving destiny', constantly posted to the websites he hacks, suggests once more that the real is being experienced as myth.

Knowledge is power: revealing truth, revealing guilt

Hussain's actions remain embedded within popular culture. In 2011, he and others develop an application to 'phone bomb' a terrorist police help number for members of the public. They record themselves, uploading the audio file with an image of the Fonejacker, at the time a popular figure on a major UK television station, who telephones people pretending to be someone else. Hussain puts on an American accent for his interaction with the officer who responds to his call:

Hussain: Do you know about TeaMp0isoN?
Officer: You hack into certain sites, certain websites.
Hussain: Yeah.
Officer: Well, what is your actual philosophy? Because I'm not absolutely familiar with it.

Hussain: Ah, well, my actual philosophy is actually pretty simple. It's Knowledge is Power. We embarrass governments, and fuck the police. (https://www.youtube.com/watch?v=PEBQoxHh1uU)

The communication is soon terminated, but the recording continues for a further few seconds. TriCk and his companions are giggling and laughing, one urges, 'TriCk, call them again, call them again bro'.' Hussain's debt to popular culture goes beyond celebrating his prowess as a phone jacker. He creates a new Facebook page to boast about his exploits (https://www.facebook.com/TeaMp0isoN/): 'Sitting on a lot of big projects – new levels will be reached when these are completed.' He portrays himself as confronting challenges and, when these are successfully met, he can progress to 'new levels', the experiential imaginary of the game.

In mid-June 2011, Hussain, as TriCk, announces through Twitter: 'Tony Blair's Private Info is getting leaked tonight, so is his Personal Advisors CV and UK MPs & Lords who supported the war in Iraq.' The information has come from accessing the personal email account of a former advisor to the prime minister. Hussain posts phone numbers and addresses of different UK politicians to Pastbin, but also includes details of an NHS doctor, a dentist as well as the CV of the advisor. The page is entitled 'Tony Blair and his sheep get owned. TEAM POISON: Knowledge is power' (http://pastebin.com/raw/mn6Dhgcd). But Hussain is not what we might consider a political activist. Six months later, he posts scanned images of the credit card, address and passport of US rapper Sean Combs, also known as P-Diddy, claiming it was obtained by hacking into a Trump hotel. He attributes Combs's success to the influence of the Illuminati, and tags the post #*Killuminati*. Here, Hussain draws on widespread conspiracy theories about the influence of the Illuminati in the American music industry, believed to be behind the success of certain artists. Through his passport, address and credit card number being posted, Combs is 'unmasked'. At the end of the post, Hussain writes once again: 'KNOWLEDGE IS POWAHH!

The structure of these actions is similar. By making something visible that powerful others want to keep private, Hussain is demonstrating his superiority. He is making visible something that others want to conceal, even if it is merely a hotel receipt or the phone number of a politician's dentist. In so doing he experiences himself as achieving an exploit and revealing a truth. He is not simply defeating a powerful person's attempt to keep something hidden; he is revealing their *guilt*.

PoisAnon and crisis

In June 2012, one year before departing for Syria, Hussain pleaded guilty to violating the Computer Misuse Act, the charges being linked to the hacking of the former advisor's email and to the phone jacking. He served four months in juvenile detention. After his release, he became involved in #OpCensorDis2, participating in a YouTube rap video wearing an Anonymous mask. The video is credited as signalling a new collaboration between TeaMp0isoN and Anonymous, who have joined forces to create PoisAnon. While not singing, nor credited, Hussain features prominently in the visual structure of this video. He is one of only two members of the group wearing an Anonymous mask, and the camera repeatedly zooms in on this, but on several occasions it cuts back to reveal brief flashes of his unmasked face.

After his period in detention, Hussain created a website, illSecure.com. It was to be a platform for updates on hacker actions, with a focus on anti-American and pro-al-Qaeda news: 'Mossad hacked by Sector404 and Anonymous', 'UPS hacked by al-Qaeda electronic army', etc. (illSecure.com archived pages). The site was intended to celebrate and promote 'attacks', the denial of service and website defacement actions modelled on those being undertaken at the time by Anonymous (Coleman 2014). It was to be a platform for #OpUSA, to be launched in May. Hussain writes breathlessly:

> As #OpIsrael fades away, the hactivists who participated in it have found a new target, The United States of America. The hacktivists involved in #OpIsrael have again united this time under the banner #OpUSA and will cause havoc in America's cyber space. #OpUSA will be initiated on 7 May 2013 and will target American websites & servers. The hackers say they are targeting the USA for its war crimes in Iraq, Afghanistan and Pakistan. (illSecure.com, archived site, 31 May 2013)

What is striking is how this model of action spills over into personal rivalries. Hussain uses the site to announce as 'news' two other hacks on the girlfriend of @Ag3nt47, the former boyfriend of his new partner, Sally Jones, who had recently converted to Islam:

Chechen Muslim hacker with the alias 'Maybezero' has released dox on anonymous member 'TruthIzSexy' under the banner of #OpUSA. In a direct message to illSecure, the hacker said the anon was targeted for her hatred towards Islamic Jihad [*holy struggle*] and for supporting America and also for trying to discredit #OpUSA, he then went on to say that 'she is a hardcore Christian who attacks women that convert to islam. (illSecure.com, archived site, 31 May 2013)

This settling of accounts takes on a comical aspect as Hussain uses his website to post still more 'news' about @TruthIzSexy: 'A new group calling themselves "40ozg00nz" made their debut in the world of bits and bytes by releasing a e-zine exposing @Ag3nt47 & @TruthIzSexy. In an email to illSecure, 400zg00nz said they targeted Ag3nt47 for spreading fake hacks & dropped dox on TruthIzSexy because she 'calls everyone on Twitter a skid' (illSecure.com, archived site, 31 May 2013). Hussain is settling scores with people only one month before he leaves the United Kingdom to travel to Syria. One of the next images of him to appear on the internet surfaces several months later; he is sitting in a hotel room, with a woman who appears to be in her early forties sitting on his lap, taking a selfie of them both by directing the camera at a mirror. Hussain is wearing the same hoodie and Anonymous mask that he wore during the video recording. The woman is wearing high heels and a miniskirt. Her name is Sally Jones.

@Pu55yGa110r3

I love being the villain, having everyone rustled. Life is beautiful.

@Pu55yGa110r3, 2 October 2012

On 28 September 2015, Sally Jones was listed for sanctions by the United Nations Security Council as a named terrorist involved in al-Qaeda in response to her social media work, urging young women to travel to Syria and offering guidance to people in the United Kingdom about how to construct home-made bombs. Before she left the United Kingdom for Syria in 2013, Jones lived in Kent, south of London. In her profile on one of the main websites that she frequented at the time, deviantart.com, she describes herself as a single mother with two children, a digital artist, involved in music, magic and witchcraft. The website functions through its users 'gifting' images to each other and commenting upon each other's art. Jones uses two names – Catgel (for cat-girl), and a magical name, Skya. Her AIM address is 'skya-kentish witch', reflecting her interest in the occult, from fairies to goddesses, evident in naming Aleister Crowley and H. P. Lovecraft as her favourite poets. Her MSN handle is 'skya-evil-temptress', intimating her interest in constructing a persona around a dangerous sexuality. She embraces a digital aesthetic drawing on classical English themes of the occult, combined with images, themes and a colour palette from the American film *Avatar*. She sells her digital images, as well as a range of cups and mugs, through an online store, and in mid-2010 she was the key figure in efforts to keep *Avatar*-inspired activities alive on the website. Jones shares in the anti-religious themes that are important in English occultism. She posts on 13 September 2010 to oppose a planned visit of the Pope to the United Kingdom, writing: 'All religion has ever done is cause wars & suffering & hurt ... I refuse to have my children believe there is a man in the sky with an invisible wand who waves it & makes it all better' (http://web.archive.org/web/20111121023811/http://catgel.deviantart.com/journal/).   She does not correspond to the 'religious zealot' model proposed by Michael Walzer (2015).

Jones's posts in 2011 underline the extent to which she, just as Hussain, shares an imaginary of conspiracy theory: the European Union (EU) is replacing the British government; the people of Britain will soon no longer be allowed by the EU to call themselves British; the United States is merging with Mexico and Canada (with a new currency, the Amero, planned); the Euro is overtaking the American dollar and will bring the United States to its knees; George Bush planned to invade Afghanistan before 9/11; there is no law obliging Americans to pay income tax, only a government conspiracy; 9/11 was an inside job; the New World Order is taking power. Confronted with this global conspiracy, 'THE INTERNET IS OUR SAVIOUR' (emphasis in original).

During 2011, Jones began interacting over Twitter with young hackers connected with Anonymous, many of whom shared a similar worldview of conspiracy, anti-government, hidden knowledge and the saving power of the internet (McDonald 2015). Hussain created an account on DeviantArt in April 2011, viewing images on the site over a period of two months. Jones did not possess any computing skills, but by mid-2012 she was photo-manipulating images and 'gifting' them to young men involved in Anonymous. These range from reworked versions of the Sony V for Vendetta mask to women in lingerie and images of Catwoman wearing latex and carrying a whip.

During this period, her Twitter handle was @Pu55yGa110r3, the seductive fictional character in Ian Fleming's *Goldfinger*, evoking her previous persona of Cat Girl. She initiates and builds relationships by designing 'avis' or profile images that she 'gifts', in particular to young men involved in hacker networks. Later in 2012, she changes her Twitter account to @Pu55yTheGod, with a username of Pu55y Hussain. Sex is central to the different personas Jones constructs, using names such as @Zer0L0v3r (with a username Pu55yTrapz). Her retweets range from condemnations of US President Obama's policy in Iraq to images of women in lingerie bending over chairs (@ Zer0L0v3r, 10 November 2012).

It is during this period that Jones and Hussain began a public feud with the girlfriend of a previous boyfriend of Jones, both of whom were involved in Anonymous. We saw above that Hussain presented the 'doxing' of this woman as 'news' on his website. At this time Jones created a fake online account that presented this woman as operating a swinger sex club from her home address, forwarding information about this to UK social services and police, as we see in exchanges in May 2013 through Jones's account @ Sukinah_Hussain: 'Social services have demanded @TruthIzSexy comes offline to save her children and she won't ... cos she don't love them' (Twitter, 25 May 2013). Jones posts a picture of herself and Hussain to her former boyfriend: 'Suki & my sexy TriCk ! (I was giving him a lovebite – so go kill yourself) @ag3nt47' (Twitter, 1 June 2013).

This provoked a response to 'dox' Jones in turn, as well as a public post of an exchange that had taken place between Jones and a (former) friend about the fake site she was creating:

Jones: hahahah...lol... gonna be lulz tonight ... I can't let her know yet . . we can on the day 'OPUSA' launches lol ... 5 more days
Jones: sweety you the only one I told cos i trust you. Love ya xxxx
Friend: What you doing to her haha?xxxx
Jones: im making up a swinger site ... shes getting them all at her door later... hahahaha ... dont say nothing fuck sake lololol. (Twitter, 2 May 2013; zhttps://archive. cyberguerrilla.org/a/2013/?p=12287)

Dozens of other posts follow similar lines. One, combined with a provocative sexual pose, is directed to her former boyfriend:

@SukiHussain: '@Ag3nt47 im a sexy nun … and the sexiest freedom fighter in the world wants me. Sorry and all. (12 May 2013)

She follows this up a month later with a bondage image, coupled with the text: 'I never wanted @ag3nt47 as my slave what he on #meth? @truthIzSexy … check it new screenshot. – Slave Me Miss'.

@SukiHussain: '@*TruthIzSexy* Maybe America should ask you about Terrorists seeing as though you called my man one you dirty whore … (Twitter, 16 April 2013)

Dangerous sex is at the centre of the persona that Jones has created, not only through her feud but also in tweets to friends. In July 2012, a friend tweets to Jones and another woman, Anon Miss Kitty, a stock photo of a woman's bum, wearing a suspender belt and stockings, asking 'who owns this?' Miss Kitty replies, saying she has a tail, so it must be @Pu55yGa110r3. Jones retweets the conversation, and for much of 2012 uses the image as her Twitter avatar.

A year later, the suspender belt and stockings have been replaced by another image, this one downloaded from a website devoted to 'girls with guns'. From February to June 2013, the conflict between Hussain and Jones and a number of members of Anonymous continued to escalate, running serious risks for them both. In April, a Twitter account under the name @illSecureFed was created, featuring an image of Hussain and accusing him of being a 'snitch' for the US FBI, where he is described as a 'fed cooperating rat'. By June 2013, Hussain and Jones had broken away from significant parts of the networks they had previously been involved with, their retorts directed not only at Hussain, but at Jones as well. She had once described herself as a member of 'TeamRo0ted', but now finds herself being attacked on Twitter by him as well as other former friends:

Ro0ted: Suki kill yourself buddy. No one cares about anything you say but you knew that. (cyberguerilla.org)

Others direct their anger at the group as a whole:

@docofcocks: @illSecure @SukiHussain @Ag3nt47 @TruthIsSezy you're all faggots who can't do shit. Ironic. (3 May 2013)

@docofrocks: remember when I said illsecure is shitty? Ya this is
        why.

In June, both Hussain and Jones were 'doxed' on Pastebin, with
Hussain also 'doxed' in Skidpaste (a site for naming and shaming
people who are regarded as 'skids') where he was accused of 'carding'
gifts to Sally Jones (i.e. fraudulently using credit card details).
Accusations were being traded on Skidpaste:

@QXL:@illSecure:	It also seem that you Junaid have been involved in cc fraud with Dillon. (29 May 2013)
@illSecure @Sukinah_Hussain:	You going dark? No more carding suki gifts?
@illSecure:	Your nothing more than a credit card scammer fact! (Twitter, 7 June 2013)

Departure

By June, this situation amounted to a complete loss of control
for Hussain, as he found himself mocked and doxed, with a fake
Twitter account bearing his photo declaring him to be a government
informer. One month after the accusation that he had been skimming
credit cards for Sally Jones, he tweets: 'I'm going away permanently
& leaving the UK to respond to the crys of the oppressed muslims,
suki will be joining me in December InshAllah' (@illSecure, Twitter,
23 July).

This tweet and the circumstances surrounding it highlight an
important development in his reinvention of self, leading to his
departure for Syria. Hussain tells his followers that he is leaving in
response to the cries of the oppressed. However, the story appears
much more complicated, even based on the fragmented evidence that
remains in cyberspace. Departure opens up the promise of resolv-
ing tensions; as Aqsa Mahmood posted, it would allow her to 'just
breathe'. In early February 2013, soon after Hussain's release from
youth detention, Sally Jones tweeted a picture of herself and Hussain
together, writing: 'Mr and Mrs Hussain #Afghanistan 2014 inshAllah <3' (Twitter, 10 February 2013). She dreamed of starting a new
life in Afghanistan. As events unfolded, they travelled to Syria, where
Hussain would play a central role in the Cyber Caliphate, while Jones

would come to play a key role in controlling young women arriving in Syria from the West.

Cyberjihad

Hussain became a central figure in the development of the Cyber Caliphate, while also encouraging individuals in the United States and Britain to undertake violent action. Much of the action he was engaged in while in Syria mirrors what he was undertaking before his departure. The Cyber Caliphate focused on 'doxing' and, despite claims that he could hack into military servers, most of the information that Hussain made public was compiled from low-security sources. On 12 January 2015, he succeeded in taking control of the US Central Command Twitter account, @Centcom, tweeting messages echoing Anonymous themes: 'American Soldiers, We are coming, Watch your back!', and 'We won't stop, we know everything about you, your wives and children.'

This kind of action is completely different from what we saw in the case of Aqsa Mahmood. She expressed little interest in the United States, being fundamentally concerned with what she sees as the threat of contamination. The logic of action evident in Hussain's posts is completely different, one that counterposes the visible with the invisible. Just as he took enormous pride and pleasure in boasting that no one knew the identity of TriCk, once in Syria as Abu Hussain al-Britani, he posts a series of images of himself on Twitter, but his face is always masked, the relationship with his audience always mediated by a gun. The pattern of action that Hussain develops while in Syria extends themes already evident while he was in the United Kingdom. He constructs relationships of winners and losers; he wants to demonstrate the superiority of the Cyber Caliphate and the powerlessness of the American military, especially in his claim that 'we know everything about you'. His experience again underlines the fundamentally social nature of the processes through which radicalization pathways are constructed and the kind of embodied imaginaries involved. It signals the importance of intimate relationships to this process, in this case that of the couple. But it also highlights an embodied imaginary of discovering hidden worlds and realities, ones where we see a radicalization pathway best approached as a game, at its core a process of dividing the world into winners and losers, those leading an epic life and those who are mere kids.

7

My Concern is Me

My concern is me.
Florida-born Moner Mohammad Abu-Salha, final video testament,
Northern Syria, 2014

The real Muslims will never accept the filthy ways of the west.
Omar Mateen, post to Facebook on the morning of the Pulse
Nightclub massacre, Orlando, 12 June 2016

A fundamental aspect of jihadist violence is that those killing actively stage their own deaths while seeking to bring about the deaths of others. Over the past two decades in France, every jihadist attack has resulted in the death of the attackers. And in three attacks involving stabbings and explosions that took place in the United Kingdom during 2017, all the attackers were killed – either by police or security staff or, in the case of the Manchester suicide bomber, as a result of detonating explosive devices. This pattern matches that of the other attacks that have taken place in the United Kingdom. In July 2005, four bombers attacked London's transport system, all dying as a result of detonating explosives in backpacks they were wearing. The two men who killed and attempted to decapitate off-duty soldier Lee Rigby as he walked across a London street in 2013 both expected to be killed by police in the aftermath of the murder. This desire to die is fundamental in any attempt to understand jihadist violence. For some observers, it is explicable in terms of Islam and the idea of the martyr. However, as Farhad Khosrokhavar (2009) insists, in Islam as other religious traditions, the martyr is someone chosen by God. In these jihadist attacks, it is the authors of the violence that either kill themselves or set off a chain of violence that can only end in their deaths. The three men who began to attack police in London's Borough Market in June 2017 all wore imitation explosive vests – making certain that they would be killed by police rather than arrested. In such cases, argues Khosrokhavar (2009), martyrdom is not longer an action of God, but has become democratized – anyone can become a martyr.

What's in a name?

Just before leaving his home to travel to Orlando, Florida, Omar Mateen declared on Facebook that he hoped his actions would save him. Mateen did not have an extensive social media profile, but he was a member of a range of online dating sites, despite being married. Those posts he did make to social media were almost all selfies. His MySpace profile consisted of a photo of himself wearing an NYPD jacket; when younger, he had attempted to join the NYPD but without success. He had then commenced training as a prison guard, but had been removed from the course because he asked about guns in class. His professional preferences appear to have been jobs that allowed him to exercise power and authority. At the time of the shootings, he was working as a security guard on the gate at a golf course.

Despite telephoning police and TV news channels during the killings he carried out at the Pulse Night Club, Omar Mateen did not once use his name, even when directly asked who he was. He initiated a first contact with emergency services through a 911 call:

Mateen: I want to let you know, I'm in Orlando, and I did the shootings.
Operator: What's your name?
Mateen: My name is I pledge my allegiance to Abu Bakar al Baghdadi of the Islamic State
Operator: OK, what's your name?
Mateen: I pledge my allegiance to Abu Bakar al Baghdadi. (City of Orlando 2017)

Mateen ended the call, and within minutes he was rung back by a police negotiator. During the communications that followed, he was asked his name on seven occasions. Each time he either remained silent or responded, 'You are speaking with the person who pledged his allegiance to the Islamic State.' This mass killing is a pivotal event for Mateen, something that brings about a total rupture with his former life. A person's name is a sign of subjective continuity; it holds a personal narrative together. Organizations that want to break that down or destroy such subjective continuity will deny the use of a name, imposing either a number, as was once done in many prisons, or a new name. A group of friends will give a new member a 'nickname', underlining that they are conferring a new identity. Jihadists who travel to Syria will take a *nom de guerre* (or *kunya* in Arabic), not simply as a sign that they are a new person but as a performative act that is part of bringing that new person into being. Almost all westerners who travel to Syria to join jihadist groups create a name beginning with Abu or Umm, father or mother. Whether or not they have children, they start to call themselves 'father of' or 'mother of' – they become the source of themselves (Benslama 2016).

Later in the evening, a police negotiator continued to insist on asking Mateen for his name:

Negotiator: What's your name?
Mateen: My name is Islamic soldier, ok! [*irritation and anger*]
Negotiator: Ok, what can I call you?
Mateen: Call me Mujahideen, that means soldier of God.

Forty-five minutes after commencing the killing, Mateen calls a local news channel. Again he does not offer a name, but insists 'I'm the shooter. It's me. I am the shooter.' At no point during the killing does Mateen offer a name, either the one given to him by his parents or the one that he has chosen. A name projects into the future. The act he is undertaking is his name, a pledge of allegiance through an act of mass killing.

I feel the pain

Negotiator: Who am I speaking with?
Mateen: You are speaking with the person who pledged his allegiance to the Islamic State, Abu Bakar al-Baghdadi, and Allah.
Negotiator: Can you tell me where you are so that I can get you some help?
Mateen: No. You have to tell America to stop bombing Syria and Iraq. They're killing a lot of innocent people. So what am I to do here? When my people are getting killed over there. You get what I'm saying? They need

> to stop the US airstrikes! … You have to tell the US
> government to stop bombing. They're killing too
> many children, they're killing too many women. OK.

In this first exchange with a negotiator, Mateen focuses on the US bombing of Iraq and Syria. He opposes the guilt of the US government to the innocence of children and women victims. Here, he parrots the majority of jihadists who describe their action as a response to the suffering of others. But while claiming to be responding to US military action, Mateen also reflects another pattern: there is no evidence that he had previously taken any action of any kind in relation to the war in Syria and Iraq. He was not a member of any solidarity group, there is no evidence of any participation in any campaigns, no sign that he wrote to his Congress member or local newspaper, nor even signed an online petition. The exchange continues:

Negotiator: Can you tell me what's going on tonight?
Mateen: What's going on is that I feel the pain of the people getting killed in Syria and Iraq, and others of the Muslim *ummah*, ok.
Negotiator: Ok. So, so have you done something about that?
Mateen: Yes I have.
Negotiator: Tell me what you did? Please?
Mateen: No! You already know what I did!
[…]
Mateen: My homeboy Tamerlan Tsarnaev did his thing on the Boston Marathon, my homeboy Moner Abu-Salha did his thing, okay, so now it's my turn, okay.
[…]
Mateen: Let it be known, over the next few days you're going to see more of this kind of action going on. Even though it's not fucking airstrikes, it's fucking strikes here, ok.

Mateen's imaginary is one of individualized violence. One homeboy 'did his thing', then another 'did his thing': 'now it's my turn'. More action will take place in the future. There is no reference to what previous attacks achieved or how the killing he is engaged in will build upon this. The violence he is undertaking is not a means but a cycle that repeats. There is no horizon pointed to beyond this. When asked 'What's going on?', Mateen responds in the first person. But he does not say 'I am killing people'. He responds, 'I feel the pain of the people getting killed in Syria and Iraq, and others of the Muslim *ummah*', placing a definite emphasis on two words: 'I' and 'pain' (recording 16-242039 CNT, 1.55 minutes into exchange). Mateen is of Afghan background, yet not once does he refer to the Taliban or to the West's role in Afghanistan.

Now you feel how it is

Mateen: Tell, tell the fucking [*pause*] that the airstrikes need to stop

Negotiator: I'm doing that, I'm passing that message along. Immediately.

Mateen: You see, now you feel, now you feel how it is, now you feel how it is.

The issue of power is at the centre of Mateen's killings. He is exercising total power in taking lives. But he portrays himself as powerless before the massacre: 'What am I to do?', as if he has no options open to him apart from killing. But through his actions he has become powerful. Once the negotiator says that he is doing as Mateen has demanded, Mateen responds to him: 'Now you feel how it is.' Killing allows him to shift from being powerless to being powerful; he is at the centre. Later, the police negotiator calls him, but Mateen no longer wants to speak:

Mateen: You're annoying me with these phone calls and I don't really appreciate it.

Negotiator: Well, I understand that, but the fact that you appreciate it or not doesn't matter at this point. We need to talk and we need to stay …

Mateen: Hey! Hey! Hey! Don't talk to me like that! No. No. No. No. No. No.

Negotiator: No. I'm treating you like an adult. We need to stay in constant contact.

Mateen: No. No. No. No. No. No. No. No. No. No.

Mateen's angry reaction is provoked by the negotiator's suggestion that whether or not he appreciates receiving phone calls 'doesn't matter'. Mateen believes he has created a space of killing where he is at the centre. He has transformed a state of lack of power to one of having power.

The filthy ways of the West

On the morning of the killings, Mateen made several posts to Facebook. In one, he wrote, 'Now taste the Islamic State vengeance'. Later, he declared: 'The real Muslims will never accept the filthy ways of the west.' He also posted 'May Allah accept me', signalling a readiness to die, together with the hope that he would be received, that he would be absolved of any fault he might have. This highlights a fundamental dimension of jihadist violence as signalled by Khosrokhavar: absolving oneself of guilt, dealing with internal conflict by turning a suicide into a mass killing. The reference to 'filth', evoking the structure of hate crime, alerts us to subjectively destructive dimensions of shame. Khosrokhavar (2017) suggests that the nature of the killings at Orlando or Nice may be closer to the mass murder committed by Andreas Lubitz, the pilot of Germanwings Flight 9525 who, having previously been diagnosed with psychosis and suicidal tendencies, flew his plane with 150 passengers and crew aboard into the side of a mountain in March 2015. In Mateen's case, the use of the term 'filth' draws attention to the element of purification that the act represents while his online search for references to the killings during the ongoing massacre highlights a quest for fame that we find across a wide spectrum of violence.

We do not know what pain Mateen was feeling. After the Pulse attack, there was extensive discussion about his sexual orientation and whether he frequented the club himself. Investigations that followed failed to determine this issue. What is clear is that Mateen had a violent childhood. He was expelled from schools for violence and was arrested, ending up with a juvenile record. Anecdotes circulated after his death about his very negative response to men kissing each other in public. The themes of innocence and guilt, combined with references to filth and appeals to Allah to 'accept me', all suggest purification is central to this killing.

There has been no evidence linking Omar Mateen to any jihadist network and no evidence that he engaged in any form of political or religious practice. In this, he resembles the author of the 14 July 2016 massacre in Nice, Mohamed Lahouaiej-Bouhlel. He too had no link to any jihadist network nor to any mosque or religious group, and he frequently drank alcohol. In his case, there is clear evidence of male and female sexual partners as detailed in his mobile phone. He was separated from his wife, had a history of convictions for violence and use of prescription drugs for anxiety. He left no written communication about the mass killing he undertook. His mobile phone, however, revealed his practice of watching beheadings and his interest in ISIS. In the days before the massacre, he took photographs of himself with a small group of friends in the cabin of his rented truck. He also searched the internet for details of the Nice celebrations, together with images of fatal traffic accidents. Approximately one-third of those he killed were Muslims, reflecting the diversity of the city of Nice.

Several observers suggest that this case may be closer to mass murder and suicide, an example of a type of violence associated with 'radical losers'. In such cases, the killers are humiliated individuals seeking scapegoats and thirsting for vengeance. This kind of person is a product not of traditional societies but of a social world increasingly divided between winners and losers, where the losers internalize their failure. In these cases, the urge to escape this is characterized by megalomania and narcissism in an attempt to impose collective punishment upon those seen as responsible for such failure (Enzensberger 2006). Violence in this case seeks the power of life and death, together with media fame as seen in Mateen's telephone conversation with the police, and also his continuous checking of social media for news about himself during the killings (Johnson 2016).

We look for all those dirty elements

It is often believed that 'recruitment' into jihadist violence is facilitated by creating outrage about distant suffering. But an interview with 'Abu X' (pseudonym), a senior leader of the proscribed organization al-Muhajiroun, suggests a quite different process, one that may throw some light onto the path followed by Mateen.

Abu X: A lot of times, there's people who have problems which exist, but they're not aware of it. Our job is to identify those problems which exist in that person's life that he's not aware of and make him aware of those problems. Once he's aware of them, then you provide the solution and then you hold his hand and you give him the action plan.

Interviewer: So basically you act as a therapist or a brainwasher?

Abu X: Yes, that's right, it's brainwashing, yeah…. We look for all those dirty elements which exist within the brain and then we wash them out. This is our brainwashing.

Interviewer: Are you looking for embarrassing elements or …?
Abu X: Anything. Whatever it is, Islam has a solution for
                everything, whatever these little problems are: he feels
                a little bit gay, we've got a solution for that, he feels
                a little bit addicted to drugs, we've got a solution to
                that.
Interviewer: Would you use those against him to get him … ?
Abu X: No, never. No. We identify the problem existing, not
                from himself, but somebody who's used and abused
                him, that he is a tool and a product of the West who's
                been exploited by the kafir. Our da'wah is based on
                two pillars: to reject all false gods [and] whatever his
                problems are, whatever he is suffering from, none of
                it is his fault, it's because he's lived within the West,
                he's accepted the law of the West, he's accepted Man
                to be in charge over him and the kafir is the one
                who's exploited him and his desires.
                     Maybe he's a victim of that. But unknowingly, he's
                laying down a path of destruction. So we're there
                to make sure he has success in this life, success in
                the hereafter, but he needs to identify what those
                problems are … When we talk of rejecting those
                false gods, it's rejecting not just the false gods of
                desires, but it's the one who dictates those desires,
                the one who legislates those desires to be permissible
                … Anything which is non-Islamic, it needs to be
                attacked. If you don't attack it, they will attack you.

What Abu X describes is not a pedagogy based on building outrage
about international politics. Most of the people he encounters know
little or nothing of international politics. The starting point of recruit-
ing someone to the group involves identifying their personal problems, such as being 'a little bit gay', 'a little bit addicted to drugs'.
An inner unease is amplified into an affect that mixes fear, anger and
self-loathing directed at something dark within, something that har-
bours a danger of destruction. Rejection of this is projected outwards
at the corrupt society that has generated this and made it possible.
For al-Muhajiroun, radicalization starts with a focus on the self.

Both Michael Adebolajo, 29, and Michael Adebowale, 22, who
murdered Lee Rigby in the street in 2013, were involved in al-
Muhajiroun, and both shared the background that Abu X describes.
Growing up, Adebolajo had been connected with local gangs,

involved in low-level drug dealing and mobile-phone theft, so much so that his family was reported to have left London to extricate him from this world. He later returned to London to study and while at university became active in jihad-supporting networks, attending protests organized by al-Muhajiroun. In 2010, he travelled to Kenya in an attempt to join the Somali-based al-Shabab. This attempt failed, following which he returned to the United Kingdom. Adebowale had a background similar in a number of respects to that of Mohamad Merah. He had grown up in a deprived area and had connections to a gang at the age of 14. At the age of 16, he was dealing crack and looking after a flat being used as a crack den. In January 2008, Adebowale and two other people were attacked by a drug user who was in a psychotic state. One person died and Adebowale suffered two stab wounds during the attack. The attacker was convicted of murder, while Adebowale was jailed for eight months in a young offenders' institution. He received psychiatric treatment for post-traumatic stress and described converting to Islam in the following year as a way of disengaging from the world of gangs and violence. When they killed Lee Rigby in the street, Adebolajo and Adebowale expected to be killed by police. They had no escape plan and, as did the attackers in Borough Market four years later, they rushed at armed police, expecting to die.

In a letter Adebolajo addressed to his children before the attack, he advised them how to survive in a world filled with danger: to beware the 'bewitching tongues of the munafiqeen [*hypocrites*]'; to be strong enough to turn away from those 'dearest to you'; and that once 'set out on this path … do not to look left or right'. He urges his children to 'seek shahada [*martyrdom*], oh my sons, so that we might be raised together'. Adebloajo expects to die but, if he doesn't, his letter to his children suggests that he is not sure about his own ability to follow the path he has mapped out, warning them: 'If I live beyond this day and you find me talking other than this, then know that perhaps Allah has left me to stray.' During his trial, he did not respond to the name given to him by his parents. Just as Mateen in Orlando, once he was arrested and in court, Adebolajo insisted that he be called Mujaahid.

Power and the mask

One of the striking traits among those who travelled to Syria to join the group calling itself Islamic State is the adoption of the mask.

Many Twitter avis incorporate a masked image, even when the person in it is widely known. Masking has a long association with images of violence. The historian Allen Feldman notes the importance of masked figures in murals in Northern Ireland during the period of 'the Troubles'. He argues that masking serves to de-individualize and depersonalize, identifying the violence of the individual actor with a generalized force. Feldman highlights the close association of the mask and the gun in such images (1991: 53).

Anthropologists note the close association of the mask with forms of power. The mask is a vehicle of transformation, of transition from one state to another, evident in particular in rituals associated with birth, initiation or death. Christian Kordt Højbjerg (2005) believes that all such transformations include an element of danger, and often the figure in a ritual who aids such transitions is masked. The mask does not conceal the identity of the person leading the ritual. Instead, the mask indicates that the person has stepped outside of himself, and that a source of power is working through his body (something similar is evident when health professionals wear a white coat in situations where this is not clinically required). For Elizabeth Tonkin (1979: 24), the mask is a 'metaphor in action': 'since masks are themselves transformations they are used as metaphors-in-action, to transform events or mediate between structures.' Kordt Højbjerg extends this argument, proposing that the mask is an expression of paradox and ambiguity, where the act of covering conceals one identity while at the same time revealing another (2005: 159). The mask is not therefore primarily a means to hide an identity but a *medium of transformation*. In traditional African societies, where much of the research on masking has been undertaken, the mask is a source of power because it gives *access to another world*, that of the power of the ancestors (Argenti 2006). That makes the mask both a metaphor and a vehicle for a particular type of power (McDonald 2013: 113).

Fighters who have travelled to Syria have invented new personas, encapsulated by their new names. And they access extraordinary power, demonstrated by both the mask and the gun. There can be rapid transformations from one mask to another, as we see in the case of Junaid Hussain, who wears an Anonymous mask in 2013 and the mask of a jihadist in 2014, metamorphosizing into Abu Hussain al-Britani. In such cases, the mask is not a disguise. It is a metaphor in action, a way of accessing power.

The 'other' is the self

In a series of twenty tweets in November 2014, Tooba Gondal describes a lecture and seminar she experienced while a university student in London. She rejects what she regards as a western version of feminism, something she sees as a dominant conformist culture shared by students and academics. She is not afraid to stand out. She rejects what she sees as weakness. She sees herself as superior to those who conform: they are 'deluded'. She says that before the seminar began, her fellow students saw her as an 'alien', completely covered from head to toe. At the end of the seminar, she says 'now I am at the centre of all hate', 'seen as more of an alien'. She is not defined by tradition; she asserts her individuality and agency. Two months later, she left the United Kingdom to travel to Syria where she came to play a key role as a 'matchmaker', facilitating the travel of young British women to Syria in order to marry western jihadists. Like many of the women who have travelled to Syria, she was a prolific tweeter, and her social media profile offers insight into a transformative experience of the self. In May 2012, she posts images of her friends, declaring college is coming to an end and that she will 'miss every day of :(' (@toobabashier, Twitter, 19 May 2012). Self-portraits are an important part of shaping and exploring who she is, something she shares with friends: smiling; 'cba to leave my bed'; enjoying home-made pizza; images of herself without make-up, 'All natural. Without any make-up I feel naked ☹' (12 November 2012).

University life brings about a shift in her social media concerns. She starts to post images of people whose houses have been destroyed by bombings, a photo of a dead jihadist fighter alongside which she declares, 'Alhumduillah! He's smiling!'. She gives advice: 'if unsure about dietary rules, don't eat it.' She posts images of heaven, and also about the dangers of shirk. She encourages people to buy bags made in Gaza, but also circulates images of behaviour that she doesn't approve of: 'Hijabi with make-up defeats the purpose of covering up for less attention' (16 February 2013). Only four months earlier, she had been tweeting that without make-up she felt 'naked'.

In Aqsa Mahmood, we saw a radicalization route constructed around the polarization of purity and impurity, the latter being Shia. For Tooba Gondal, this is not the case. The contamination is much closer, and not so easily turned into an object of humour and grotesque ridicule. For Gondal, *the 'other' is herself* – or the self she previously was. Two days after her tweet about the incompatibility of make-up and wearing the hijab, Gondal posts three audiofiles to Audioboom (https://audioboom.com/posts/1220814-dangers-of-the-duniya-part-1?t=0). In these, she tells a story about the Prophet Muhammad walking with his followers and seeing the carcass of an animal. She affirms that 'the material world and everything in it means nothing less to Allah than that dead carcass'. That carcass evokes the 'dunya' or 'material world', something that Gondal describes in terms of four evils: 'taking ribat [*accepting interest*], using intoxications, going gambling, going to clubs'. Muslims, she argues, 'must be slaves of Allah, not slaves of our desires'.

This appears close to what sociologists have termed 'religious rejections of the world' (Weber 1991 [1948]), the idea that salvation requires distance from the world and its pleasures. But there is something more here. By disapproving of intoxication and clubs, Gondal is rejecting the party life that her earlier social media feed suggested she was leading. She is making a break from her previous self, living a 'born-again' experience. This rejection is associated with guilt. When Abu X details the pedagogy of al-Muhajiroun above, he emphasizes that the source of guilt is a society with man-made laws. But Gondal does more than look to others to explain this. The metaphor of *carcass* suggests the theme of *contamination* that we observed in Mahmood.

Gondal made an audio recording about her experience of transformation, circulating it to her Twitter followers in 2013. British criminologist Simon Cottee quotes part of it:

> I will give some background on how I used to think and behave, without revealing my sins too much. Year 9 [*age 13 to 14*] where I started to, you know, go totally off track. I started smoking, got into the habit where it became addiction. And then hanging around with bad company and guys and doing all sorts of haram [*forbidden*] things. But it wasn't to such a bad extent until I got to college. Then I had that freedom, you know? I wore whatever I wanted. As time went on it was getting worse – piercings – without even thinking what I was doing. You know, there was no haya [*modesty*], no limit. (Cottee 2016)

She then goes on to describe an event that was a turning point for her: a debate in a university class about humane ways to kill animals, where she found herself opposed to her 'atheist teacher'. She is defending halal as the best approach, but the teacher rejects this, escalating the confrontation, and according to Gondal:

> He says these exact words, which I cannot forget. Ever. To this day I remember, and every day I think it sinks in my heart so deep. He goes:

'Who are you to say anything about Islam when you choose what you want to follow and disregard everything else?' Next thing he said: 'Do you pray five times a day?' – this is in front of the whole class – and I sit there shocked. And then I'm like, 'How dare you ask me this question? I will not answer to you, I will not answer to you. I will only answer to Allah on the day of judgment!' (Cottee 2016)

According to Gondal, she then burst into tears:

Never have I said these words before. As soon as these words came out of my mouth my heart sank, and then straight away, at that moment, the bell went and I quickly left the classroom alone. I looked down at what I was wearing and I started thinking, 'How will I stand in front of Allah like this? I've never done anything good in my life.' (Cottee 2016)

Gondal then goes on to describe throwing away her cigarettes, going to a toilet to remove her piercings and later speaking to a veiled classmate about her faith and what she was wearing. She liked the jilbab (loose-fitting over-garment) her classmate was wearing which she found nicely 'tailored', and the next day her classmate brought her one, as well as a headscarf, to try on. Gondal did so, looked in a mirror, and describes her feelings: 'I literally fell in love. I feel like a new person ... I felt so pure and clean and happy' (Cottee 2016).

This is Gondal's reconstruction and reinterpretation of events a year later. But there is evidence in her Twitter feed to back up the timeline she suggests. She dates this classroom confrontation to 16 November 2012, and the following day she does in fact post an image, for the first time, of 'my favourite hijab' (@toobabashir, Twitter, 17 November 2012). There is, however, more going on here than abandoning cigarettes and piercings in order to embrace a more pious lifestyle. We can glimpse this when Gondal describes herself as 'pure and clean'. She is contrasting this with her former self who by implication was not pure and clean. But as we saw with Abu X and the recruitment strategy of al-Muhajiroun, guilt experienced in relation to one's previous life can be passed onto others.

Gondal was born in Paris, and migrated to the United Kingdom with her family when she was young. Two months before departing for Syria, she tweets:

Out of all countries to be born in, I was born in the disgusting scum France. I hate the racist French, who oppress any practising muslim and liberate those Arabs who have shamed Islam (drinking, prostitution ...), filth. When 'muslims' say they love France as a country. WaAllahi

Figure 7.1   SisterTooba. Tumblr, 9 September 2014.

shame on you! That country has oppressed our niqabi sisters, shamed Islam! They oppressed my mother, they stopped me from wearing the hijab in school when I was young living over there. Alhamdullilah we made Hijra! Where we used to live, in Paris, Arabs drinking alcohol used to try to humiliate sisters who are covered by calling them for prostitution! Filthy scummy French imbeciles. (Twitter, 22 November 2014)

The theme of filth appears again in a tweet she posts once she has successfully left the United Kingdom: 'Hey UK security, how do you feel that your citizen left your filthy country whilst listening to Salil as-Sawarim [*jihadist nasheed*] on the plane? Pathetic' (Twitter, 15 February 2015).

Gondal's pathway is not a linear one. Five months before departing the United Kingdom, she created a blog entitled SisterTooba (Figure 7.1), promising 'My unique and very much emotional story of how I came to Islam will be released. Stay tuned guys ...' She subtitles her blog 'A student, a sister and most importantly a muslimah' (sistertooba.wordpress.com). She announces that the blog will be about her journey 'from darkness to light'. Significantly, she chooses an image of sunrise over Paris to visually capture the story she intends exploring.

The visual theme suggests the beauty of a religious experience. Significantly, she describes herself as a student, an identity that she would turn her back on some four months later. Just over two months later she tweets about the 'scummy French'. She created the page in September but did not proceed to tell her story then. It remains on the Web, empty. As 2014 progresses, her social media feed becomes more and more defined by the conflict in Syria. She posts images of dead jihadists who are smiling, jihadists at prayer, images of ISIS fighters pillaging booty; she affirms that Islam is about justice, not equality (26 October); she feels like a soldier (18 November); an imaginary of war takes over her social media profile, one where war is inevitable (11 November); 'for every drop of blood, we will take revenge' (29 November); she retweets images of the executions of those who cursed Allah (26 October); she retweets a British jihadi who affirms that Allah does not need jihad, 'we need these things for ourselves' (1 October). Apostates are killing brothers in Islam, God prefers those who go rather than stay behind. One of her last tweets of 2014 points to the fact that she has decided her path: 'All sins forgiven to those who make sincere Hijra [*migration*]' (25 December 2014). This communication evokes that of Omar Mateen: purification and forgiveness will follow from the action to be taken.

Order and chaos

In the six months leading up to her departure, Tooba Gondal tweets between thirty and forty times each day. She uploads photos and videos from Syria; she campaigns for women not to have their faces in Twitter profiles; she mourns the death of British fighters in Syria. All these momentous events enter the intimate space of her Twitter feed, once focused on how she felt without make-up or on her upcoming exams. A great proportion of these tweets and images involve a tension between *order* on the one hand and threatening *danger* on the other. Danger is present in constant tweets describing ad-Dajjal, a huge one-eyed figure, with white/red skin; she decries the oppression of the Muslim community who have become so abased that they vote in elections. Death, she warns, comes unannounced; she appeals to all on her Twitter feed to pray for protection from the evil eye. Western culture is destroying Muslim families; the Muslims have become corrupt.

Gondal's fundamental preoccupation is that this chaos and danger is at work in the disorganization of gender relations. We can see this in her posts calling on women to remove their faces from their Twitter profile, or 'avi: 'Take down your Avis with faces, eyes, lips, feet, and the rest of that fitnah [*strife*]. Women are forgetting how much sins they are accumulating' (3 November 2014). 'The biggest fitnah for ahlul twitter [*house of Twitter*]) is free mixing and photos. Avoid that and then give reminders, that will confirm your sincerity' (9 November 2014). This is also destroying what it means to be a woman:

RT: That awkward moment when a woman with fake hair,
           fake nails, fake butt, fake breasts, and drawn-on eyebrows
           says she wants a 'real man'. (9 November 2014)

#PRT: Yeah that's the state of the majority of these westernised
           women. Only a saleh Muslimah knows how to keep it real.
           (9 November 2014)

For Gondal, there is more at stake here than authenticity: 'Lowering
your gaze is a COMMAND from Allāh before He told us to cover.
Face avis go against this' (5 November 2014). This divine imperative
must be enforced: 'How can a practising muslim akh [*brother*] allow
his wife to leave the house with make-up on? How is this even possible? Ya3ni I don't get it' (11 November 2014).

Women are responsible for enforcing this as well: 'Oppressing
your nafs [*self/desires*] that is what the Niqab does. No wonder all
these non-muslim men are irritated when they see a proud Muslimah
covered' (11 November 2014). The concept of 'nafs' within Islamic
tradition has various meanings, all associated with the 'self'. In the
way that Gondal is using the term, 'naf' appears to be uncontrolled
desire, in this case female desire.

My eyes are filled with tears

Two months before her departure, Gondal tweets 'My eyes are
filled with tears and everybody is looking at me on this train.' She is
responding to the news of the second British jihadist to be killed in
Syria, Abu Abdullah al-Habashi, and has just read and circulated the
video message he recorded before the fight in which he was killed.
Later in the day, she tweets 'I haven't eaten all day … since I heard
the news of my brother's shahadah.' Gondal refers to al-Habashi as
'my brother', rather than 'the brother', this use of 'my' signalling a
level of familiarity that it is important to understand. It alerts us to
the intimacy of social media communications, in particular those
associated with the mobile phone, which is a very personalized technology – often decorated and adorned, kept close to the body with
other items that have an affective charge. There is no evidence that
Gondal ever met al-Habashi, but she is crying because of his death
and shares this with her followers.

Gondal has constructed an account of a radical personal shift, of
a 'before' and 'after'. She experiences this transformation between
one day and the next, as she describes in the audio tape I referred to

above, and also when asked about her personal experience, as in this exchange on ask.fm:

> When did you start practising?
> In 3 days, it will be 2 years exactly Alhamdullilah. (13 November 2014)

Why the repeated reference to a date? The date implies a radical break with the past, rather than a gradual development or evolution. Gondal constructs an experience of her selfhood in terms of a 'before' and an 'after'. But why should this transformation, associated with many experiences of religious conversion, lead her to celebrate violence? Gondal's response to France and the French offers us some insight. The image on her blog is a beautiful sunrise in Paris, one that captures the subtitle of her blog – *from darkness to light*. But in the period since commencing the blog she has known the proximity of death and a cluster of themes grouped together as both mystical and dangerous. Gondal insists that the way to reduce this danger is to exercise power: the power of the husband to ensure that his wife does not leave their home wearing make-up; the almost magical power of the niqab to suppress desire. But for Gondal, this danger is above all present in the day to day. This is where the danger is most threatening and immediate in daily life in the West. This is where the menace of filth is to be found, as she tweets on the anniversary of her transformation: 'The blessed are those living under the Shari'ah of Allāh ﷻ; the unfortunate ones are we … surrounded by all this zina [*promiscuity*] and filth. Sigh. (16 November 2014).

A structure of feeling

Part of the challenge we face when attempting to understand radicalization is how major paradigms in the social sciences struggle to capture what is at stake. Much sociological work tends to look at the actions that people take as 'caused' by a social structure. In the case of radicalization that has meant researchers looking for 'causes' in social marginalization or isolation, poverty or outrage against areas of government action such as foreign policy. Other approaches, grounded in paradigms of cost and benefit, such as strategic action theories, examine how social actors might benefit from their involvement, whether in terms of prestige, excitement or honour. Both these approaches remain embedded in a cause–effect framework.

More contemporary social science is not only alert to social structures but also to the creativity and purposeful action of social actors (Touraine 2007). In part, this involves attempting to understand and respond to what people believe. And, increasingly, social scientists are aware of the extent that believing is linked to feeling, and that, in order to be able to *believe* certain things, we have to be able to *feel* certain things. We are now much more alert to the ways our humanity and agency are constituted through shared embodied experience. What the British cultural theorist Raymond Williams (1977) called 'structures of feeling' are at the centre of how we produce ideas and act together. Amin and Thrift define such 'structures of feeling' as 'inexact but powerful constellations of affective account and evaluation running through the mill of everyday practice', a 'shorthand for orientation to the world' where 'the world takes on shape as a form of emotional constitution' (2013: 174). The timelines and social media communications of many of the people described in this book constitute such a 'structure of feeling'.

In Tooba Gondal's case, understanding this is necessary to get any sense of the kind of transformation she experiences. In her audio recording where she recounts her transformation, she is crying (Cottee 2016). In the Audioboom that she uploads, her voice trembles and it is clear that at times she is dealing with something vast and powerful – the *danger of the dunya* (this world). There is some sort of 'structure of feeling' here, but how can we understand it? From what we can deduce from her social media profile while at secondary school, Gondal went to parties, wore make-up and may have drunk alcohol. She feels guilty about this. But guilt about clubbing and make-up is hardly sufficient motivation to embrace ISIS and call for the beheading of 'kaffirs' while still a university student in London.

We saw that school shooters attempt to 'fracture' reality through the scale of the violence they attempt, by doing something that is unimaginable. There is a possibility that the war in Syria fractures Gondal's reality in a way that is somewhat similar. The war is momentous and ominous, the scale of violence is terrible but, above all, it has entered her intimate world through becoming part of her timeline. This violence puts into question the life a person is leading; it makes the day to day appear small, unauthentic and contingent once confronted with the enormity of what is happening. As Gondal tweets, 'death can come at any time'. But how does she move from this to calling for beheadings? It could just as easily lead to a new appreciation of the vulnerability of life, or to her campaigning for peace and an end to war.

In Mahmood's case, we can see a trajectory focusing on *the 'other'*. In Gondal's case, this is much more about *herself*. Unlike Mahmood, for whom the danger is the existence of Shia Muslims, for Gondal the danger is within herself. The fracture in Gondal's day-to-day security is evident in her preoccupation with danger, in an unease and sense of danger, evident in her tweets about the Dajjal (the Antichrist), her prayers for protection from the evil eye and her constant tweets about death. On any reckoning, her personal guilt is concerned with small matters – clubbing, smoking, drinking. But these link her to a chasm in reality, one inhabited by forces imagined as a one-eyed giant Antichrist and to the proximity of death – something very distant from the comfortable London suburb where she lives, but which stalks her through its presence on her social media timeline. In her posts and her fixation with Muslim women in the West, in combating what she sees as the deregulation of gender relations, she sets out to overturn who she is. This explains why she constantly refers to a particular date when she 'transformed'. In her case, there is no gradual change. She has to reconstruct her personal trajectory in terms of a before and after, a then and a now. And these are at war.

Gondal is less concerned with creating a sisterhood than with dealing with the danger that she feels is pervasive. She uploads a picture of her phone's ear buds, listening to a jihadist nasheed: 'Chilling mornings with this in my ears – I feel like a soldier'. The suffering of Syrians rarely features in her timeline. What counts are jihadist fighters and the epic events that make Syria a momentous place, a place that will allow her to remove her guilt and escape the dangers of the dunya: 'All sins forgiven to those who make sincere Hijrah [*migration to the land of Islam*]' (25 December 2014). We saw that Gondal described wearing the niqab as feeling clean and pure. It washed away her sins. But it has not solved the problem of danger. This needs to be solved by power. She tweets approvingly a picture of the execution of three men in Raqqa. She comments in support: 'These three men cursed Allah SWT in front of people and dealt with according to the Sharia' (26 October 2014).

Despite her constant concerns about the dangers of the dunya, Gondal is not immune to the attractions that hijrah will have to offer. Two months before leaving, she posts a picture of a jihadist fighter driving a luxury BMW: 'After having an Audi as his car back home, this bro seems to have adjusted well' (14 November 2014). She takes great pleasure in posting two images of herself within a month of arriving in Syria. She shows off her new luxury car that has been taken from someone, celebrating the fact that she can drive it without need of a driving licence. She also posts an image of herself with an AK-47 – making a point, however, of blocking out her eyes so that they can't be seen.

Life sucked

On 25 May 2014, a young American, Moner Abu-Salha, exploded a fortified lorry that he was driving near the Syrian city of Idlib. While many jihadists who travel to Syria leave a large social media footprint to explore, Abu-Salha's is more modest, essentially consisting of his Facebook wall and his final testament video. On Facebook, most of the material he posts takes the form of images, and almost all of these have an 'otherworldly' character. In 2011, he mostly posts videos of nasheeds, or devotional recitations. One is entitled 'Don't be sad beautiful nasheed – heart touching', another 'For those going through a tough time or sadness'. He posts a commentary: 'um, just one thing I want to put in that this video will not cure you only allah can salam awlycum' (25 December 2011). Earlier in that week, he posted: 'Dear allah I have one word for you subhanallah thank you for everything you have given me I love you allah and I allways will. For all my brothers and sisters remember allah, fear allah, love allah, worship allah, and love allah ☺.'

What is striking is the ordinariness of his Facebook page. His apps and games include Xbox, *Call of Duty* and NBA games. His 'likes' are core aspects of American culture: Pizza Hut, McDonalds, sports, the film *Shrek*. He is a member of one group, an Arabic-speaking group for 'lone singles'. What is striking is the absence of others. His photos consist of devotional images – prayers at Mecca, magical representations of Jannah [*Paradise*] where animals frolic in the sun. There is one photograph of a street scene in a Middle Eastern city, but Abu-Salha's face only appears in two photos and in both of these he is alone. He has posted an image of a Florida beach from Florida Parks service, but again this is an image of bright sun, sand and waves, but the beach is empty.

Abu-Salha features in a video made in the period immediately before he died. In it, he doesn't speak about politics or the civil war in Syria. He speaks about himself. The video begins with him happy and smiling as he takes out his US passport, rips it apart and sets it alight. This is an irreversible event. He then speaks to camera, this time holding his AK-47:

I made my hijrah [*migration*] with only $20 in my pocket. Twenty dollars in my pocket. Only enough to buy a visa. From there I had no money, I had nobody to even help me get to Syria. I came to Istanbul looking for the mujahedeen because its very hard from where I come from. I want all the brothers to understand and to listen to my story.

This [*USA*] never was a place for a Muslim, this never was a place for me [*touches his chest*] … it can cause a Muslim to go astray from the path of Allah.

There is a strong sense of being out of place. The isolation suggested by Salha's Facebook posts is reinforced by the story he tells:

I lived in America, I know how it is. You have all the fancy amusement parks and the restaurants, and the food and all this crap, and the cars and you think you're happy? You're not happy, you're never happy! I was never happy, I was always sad and depressed. Life sucked. I had to walk from my work to home, I begged Allah, crying a lot, to get me out of this land. All you do is work 40, 50, 60 hours a week, and then you go waste it on garbage, and then you do the same thing over – this is what you do your whole life. When I was living by myself I had, I hardly had any food, sometimes I almost went to dumpsters behind restaurants to eat food out of dumpsters.

He comes to his central theme: 'My concern is me being a true Mujahid for Allah; me fighting for Allah; me dying a shaheed for Allah, inshallah, me lifting the banner of Allah.' He then tells a story:

This martyr operation, it's not an easy thing. I asked Allah for it. When I first came to Syria, I seen a video, and I want to share this video with you, it's a very inspiring video. There's an 'ahi' [*brother*] that I knew, he showed me a video of a good brother that he knew. He did a martyr operation. In this video, he is driving towards the enemies, and if you can see ahead of him, on the left side, there is a little light, a noor [*light*] peeking and going back. While he's driving very slowly, peeking and going back. This noor is waiting for him. Once he reaches 20 metres away from the kuffars, this noor enters into his car, drives, and explodes Allah akbar! This person who filmed this brother, had a dream the next night – brother we filmed you, we took pictures of you, we saw this light go in your car, what was this. This brother was laughing, saying 'This was my wife of jannah! This is my wife of jannah! Who entered my vehicle!

While he had nothing in the United States, the heaven that awaits Abu-Salha is a place of bountiful food and beautiful women. He concludes his video, speaking of himself: 'The mujahedeen leave their homes, their wealth, their families, they leave everything behind. They do it all for Allah, they don't care about you, they do it all for Allah, they do it all, er, because they want eh, ah, er, they want to gain the biggest reward! They don't care what man thinks about them.'

Here, we have a justification for martyrdom that is totally focused on the self. It is a passage from a life spent eating out of dumpsters to a life of abundance, where trees pick their fruit and where sex is freely available. This kind of martyrdom is rare in the cases we have explored – its composition appears fundamentally suicidal, directed towards killing the self to escape a life experienced as intolerable.

You will never be anybody!

On 1 July 2014, Abdelhamid Abaaoud, while still in Syria, sent a message via Facebook to Brahim Abdeslam, a friend he had grown up with in Brussels and with whom he shared a past in low-level crime. Seven messages were exchanged:

> *Abdeslam*: Peace brother. Mabroek Ramadan [*greeting at time of Ramadan*].
> *Abaaoud*: The Caliphat has been declared. Allah Akbar.
> *Abdeslam*: Allah Akbar. I'm on my way, inshallah. See you soon, brother.
> *Abaaoud*: Inshallah.
> *Abdeslam*: I love you brother and may Allah be with you. Amen.
> *Abaaoud*: I love you, for Allah's sake. May Allah guide you in the path to jihad and accord you martyrdom. Destroy these kuffars, take as much as you can from these pigs and come join God's army.
> *Abdeslam*: OK, brother. Inshallah. I'll contact you soon. God protect you. (Katz 2017)

In this exchange, we read declarations of brotherly love that are made possible by what is shared, not a shared family past but something experienced as even more important – a commitment to jihad. The exchange demonstrates the extent to which such shared experience can provoke and sustain the kind of intimacy that allows one to say to another, 'I love you.' But despite Abdeslam's promise to leave and travel to Syria, his departure was not fast enough for his friend, who later mocked him on social media for still being in Brussels: 'What will you get out of staying there? You will never be anybody!'

Late in 2014, Brahim Abdeslam did depart for Syria, but his time there was short. He was back in Brussels by February 2015. But while in Syria he was filmed for a propaganda video when at target practice. He turns to camera and declares 'This is for you, François Hollande! [*president of France*]', then fires off rounds. On his return to Brussels, many of those who knew him describe him sitting at the bar of Les Beguines café that he co-managed, smoking joints while he watched execution videos, commenting: 'That one is a non-believer – he should be killed!' (Ait Akdim, Chemin and Vincent 2015).

The propaganda video, which featured Abdeslam looking threatening and shooting rounds of ammunition, was released in November 2015 after the Paris attacks. But Abdeslam had appeared on television six months earlier, filmed in Brussels after his return from Syria. In May of that year, a television crew was making a documentary about urban police, following a local squadron around Brussels. These police, together with the camera crew following them, came across Abdeslam in the process of robbing a bar. The police enter the bar as the robbery was taking place and Abdeslam took refuge in a building. The bar owner called the police who cornered him at the top of a stairway. The chase was filmed by the television crew, who later broadcast the interaction between the arresting officer and Abdeslam:

Police officer: Is this your money?
Abdeslam: Yes, it's mine. I haven't taken anything at all, sir.
Police officer: Where does it come from?
Abdeslam: I haven't taken anything, I haven't stolen anything [*looks down*]. I haven't stolen anything sir. (https://www.youtube.com/watch?v=WtYfW-_-E_A)

Abdeslam's demeanour is completely different from the menacing figure filmed firing off rounds in Syria a few months earlier. He looks down, shoulders hunched, and addresses the officer as 'sir'. He appears nothing like a gangster, more like a schoolboy or a character from the British comedy film *Four Lions* about incompetent jihadis. After returning from Syria, Abdeslam had returned to his previous life of petty theft. Six months later, during the 13 November attacks, Abdeslam was dropped off alone outside a café in the east of Paris. It is not clear if he had participated in earlier killings on the terraces. What happened next was filmed by the café's security camera. He walked inside, and standing at the bar ordered a drink; not one of the patrons engaged in conversation looked up at him. He took a step back, put his head in his hands for a moment, then released a trigger to blow himself up. No one else was killed, although 15 customers were injured, one seriously. At the moment when he took his own life, Abdeslam was not shouting a message, he was not decrying the debauched ways of those around him, looking to instil fear and horror in those he was about to kill. Instead, he was standing silently, unnoticed, alone in a crowded bar, head in hands.

Brahim Abdeslam's death leads us to ask if it was an act aimed at killing others, sacrificing his own life in the process, or if is better understood as an act of killing himself while taking others with him. It is significant that he killed himself in a café, setting out to destroy it and its occupants. A week earlier, he had been the manager of a similar café that sold alcohol, where he spent much of his time seated at the bar, watching videos and reportedly smoking hashish. The lease of the bar that he and his brother managed in Brussels had been suspended only nine days before the Paris attack because of drugs being sold (Vincent 2016). Soon after his death, a video filmed some months earlier began to circulate. It showed Brahim and his brother Salah dancing in a crowded Brussels nightclub; both are smoking, and Brahim is filmed flirting with women, despite the fact that he was married. His act of obliterating himself while attempting to demolish a café and its customers suggests a type of violence directed at himself and at the life he has led. His death suggests something closer to suicide–murder than the violence of war.

The manner and context of his death also raises the possibility that he had depression – smoking hashish, watching execution videos, not looking at the intended victims but closed in on himself. As the French psychiatrist Fethi Benslama argues, radicalization presents a powerful cause, offering a meaning to life that may not otherwise be there. In some cases, the person can see himself or herself transformed from nothing into a saviour figure (Benslama 2016), a transformation also seen in the school shooters. In this case, however, there is little of the narcissism of the saviour. Abdeslam's death suggests that he is obliterating himself and the life that he has led. He, like others discussed in this chapter, is fundamentally concerned about himself.

8

Radicalization: Experience, Embodiment and Imagination

The vulnerability paradigm

We began this book considering the origins of the current use of the term 'radicalization'. This focused on vulnerable people being manipulated through a process of indoctrination, a model of linear stages moving from vulnerability to action. Radicalization from this perspective was something done to a person. One of the conditions of their vulnerability was the presumption that they were socially isolated, later framed as lacking integration into society. And radicalization was fundamentally understood in terms of *ideas*. This reflected understandings of propaganda and indoctrination, but it also reflected a modern, western understanding of religion as a collection of beliefs (Asad 1993). In the years since this model of radicalization was articulated, it has taken on different emphases. Government prevention policies have embraced the model of the vulnerable person who lacks social assimilation, believing that social isolation makes people vulnerable to messages and manipulation. This largely reworks the understandings of media manipulation that had been influential in the second half of the twentieth century associated with theories of what was called 'mass society'. The structure of this 'messages to vulnerable people' argument was not only familiar; it invited what seemed to be a clear path of action: counter-messaging.

We have explored experiences of radicalization in an attempt to identify pathways and understand transformations at stake. We have attempted to understand the 'affect', or what Margaret Wetherell calls 'embodied meaning making' (2012: 4) at the heart of radicalization.

This has meant seeking to capture the transpersonal intensities (Stewart 2007) through which radicalization is constructed as a social experience, practices rooted in social life and concrete activities (Pilkington 2016: 202), in particular intensities constructed and shared through social media.

On the basis of what we can draw together from his social media communications, Moner Abu-Salha appears to correspond to the person who is isolated and vulnerable. We can compare his violence with that of the school shooter. He wanted to transform his life, and the way to do that was through his death. However, he was not driven by desire for fame or by a compulsion to demonstrate his superiority through an act that would reverse what he experienced as an unbearable social hierarchy. The school shooters wanted others to know how great they were; they wanted to reveal a truth through the immensity of violence. Abu-Salha wanted to taste food, to have sex, to be loved, all things that to him appeared possible only in death. He did not consider the impact of his death on the living, much less on those he would kill. His aim was not to kill others and to die in the process. His aim was to kill himself. He became a victim of a murderous regime that fed on human sacrifice – not of its leaders, but of the people who manifest a vulnerability associated with modern, individualist societies, evident in the high incidence of depression that characterizes them (Ehrenberg 2010).

This vulnerability may well also shape the trajectory of Brahim Abdeslam, who walked into a Paris bar and obliterated himself only nine days after the bar that he and his brother managed in Brussels was closed because of its association with drug use. He was unemployed and a heavy user of hashish. He had failed to respond to the first call to travel to Syria, despite affirming 'I'm on my way,' only leaving after being taunted 'You will never be anybody.' He did not stay long in Syria, and once back in Belgium he had returned to a life of largely unsuccessful small-time crime. The manner of his death, standing alone in a bar with his head in his hands, is the opposite of the 'ecstatic violence' we explored in relation to school shooters. It suggests a kind of depressive violence, aimed at obliterating himself and the life that he led.

But these cases of isolated or depressed individuals cannot be presumed to be the paradigms of radicalization. And even where we recognize their importance, we need to underline the limits of a 'counter-messaging' paradigm as a response. Brahim Abdeslam was part of a criminal world where time spent in Syria was a badge of respect, a means to acquire a reputation. The manner of his death suggests that ultimately he did not succeed. But to understand this, we need to be able to see the kind of agency he was exercising and the world of relationships and imaginaries in which he lived. Such relationships and imaginaries have been closely associated with a number of recurring tensions.

Strangeness and the uncanny

A recurring theme in these accounts is that of strangeness, of events out of place, of hidden meaning. Ahmed talks about his dreams. The chat groups that emerged around Diaby's movies make constant reference to being 'unsettled' and disturbed. Often this strangeness is lived as the irruption of unknowable events, a breaking of limits, the sublime. But this can also be lived as the uncanny, where the familiar is defamilarized, turned into something strange, harbouring hidden and dangerous meanings. Anthropologists, exploring fear of children as witches, argue that we need to locate this fear in a wider context of the loss of authority of parents in a world that is increasingly unintelligible and experienced as dangerous (Geschiere 2013). In modern western society, this may be associated with social phenomena such as the widespread development of conspiracy theories or the loss of trust in experts, in the repetitive, almost addictive, experience of groups exploring hidden meanings and danger, from chemtrails to the pervasive presence of the Illuminati.

The danger of these hidden 'realities' is the source of the thrill, the frisson or sudden rush of intense feeling associated with discovery. This delivers awe and shock at the scale of the conspiracy. Such discovery may create a feeling of vulnerability or nourish a sense of narcissism, power or superiority because one is able to look in the face what others prefer not to see. This is central to the experience of Junaid Hussain, who moves from the world of games and its competitive search for clues and meanings to discovering the power of the Illuminati, and who then begins to perceive his life as 'destiny'. His hacking is focused on demonstrating his power, his ability to make visible what is otherwise hidden, such as the electronic diary of a prime minister's aide or the credit card of someone he believes owes their career to the power of the Illuminati. In these cases, the act of revealing what is hidden demonstrates not only power but truth.

Strangeness, occult forces and hidden meanings recur in other contexts. The dark danger represented by 'shirk' and 'black magic' is radicalized by jihadist actors, often by relying on popular culture, as we saw in the case of the murder of a local imam in the north of England who was believed to be accessing the power of spirits. The group involved in this referred to him as Voldemort, photographing themselves as they followed him and posting the images to social media. In this case, there is a kind of unreality as the protagonists pose for pictures wearing Kevlar vests or altering street signs, their constant smiles suggesting that humour plays an important role in allowing this to happen. This same focus on 'shirk', or sorcery, was shared by young British jihadists in Syria, who posted to social media admiring pictures of the execution of sorcerers.

This preoccupation with the occult is a fundamental dimension of contemporary jihadist culture. In the years before it was blocked, the French-language website Ansar Al-Haqq.net was the principal forum frequented by French jihadists (Abdul 2013). The culture of this forum is fundamentally one of deciphering hidden meanings, from conspiracies against Islam to the pervasive reality of sorcery in contemporary society. One senior member details the 'symptoms of sorcery', which include loss of appetite, chronic constipation, stomach ache, failure to marry, inability to have sexual relations with one's spouse, sterility, social isolation and so on. A visceral fear of contagion is evident when participants ask if it is possible that sorcery can be transmitted down the generations; another declares that he has become ill after a sorcerer, who is a neighbour, poured contaminated water in front of the window of his home; this same participant declares in a separate post that he and his family are constantly ill because of the sorcery of their neighbour; another asks for help to overcome possession. A thread addresses the theme 'sorcery prevents me having relations with my wife' (http://web.archive.org/ web/20150516162942/http://ansar-alhaqq.net/forum/showthread. php?t=7358). On this same site, there are extensive threads addressing the 'Illuminati New World Order', with flow charts linking the Illuminati with the Vatican, the Bildberg Group, the Trilateral Commission, the World Economic Forum, the World Bank, the European Commission and so on (http://le-nouvel-ordre-mondial-illuminati.over-blog.com/page/39). These discussions juxtapose intimate personal problems with vast global conspiracies, resembling the videos produced by Omar Diaby, where personal problems and questions are answered by stories of portentous power and hidden meanings. Here again, we can appreciate the fundamental debt of this experience to popular culture, from *The Lord of the Rings* to Hollywood B movies. We see this also in the tweets of Ifthekar

Jaman, who posts images of the vastness of the universe which takes his breath away, alongside images of cute kittens.

This is a distinctive dimension of jihadist culture: the intimate and the vast, in a way reflecting the encounter with the sublime. Discussing this in relation to witchcraft, Geschiere draws on Kant's exploration of the sublime, which he understands as 'the reaction people may have to nature and the sensation it can give of awe and the lack of words to express it' (2013: 174) where 'confrontations with the sublime and the subsequent struggle to define the limits of one's powers of cognition' become 'vital to the crystallization of self-consciousness'. But, argues Geschiere drawing on Freud, 'when people are not capable of bringing closure to the experience of the awesome, the sublime turns into the uncanny' (2013: 174).

The idea of the uncanny brings together the cognitive and the sensory. In this case, we are aware of something so immense and powerful that words fail us, leaving us sensing the unsettling presence of danger. That danger can be present in the action of a neighbour, who is most frequently the sorcerer. Or a parent, demanding we settle down and make money. Or it can take the form of a huge conspiracy, uniting sinister forces ranging from the Illuminati to the European Commission. It can even take the form of oneself. When the principal danger to oneself becomes oneself, the only way to free oneself is to create a rupture between one's past and one's present, a kind of separation that is experienced as a radical break. For Tooba Gondal, 'the material world is nothing more than a deception.' It is the world that represents danger, above all a danger of contamination. The danger can be represented by one's family: 'Even if our family want us to do something that goes against the Shari'a we have to keep strong and firm and, er, we have to let them know that we must obey Allah (SWT) and his Messenger, even if it's against our own selves' (Tooba Gondal, Audioboom, 18 February 2013). Or it may be the world itself that is the source of danger: 'Now this Dunya is very, very dangerous, because it's fulled [sic] with traps and deception that can cause us to go astray and forget about Allah. Um, er, to be honest it's one of the easiest ways to get destroyed and lose ourselves in this life and the hereafter (Tooba Gondal, Audioboom, 18 February 2013).

In Gondal's case, the danger of the world was at work in her *past* and to the extent that this has shaped who she is today. This helps understand her focus on self-transformation and issues of gender – veiling, appropriate way to wear hair, use of eye make-up and so on. It also helps us understand the significance of her reaction to the attacks in Paris, the city where she was born:

Burn Paris burn. Can't believe that is my birthplace. LOL HOW SCARED ARE THESE KUFFAR EXPLOSIONS AND SHOOTINGS ... 80 dead. And all praise is due to Allah Almighty. #ParisUnderAttack ... Wish I could have seen the hostages being slaughtered last night with my own eyes. Would have been just beautiful.

In her case, destroying her past is intimately linked to the destruction of Paris.

Purity and impurity, desire and repulsion

A fundamental experiential structure we have met throughout this book is the tension between purity and impurity, lived in different ways, but always as a social construction. This tension is at the heart of Aqsa Mahmood's transformation, where we see the opposition between good and evil mutate into one of innocence and guilt, and then true and false, pure and impure. This construction takes place in the world of networked intimacy and affect that she shares with her 'fam' in games, pleasure and relationships of inclusion and exclusion. Violence entered this intimate world in the form of Gaza 2012, prompting an initial response shaped by the #Kony2012 social media campaign that had taken place earlier in the year. This was a Twitter campaign in support of children kidnapped by the Lord's Resistance Army in Uganda to become child soldiers. But in Mahmood's case, this suffering makes her question who she is and what matters to her, bringing with it a quite new danger that had never before been part of her timeline: hypocrisy and corruption. The threat of this danger on the one hand and the serenity and power she finds on the other create a completely new experience which leads her to progress from a concern with the potential for her own corruption to a focus on the corruption of the 'other', framed in terms of fear of penetration and collapse of sexual borders separating human beings from other animals, adults and children, as evoked in her images and themes of disgust. Her timeline becomes fixated on an extraordinary imaginary of sickness, impurity and ultimately death. She creates a sensory field not only of purity and impurity, but also of beauty and the grotesque. The overwhelming presence of these two themes, desire and repulsion (reflected in the juxtaposition of beauty and the grotesque) suggests that the strength of this tension serves as a way to connect with reality itself. Humour plays a fundamental role in this process – it allows her to say something in a register other than that of truth and falsehood, and it allows others, through the act of laughing (*lol*) or sharing disgust (*eww!*) to become active participants in this process. The centrality of impurity to the experiential world Mahmood constructs, and her constant use of humour as a strategy of inclusion and exclusion, underlines the extent to which her radicalization evokes racism, which is also constructed though an imaginary of purity versus impurity, filth and dirt. Here, disgust becomes a strategy for dehumanization (Speltini and Passini 2014), one constructed collectively through the inclusive medium of humour. Humour does more than integrate others into an action; it also makes possible forms of communication that otherwise would not be possible. Humour allows Mahmood to say the unsayable. She does more than turn Shia Muslims into objects of ridicule – they become less than human. She was still a university student in Glasgow when she posted that Shias were something to be hunted and killed. After a year in Syria, she has reached the point where she justifies the sexual slavery of Yazidi women.

We noted the disgust registered by a group responding to an online video in which a young man from the United Kingdom holds a severed head up to camera. This is also shared using humour about an act of violence that not only destroys life but humanity itself, reducing the victim to an 'it', an object of grotesque horror and ridicule.

The tension between purity and impurity takes other forms as well. Rather than identify the polluting filth of the 'other', other actors focus on the purification of the self. This is true of Tooba Gondal, profoundly shaped by her fear of the danger of the 'dunya', or this world, above all that of disordered gender relations and the threat of uncontrolled sexual desire that this makes possible. This shapes her online presence, which, rather than ridiculing Shia Muslims, admonishes her followers for wearing make-up, having their hair in buns under their niqabs, using their faces as avis and showing their eyes in photographs. We do not have access to Gondal's inner world, but a year earlier she had been tweeting selfies while not wearing make-up, declaring that she felt naked without it. Now she is fearful of the danger that lurks within, and her response is to stamp it out in others. Everything she does is aimed at imposing order on the potential for disorder that lies in 'free mixing'. She was born in France, and this is above all what she hates, an exemplar of filth: 'I hate the racist French, who oppress any practising muslim and liberate those Arabs who have shamed Islam (drinking, prostitution ...) filth. Out of all countries to be born in, I was born in the disgusting scum France' (22 November 2014). This is why she takes such pleasure in the Paris attacks of November 2015, which targeted people in bars, restaurants, concert halls and cafés – attacks meant to cleanse and purify.

Gondal may not remember her life in Paris, but it is part of her narrative. When we explored fragments of the experience of the three young girls who travelled to Syria from London in 2015, we found something similar to what Alison Landsberg (2004: 2) calls 'prosthetic memory', a kind of 'networked memory' (Garde-Hansen 2013) associated with the circulation of images, where a person's subjectivity can become shaped by a 'deeply felt memory of a past event through which he or she did not live' (Landsberg 2004: 2). Conceptual tools, such as networked memory that becomes part of who we are through embodied experiences such as grief, shock or bliss, may offer a way of approaching the significance of vulnerable and innocent beauty in the social media communications of these girls, and its role in uniting a group into a sisterhood who share the love of a common protector. Rather than Mahmood's transformation of the horror of suffering into the horror of the grotesque, in the social media communications of the 15-year-old girl that we explored, beauty and bliss come to shape a radicalization pathway. We also considered other examples of fusion relationships, in one case in claustrophobic couple relationships. Here, there is no reference to a 'great Other, common to you and me' (Gutton 2015: 17), but the eroticization of power relationships built on the tension between anticipation and release, and what Seelow (2016b) describes as 'reality fatigue combined with deadly delusion'.

A sociology of experience

Earlier in this book, I introduced the idea of a 'sociology of experience' as a way to think about the multiple and overlapping dimensions of how people act, what social scientists call 'agency'. Drawing on the work of Alain Touraine (2007) and François Dubet (1994) who shaped this approach, I have explored three relational dimensions of agency. The first is an experience of community – this may be our nation, our identification with neighbourhood, social class, race or ethnicity, where we experience the world in terms of 'us'. A second type of social experience is less focused on ourselves and more on the ways we enter into relationships with others. Good examples of this are markets, configured in terms of competition, or workplaces – not because of how they may establish some sort of collective identity but in the ways they are structured as meritocracies, giving reward for effort. Here, what counts are rules that apply to all. A third type of agency is not focused on 'us' as a community, nor interaction with others on the basis of abstract rules of exchange, but on the subjective experience of the actor. This can involve freedom and dignity or a capacity to experience vulnerability to the 'other'. In this book, I have shown these three kinds of agency mutate. We have seen the extent to which radicalization is a social activity, one that is communicative, involving networked affect, memory, embodiment and imagination. As all research, this book is based on incomplete data. There are gaps and uncertainties which are unavoidable. But the tensions identified, embedded in and between different kinds of affect as social practice, allow us to identify pathways that intersect and overlap, more like tracks than clear roads.

Focus on 'I'

While all the experiences explored here engage with the 'I', they do so in very different ways. When Jamal describes his experience, he constructs an account of personal transformation, framed in a shift from a dangerous world of disorder (war on the estate) to one where he finds himself integrated into a hierarchical community, one that offers security and confidence in the relationships that surround him. Very close to the experience of the gang, the world he details is one where internal loyalty is generated through external conflict. What is striking is the extent that his involvement in al-Muhajiroun reproduces his previous life. In the past, he was involved in war on the estate. Now, he is seeking to make a break with a world experienced as chaotic and dangerous, one from which the structure, loyalty and purpose of al-Muhajiroun offer a refuge.

While Jamal had spent half his life in prison, Tooba Gondal grew up in a comfortable middle-class part of London. But her extensive social media profile demonstrates how much she too is centred on herself and on making a break with a past experienced as threatening. The danger she describes is not gang violence, but gender disorder, an experience she captures with constantly recurring images of corruption and death (her long Audioboom narrative about the carcass, the recurring frightening images of ad-Dajjal that appear on her timeline, her fascination with the apocalyptic musings of al-Awlaki). She has constructed an experience of personal guilt that is critical for the transformation she undergoes, one to which she accords a date which allows a clear division between a before and an after. Her past is corrupt, her experience of transformation one of becoming pure, clean and happy. The 'other' is unclean, just as she was: 'scummy French', 'filthy Arabs'. She rejoices in the death of hostages in Paris, their death being part of obliterating her past.

Suicide by murder

A quite different focus on the self appears in the violence associated with spree killing, where the killer is certain of his own death. We saw the importance of mediation in this kind of death, the search for fame and an imaginary where the scale of violence will be such as to fracture reality itself. In the case of the school shooter, death is the pathway to becoming someone. The act of killing *reveals a truth* that up to now has been hidden, in this case the greatness of the killer. Killing will turn the world upside down, evident in these killers' recurring references to previous experiences of humiliation and suffering. Within this imaginary, the humiliation of capture and imprisonment is inconceivable, and so this kind of violence can only be imagined with its end point being the death of the killer.

Mateen's mass killing in Florida, framed as a rejection of western filth and as an act of self-purification, is a deed that he hopes will make him 'acceptable to God'. He constructs this as a response to distant suffering, something that he says is the source of the pain that he feels and that he intends to inflict upon others. But it is far from clear that his murderous rage is in fact a response to the suffering of Syrians. He has never done anything in relation to Syria at all. His online presence is focused on dating sites where he presents himself as something that he is not. His killings are directed towards taking power as well as lives, and his inability to use his own name suggests that he can no longer imagine beyond an act that must end in his death. Capture and arrest would mean a loss of control and power, and the extent to which this is unthinkable to Mateen underlines the extent to which this killing shares with those of the school shooters a murderous desire to reverse an experience of humiliation. Where the school shooter seeks fame, Mateen seeks purification. They are both acts of murderous narcissism.

Criminal pathways

While often associated with claims of transformation, what appears most striking in criminal pathways into jihadist violence is the theme of continuity. As Khosrokhavar (2017) argues, the pleasures involved in criminal violence and the exercise of power over the 'other' are sacralized, and theft becomes legitimized as 'booty'. In this we have an imaginary of 'soldiers' and 'the front', images of war that frame organized urban criminality. This is not primarily driven by the search for economic resources but for pleasure, camaraderie, relationships of trust and respect, securing the status and admiration due to the anti-hero. While often celebrated as wiping away a past, in almost all respects this past is reproduced, from the narcissism of the 'tourist terrorist' to Abaaoud's practice of wearing a GoPro camera, filming his life and turning himself into a celebrity, one who promises to 'personally' welcome those from his neighbourhood who travel to Syria. As seen with the young men from London who made up Rayat al-Tawheed, jihad is framed in terms of 'leaving the gangster life'. But it is among this group that a young man is posting to social media about 'his first time', presenting bloodied hands to camera, being celebrated by those who contribute to the timeline as having undergone a rite of passage, the 'first of many'. Organized violence continues to offer status, respect and honour, achieved by stripping this from others. It offers the possibility of becoming 'someone'.

Focus on 'you'

While some pathways appear more centred on 'I' or on 'us', others appear more focused on a relationship with another, formulated as 'you'. This is most evident in the world of gamers, who uncover hidden meanings, and in the process, progress through levels of achievement, as seen in the case of Junaid Hussain. We explored his origins as a hacker and the extent to which his search for respect focused on making his opponent visible, thus demonstrating his superiority. This is at the centre of the practice of 'doxing' within hacker culture (McDonald 2015), and by taking control of others' websites Hussain demonstrates their lack of skill and his superior ability, something that he comes to frame as 'destiny'. Themes such as purity and the grotesque are not part of this trajectory. He is involved in what Wagner (2012) calls 'metaphysical sorting', dividing the world into winners and losers. He may call the Indian Cyber Army 'filthy', but this is not central to the kind of pathway he is constructing. He wants to demonstrate his power through rendering the 'other' visible, and thus vulnerable. As he gleefully proclaims when ringing an anti-terror hotline, 'Knowledge is power.'

It is important to understand how someone can progress in a few months from wearing an Anonymous mask to travelling to Syria to join ISIS. Hussain tweeted that his departure was in answer to the cries of the oppressed. We saw that the context of his departure was more complex – he had been 'doxed'. Someone linked to Anonymous had created a fake Twitter account in his name, declaring him to be a government informer; another former collaborator had accused him of skimming credit cards for his girlfriend, Sally Jones. Two years earlier, Jones had been exploring esoteric art online and had been posting against organized religion, eventually boasting about her success in 'cybering dudes', reflected in her Twitter handles such as @Pu55yGallor3 or the avi she used for much of this period. Before she met Hussain, she was embedded in a world of the esoteric and hidden meanings, fascinated by the English occult tradition and by conspiracy theory.

Conspiracy theory can be seen in other experiences explored in this book, but it is fundamental to Jones and Hussain and to the world of gamers and hackers from which they emerge. It is not about purification of the self, nor the sickness of the 'other'. It has nothing to do with the suffering of the victim. It is about the frisson and fascination of discovering hidden meanings just around the corner. It is based on power and its unmasking, as in Hussain's and Jones's belief that the attacks of September 11 were the action of the United States government. The paradigm is a game, where it is not necessary to believe that something is real, only that it could be. There is a blurring of categories of the real and the not real, as we saw with Aseel Muthana in his pretend 'operation' in Cardiff, or in the filming and uploading of the explosion of an improvised device in a back garden in Britain.

Other radicalization pathways are shaped by the desire for power and prestige, as in the figure of the anti-hero embodied by Abdelhamad Abaaoud. He leaves his life working in his family's clothes shop to become a 'Caïd', a leader of a battalion who will 'personally' welcome those believers coming to Syria. While Hussain demonstrates his power by staying invisible, Abaadoud lives his life as a kind of jihadist celebrity, wearing a GoPro camera and filming his exploits. He lives in a world of honour and prestige, constantly affirmed by the humiliation of the 'other' and by his capacity, like Hussain, to make this humiliation visible – in its extreme form to turn the object of his violence into a figure of disgust and ridicule. We saw this at work in the gruesome film uploaded to social media by British jihadists, who hold decapitated heads up to camera, and who are celebrated as 'so brave' by their audience.

Radicalization as 'us'

An important number of the experiences I have outlined involve ways of structuring community. But rather than tradition, history or pride, the model of community here is inverted, organized around two types of dangers: from within, disorder; and from without, contamination. The theme of contamination is most evident in the type of community constructed by Aqsa Mahmood, which opposes purity to impurity, beauty to the grotesque, until she experiences this opposition as one of life and death, where the very existence of the 'other' contains the threat of contamination and sickness. Her transformation is not fundamentally at the level of ideas, but is visceral and embodied, accomplished through affective experience such as disgust and humour, and her imaginary of cleansing. Here, we find a kind of pathway where incompleteness and the existence of the 'other' can only entail a threat of death.

Jamal, the former gang member who joined al-Muhajiroun while in prison, is also seeking a strong community. But in his case, community offers security and structure in a world where this is absent and where there is an ever-present threat of violence, not only the violence of others but also his own. He is looking for a principle of order that will contain and control the threat of disorder. While Mahmood sees danger in the 'other', Jamal experiences this much more in himself, as something that can be controlled only by a community that will give him a place and role. It is not surprising that Jamal joined a group offering structure and identity in one of the most dangerous places that exist in the United Kingdom: prison.

Transforming disorder into order is also central in the story recounted by Ahmed. He is drinking, he has been abandoned by his girlfriend. He apprehends the world in terms of the disorder of his life. So too does Tooba Gondal, but in her case the dangers of her past link her to what is a potentially cataclysmic danger of the potent mystical forces she sees unleashed in Syria. Rather than a gang-type organization, Ahmed is looking for order in law, in what he experiences as the surety of the criminal's hand being cut off. Gondal appears much more threatened by her past and the danger that it still represents. Fear, and its transformation into anger, is at the centre of her trajectory.

Pathways, affect and imagination

Theory helps us to explore processes, transformations and relation-ships at work in human experience. It can allow us to capture realities that otherwise appear too complex to grasp. Theory can alert us to the different ways embodied meaning is created and shared. It can highlight things that we may otherwise miss, or alert us to the signifi-cance of something that we might not notice. At the same time, it is important to recognize that there will always be dimensions of human experience that theory will miss. With that proviso in mind, we can draw together key aspects of the pathways we have explored, rec-ognizing that what we arrive at is a tool for analysis, not a complete representation (Figure 8.1).

The categories identified above are analytical – they aim to sepa-rate different dimensions of radicalization in order to understand experiences that actors are inventing and combining in different ways. These pathways are not *caused* by social, political or religious 'factors', but are created by the way actors experience realities and respond to them. They are social constructions, produced by the embodied interactions and imaginaries of social actors, and involve different affective registers which allow certain feelings to be pro-duced. From there, certain ideas become possible, for example in the way that Mahmood transforms her horror of violence and her personal fear into a shared production of the grotesque. Horror combines with humour to allow the opposition of good and evil to be transformed, first into innocence and guilt and then into purity and impurity, with its imaginary of contamination and its call for purifica-tion through cleansing.

Radicalization, politics and religion

I began this book by considering the claim that the origins of radicali-zation lie either in religious enthusiasm or political action. The argu-ment about religion has tended to be framed in terms of large-scale movements having religious origins, as we saw with Michael Walzer (2015) in the introduction. Among European social scientists, the most active debates about the religious nature of radicalization have taken place in France, where political scientists such as Gilles Kepel argue that the growth of jihadist movements in Europe and North America is a response to the appeals of what he calls Salafi-jihadist

Field of experience and relationship	Radicalization as mutation and rupture	Meaning of violence	Affect	Objective of violence
I: Subjectivity freedom, dignity, vulnerability, incompleteness	Impurity of self; rupture of personal biography; depression; fear and unease at the uncanny; not belonging; claustrophobic fusion; a new self through hijrah	*Purification* of self; *individuation* through death; *fusion* with vastness through death; ecstatic violence; depressive violence; intensity shared within couple	Rage, fear, anger, relief, decompression, desire, bliss	Purification or relief through death of self; obliteration of self; erotic anticipation
You: Justice fairness, equality, opportunity, competition, cooperation	Gamification of life as myth; epic imaginary; anti-hero and imaginary of power and gun; sacralization of violent crime as jihad	Reversal of humiliation; no limits; experience of power; reveal hidden meanings; celebration of superiority and its benefits (booty)	Fascination with hidden meaning; pleasure, intensity, excitement, frisson, visibility, fame	Humiliation of other; transform humiliation into honour; fame, power and celebrity; conquest
Us: Community Experience of 'us': tradition, memory, ritual, place	Impurity of the 'other'; *Other within*: fear of disorder (free mixing, black magic, democracy, personal potential for violence); *External other*: contamination, sickness, hypocrites	Separation; demonstration of impurity of other; cleansing	Encounter with mediated suffering; humour, tenderness, disgust, fear, hate, grotesque	Obliterating difference; turning disorder into order; rite of passage; purge and cleanse

Figure 8.1   Radicalization pathways

thinkers (Kepel 2015: 33). We may find references to jihadist thinkers, but these cannot be understood as the source of the experiences
I have explored.

The different pathways explored here demonstrate a kind of
reworking of the uncanny, involving the experience of hidden
meaning in which the familiar becomes defamiliarized and dangerous. This opens up something that is enormous and threatening,
so powerful that it risks engulfing subjectivity, where an imaginary
of fusion into something all-encompassing is reworked as a death
fantasy. This can be seen at work in the social media posts of Ifthekar
Jaman in the period immediately before he left the United Kingdom.
Paradoxically, this shapes the reception of the martyr as having
achieved something otherwise unattainable, and thus it becomes a
path to individuation in a way that resembles the path of the school
shooters, who are widely treated on fan sites as martyrs who gave
their lives to a greater cause. As we have seen, some school shooters
also use religious metaphors to explain their killings. But the claim 'I
die as Jesus Christ' does not make an action intelligible in religious
terms, pointing instead to a kind of pathological narcissism.

The radicalization pathways explored in this book show a parasitic
relationship with religious traditions. Practices around purity are
part of many religious traditions, but we see these appropriated and
reworked here as purification through suicide/murder, or the production of disgust at the 'other' where religious themes serve to sacralize
an imaginary of genocide, the proposition that a group deserve to die
because of what they are. Religious traditions can also be interpreted
within an imaginary of power and prestige, as we see when Abaaoud
returns to Brussels from Egypt as a possessor of knowledge, or in
the kind of narcissism demonstrated when Omar Diaby constructs
his mythical history of humanity, something that pivots on his arrest
for petty crime. Jaman is fascinated by loss of self in something
immense and awesome, while participants in the Ansar al-Haaq
website explore contemporary experiences of unease, evident as well
in the actions of a small group of young men in Britain, which led to
the killing of an imam whom they codenamed Voldemort.

Implications for prevention and disengagement

The focus of this book has not been radicalization prevention policies
and practices, nor what has come to be called 'de-radicalization'. The
development of these fields is simply too large to encompass within

this book. However, the experiences explored here have implications for these areas. Much of what is called 'counter-radicalization' policy is premised on the proposition that radicalization is something done *to* a person, principally through the vulnerable-victim model, often seen as an isolated person in front of a computer screen. As a result, 'de-radicalization' is conceived of in similar terms, as something also to be done *to* a person, to be 'delivered' by programmes and professionals in a one-to-one relationship. My starting point has been that radicalization is not something done *to* a person, but a form of communicative agency, fundamental to a person's biography. Rather than focus on 'indoctrination' or narrative, I have explored affect, or communicated embodied experience, from disgust to humour. This has important implications. De-radicalization equally needs to be approached as something that a person *does*, a form of agency. Actors have to be supported to understand what has happened to them and what they have done, said and thought, as well as what they have felt. They can then construct affective registers that will allow them to experience feelings that will make it possible to disengage from a pathway that might otherwise be dangerous or disorienting. Radicalization pathways in prison, for example, such as that experienced by Jamal, represent a tension between order and disorder, a fear and danger experienced in a world of unpredictable violence (the source being oneself or the 'other'). Jamal expresses a desire for the security of family life and community that he finds in al-Muhajiroun and which offers him a future. Here, support for de-radicalization is not primarily an issue of counter-messaging but of addressing emotions such as fear, hope, anxiety and desire. This is all the more so when radicalization is created through, and in turn sustains and amplifies, transpersonal intensities such as those described in this book: the shared humour that makes it possible to say the unsayable; the fascination and repulsion at the heart of experiences of disgust; the destabilizing unease provoked by the uncanny; the narcissism of ecstatic violence; the pleasures in demonstrating one's superiority; the fusion experiences of adolescents and couples; the metaphysical sorting of the gamer; the imaginaries of purification in the aching desire for death of the self, of one's past, or of the 'other'.

I began this book by arguing that the term 'radicalization' unifies often very different experiences and meanings, while separating these from other kinds of violence characteristic of contemporary societies. The experiences explored in this book affirm the extent of such differences, when we compare for example radicalization trajectories that begin in prison with those of an adolescent girl. Such differences underline that there is not 'one' radicalization, a proposition often implicit in the suggestion that radicalization is caused by propaganda. But while recognizing such varied pathways, we are not reduced to saying that 'every case is unique', with radicalization becoming little more than a word we use to describe something we don't understand.

The intensities and imaginaries discussed in this book are embedded in social, communicative practices that we can understand and analyse. Disciplines such as sociology in particular offer us tools to recognize the ways radicalization experiences are constructed around an 'I', a 'you' or an 'us'. Understanding this is fundamental to constructing tools to assist families and communities, friends and also those directly concerned to recognize and understand what is happening in such experiences. This is a critical contribution to overcoming the fear, loss and bewilderment hinted at in some of the accounts we have explored. It goes without saying that such tools are vital to those professions seeking ways to support prevention and disengagement from radicalization pathways.

To a significant extent, the professionalization of counter-terrorism has resulted in the domination of this field by security consultants and by what intellectually has come to be known as security studies, which pays little attention to the fundamentally social, embodied and affective dimensions of radicalization. It is these, however, that need to be placed at the centre of de-radicalization strategies. Our ability to understand different radicalization pathways and the affective registers these involve is a critical first step in constructing responses that may support individuals to explore tensions in other ways and to construct different types of futures for themselves – and, ultimately, for us all.

References

Abdul, S. (2013). Ansar Al-Haqq, site préféré des djihadistes. *Le Monde*, 20 September.

Adorno, T. (1991). *The Culture Industry: Selected Essays on Mass Culture*. London: Routledge.

Ahmed, S. (2004*). The Cultural Politics of Emotion*. London: Routledge.

Ait Akdim, Y. Chemin, A. and Vincent, E. (2015). Les Abdeslam, frères de sang. *Le Monde*, 23 November.

Amin, A. and Thrift, N. (2013). *Arts of the Political: New Openings for the Left*. Durham: Duke University Press.

Appadurai, A. (2006). *Fear of Small Numbers: An Essay of the Geography of Anger*. Durham: Duke University Press.

Argenti, N. (2006). Remembering the Future: Slavery, Youth and Masking in the Cameroon Grassfields. *Social Anthropology* 14(1): 49–69.

Asad, T. (1993). *Genealogies of Religion: Discipline and Reasons of Power in Christianity and Islam*. Baltimore: Johns Hopkins University Press.

Asad, T. (2012). Thinking about Religion, Belief, and Politics, in R. Orsi (ed.), *The Cambridge Companion to Religious Studies*. Cambridge: Cambridge University Press, pp. 36–57.

Ashuri, T. (2011). Joint Memory: ICT and the Rise of Moral Mnemonic Agents, in M. Neiger, O. Meyers and E. Zandberg (eds), *On Media Memory: Collective Memory in a New Media Age*. Basingstoke: Palgrave Macmillan, pp. 104–13.

Aubenas, F. (2016). Attentats de Paris: la bande de Molenbeek. *Le Monde*, 4 May.

Auvinen, P. E. (2007). *Natural Selector's Manifesto*. http://zami.pp.fi/jokela/files/

Bamman, D., Eisenstein, J. and Schnoebelen, T. (2014). Gender Identity and Lexical Variation in Social Media. *Journal of Sociolinguistics* 18: 135–60.

Bataille, G. (1986). *Eroticism: Death and Sensuality*. San Francisco: City Lights Books.

Beijers, J., Bijeveld, C., van de Weijer, S. and Liefbroer, A. (2017). All in the Family? The Relationship between Sibling Offending and Offending Risk. *Journal of Developmental and Life-Course Criminology* 3(1): 1–14.

Bennett, Lance W. and Segerberg. A. (2015). *The Logic of Connective Action: Digital Media and the Personalization of Contentious Politics*. Cambridge: Cambridge University Press.

Benslama, F. (2016). *Un furieux désir de sacrifice: le surmusulman*. Paris: Seuil.

Bjorgo, T. (2014). *Terror from the Extreme Right*. London: Routledge.

Boltanski, L. (1999). *Distant Suffering: Morality, Media and Politics*. Cambridge: Cambridge University Press.

Bourgois, P. (1996). *In Search of Respect: Selling Crack in El Barrio*. Cambridge: Cambridge University Press.

Burke, E. (2008 [1757]). *A Philosophical Enquiry into the Origin of our Ideas of the Sublime and Beautiful*. Oxford: Oxford University Press.

Campion-Vincent, V. (2005). *La société parano: Théories du complot, menaces et incertitudes*. Paris: Payot.

Castells, M. (2013). *Communication Power*. Oxford: Oxford University Press.

Channel 4 (2013). Britons Fighting with Syria's Jihadi Band of Brothers. https://www.channel4.com/news/syria-war-rebels-jihadi-ibrahim-al-mazwagi

Chomsky, N. (1965). *Cartesian Linguistics*. Cambridge: Cambridge University Press.

City of Orlando (2017). Pulse Tragedy Public Records. http://www.cityof orlando.net/cityclerk/pulse-tragedy-public-records/

Clough, P. (2007). Introduction, in P. Clough and J. Halley (eds), *The Affective Turn: Theorizing the Social*. Durham and London: Duke University Press, pp. 1–33.

Coleman, G. (2014). *Hacker, Hoaxer, Whistleblower, Spy: The Many Faces of Anonymous*. London: Verso.

Collins, R. (2008) *Violence. A Micro-Sociological Theory*. Princeton: Princeton University Press.

Coolsaet, R. (2016). *Jihadi Terrorism and the Radicalisation Challenge: European and American Experiences*. London: Routledge.

Cottee, S. (2016). How a British University Student Became an ISIS Matchmaker. *VICE*. https://www.vice.com/en_uk/article/pgpvxn/how-a-british-college-student-became-an-isis-matchmaker

Couldry, N. (2012). *Media, Society, World: Social Theory and Digital Media Practice*. Cambridge: Polity Press.

Dabiq (2015). Interview with Abū 'Umar al-Baljīkī'. *Dabiq* 7: 72–5.

Deleuze, G. (1981). *Francis Bacon – the Logic of Sensation*. Minneapolis: University of Minnesota Press.

Della Porta, D. (2013). *Clandestine Political Violence*. Cambridge: Cambridge University Press.

Devji, F. (2005). *Landscapes of the Jihad: Militancy, Morality, Modernity*. London: Hurst.

Douglas, M. (1966). *Purity and Danger: An Analysis of Concepts of Pollution and Taboo*. London: Routledge.

Dubet, F. (1991). *Les lycéens*. Paris: Seuil.

Dubet, F. (1994). *Sociologie de l'expérience*. Paris: Seuil.

Durkheim, E. (1951 [1897]). *Suicide: A Study in Sociology*, trans. J. A. Spaulding and G. Simpson. New York: The Free Press.

Ehrenberg, A. (1991). *Le culte de la performance*. Paris: Calmann-Lévy.

Ehrenberg, A. (2010). *The Weariness of the Self: Diagnosing the History of Depression in the Contemporary Age*. Montréal: McGill-Queen's University Press.

Enzensberger, H. (2006). *Le perdant radical: Essai sur les hommes de la terreur*. Paris: Gallimard.

Europol (2017). *European Union Terrorism Situation and Trend Report 2017*. www.europol.europa.eu

Feldman, A. (1991). *Formations of Violence: The Narrative of the Body and Political Terror in Northern Ireland*. Chicago: University of Chicago Press.

Filiu, J.-P. (2012). *Apocalypse in Islam*. Berkeley: University of California Press.

Garde-Hansen, J. (2013). Friendship Photography: Memory, Mobility and Social Networking, in M. Sandbye and J. Larsen (eds), *Digital Snaps: The New Face of Photography*. London: I. B. Tauris.

Garde-Hansen, J. and Gorton, K. (2013). *Emotion Online: Theorising Affect on the Internet*. Basingstoke: Palgrave Macmillan.

Geschiere, P. (2013). *Witchcraft, Intimacy and Trust*. Chicago: University of Chicago Press.

Gibbs, N. and Roche, T. (1999). The Columbine Tapes. *Time Magazine*, 20 December.

Giddens, A. (1999). *Runaway World: How Globalization is Reshaping our Lives*. London: Taylor and Francis.

Ginsborg, H. (2014). Kant's Aesthetics and Teleology, in E. Zalta (ed.), *The Stanford Encyclopedia of Philosophy*. https:/plato.stanford.edu/archives/fall2014/entries/kant-aesthetics

Guardian (2016). Aseel Muthana and Kristen Brekke Brandish Replica Gun in Cardiff – video. https://www.theguardian.com/uk-news/video/2016/feb/10/aseel-muthana-kristen-brekke-brandish-replica-gun-cardiff-isis-video, 10 February.

Gutton, P. (2015). *Adolescence et djihadisme*. Paris: L'Esprit du temps.

Habermas, J. (1984). *The Theory of Communicative Action: Reason and the Rationalization of Society*. Cambridge: Polity Press.

Hong, S. (2015). When Life Mattered: The Politics of the Real in Video Games: Reappropriation of History, Myth, and Ritual. *Games and Culture* 10(1): 35–56.

Huntington, S. (1996). *The Clash of Civilizations and the Remaking of World Order*. New York: Simon and Schuster.

Ito, M. (2005). Intimate Visual Co-presence. 2005 Ubiquitous Computing Conference. pfds.semanticscholar.org

Jenkins, B. (1975). International Terrorism: A New Mode of Conflict, in D. Carlton and C. Schaerf (eds), *International Terrorism and World Security*. London: Croom Helm, pp. 15–31.

Johnson, M. (2007). Gunman Sent Package to NBC News. http://www.nbcnews.com/id/18195423/ns/us_news-crime_and_courts/t/gunman-sent-package-nbc-news/#.WmNg25OMjjA. 19 April.

Johnson, R. (2016). Letter to Mark Zuckerberg. United States Senate Committee on Homeland Security and Government Affairs. https://assets.documentcloud.org/documents/2863236/2016-06-15-RHJ-to-Facebook-Re-Orlando-Attack.pdf, 15 June.

Juergensmeyer, M. (1996). *Terror in the Mind of God: The Global Rise of Religious Violence*. Los Angeles: University of California Press.

Kant, I. (2007 [1914]). *Critique of Judgement*, trans. J. Bernard. New York: Cosimo Classics.

Katz, J. (2017). Attentats de Paris: la conversation entre Abaaoud et Abdeslam passée entre les mailles du filet. https://www.rtbf.be/info/societe/detail_attentats-de-paris-la-conversation-manquee-entre-abdeslam-et-abaaoud?id=9584392

Kaufmann, J.-C. (2010). *The Meaning of Cooking*. Cambridge: Polity Press.

Kendler, K. S., Morris, N. A., Lönn, S. L., Sundquist, J. and Sundquist, K. (2014). Environmental Transmission of Violent Criminal Behavior in Siblings: A Swedish National Study. *Psychological Medicine* 44(15): 3181–7.

Kepel, G. (2015). *Terreur dans l'Hexagone: Genèse du djihad français*. Paris: Gallimard.

Khosrokhavar, F. (2009). *Inside Jihadism: Understanding Jihadi Movements Worldwide*. Boulder: Paradigm.

Khosrokhavar, F. (2015). Le jihad des femmes: une expérience post-féministe. *Sciences Humaines*. https://www.scienceshumaines.com/le-jihad-des-femmes-une-experience-post-feministe_fr_34038.html

Khosrokhavar, F. (2017). *Radicalization: Why Some People Choose the Path of Violence*. New York: The New Press.

Kordt Højbjerg, C. (2005). Masked Violence: Ritual Action and the Perception of Violence in an Upper Guinea Ethnic Conflict, in N. Kastfelt (ed.), *Religion and African Civil Wars*. London: Hurst and Company, pp. 147–51.

Kovacs, E. (2012). Hackers Around the World: It's No TriCk, He's Among the Best in the UK. *Softpedia News*, 18 February.

Kuntsman, A. (2012). Introduction: Affective Fabrics of Digital Cultures, in A. Karatzogianni and A. Kuntsman (eds), *Digital Cultures and the Politics of Emotion: Feelings, Affect and Technological Change*. London: Palgrave Macmillan.

Landsberg, A. (2004). *Prosthetic Memory: The Transformation of American*

Remembrance in the Age of Mass Culture. New York: Columbia University Press.

Lasén, A. and Gómez-Cruz, E. (2009). Digital Photography and Picture Sharing: Redefining the Public/Private Divide. *Knowledge, Technology, Policy* 22(3): 205–15.

Levi, P. (2017 [1986]). *The Drowned and the Saved*. New York: Simon and Schuster.

Libération (2012). Transcription des conversations entre Mohamed Merah et les négociateurs. *Libération*, 17 July.

McDonald, K. (1999). *Struggles for Subjectivity: Identity, Action and Youth Experience*. Cambridge: Cambridge University Press.

McDonald, K. (2003). Marginal Youth, Personal Identity and the Contemporary Gang: Reconstructing the Social World, in L. Kontos, D. Brotherton and L. Barrios (eds), *Gangs and Society: Alternative Perspectives*. New York: Columbia University Press, pp. 62–74.

McDonald, K. (2006). *Global Movements: Action and Culture*. Oxford: Blackwell Publishing.

McDonald, K. (2013). *Our Violent World: Terrorism in Society*. London: Palgrave.

McDonald, K. (2015). From Indymedia to Anonymous: Rethinking Action and Identity in Digital Cultures. *Communication and Society* 18(8): 968–82.

McGonical, J. (2011). *Reality is Broken: Why Games Make Us Better and How They Can Change the World*. New York: Penguin.

Mellor, A. (1993). *Romanticism and Gender*. Abingdon: Routledge.

Mellor, A. (1996). Immortality or Monstrosity? Reflections on the Sublime in Romantic Literature and Art, in F. Burwick and J. Klein (eds), *The Romantic Imagination: Literature and Art in England and Germany*. Amsterdam/New York: Rodopi, pp. 225–39.

Miller, W. (1998). *The Anatomy of Disgust*. Harvard: Harvard University Press.

Mishra, V. (1994). *The Gothic Sublime*. New York: State University of New York Press.

Mitchell, W. (2005). *What Do Pictures Want? The Lives and Loves of Images*. Chicago: University of Chicago Press.

Neumann, P. (2016). *Radicalized: New Jihadists and the Threat to the West*. London: I. B. Tauris.

Paton, N. (2015). *School Shooting*. Paris: Maison des Sciences de l'Homme.

Perry, A. (2015). On the Trail of Britain's Homegrown Jihadis. *Newsweek*, 15 January.

Petersen, S. (2008). Common Banality: The Affective Character of Photo Sharing, Everyday Life and Produsage Cultures. Doctoral dissertation, Copenhagen: University of Copenhagen.

Pilkington, H. (2016). *Loud and Proud: Passion and Politics in the English Defence League*. Manchester: Manchester University Press.

Piot, C. (2010). *Nostalgia for the Future: West Africa after the Cold War*. Chicago: University of Chicago Press.

Polychroniou, C. and Chomsky, N. (2015). The Empire of Chaos: An Interview with Noam Chomsky. *Truthout*. http://www.truth-out.org/news/item/33519-the-empire-of-chaos-an-interview-with-noam-chomsky

Read, M. (2013). #FreeJahar: When Conspiracy Theorists and One Direction Fans Collide. *Gawker*, 25 April.

Rose, G. (2016). *Visual Methodologies: An Introduction to Researching with Visual Materials*, 4th edn. London: Sage.

Roston, M. (1996). The Contemplative Mode, in F. Burwick and J. Klein (eds), *The Romantic Imagination: Literature and Art in England and Germany*. Amsterdam: Rodopi, pp. 377–97.

Roussinos, A. (2014). The Social Media Updates of British Jihadists in Syria Just Got a Lot More Distressing. *VICE*. https://www.vice.com/en_us/article/qbejwx/british-jihadis-beheading-prisoners-syria-isis-terrorism

Roy, O. (2014). *Holy Ignorance: When Religion and Culture Part Ways*. Oxford: Oxford University Press.

Roy, O. (2017). *Jihad and Death: The Global Appeal of Islamic State*. Oxford: Oxford University Press.

Seelow, S. (2016a). L'orientation sexuelle à l'épreuve du djihad. *Le Monde*, 26 July.

Seelow, S. (2016b). Ines Madani, la djihadiste qui se faisait passer pour un homme. *Le Monde*, 8 November.

Serazio, M. (2010). Shooting for Fame: Spectacular Youth, Web 2.0 Dystopia, and the Celebrity Anarchy of Generation Mash-up. *Communication, Culture and Critique* 3(3): 416–34.

Siegel, J. (2005). *Naming the Witch*. Stanford: Stanford University Press.

Silber, M. and Bhatt, A. (2007). *Radicalization in the West: The Homegrown Threat*. New York: New York Police Department.

Silvestri, L. E. (2015). *Friended at the Front: Social Media and the American War Zone*. Lawrence: University of Kansas Press.

Speltini, G. and Passini, S. (2014). Cleanliness/Dirtiness, Purity/Impurity as Social and Psychological Issues. *Culture and Psychology* 20(2): 203–19.

Stewart, K. (2007). *Ordinary Affects*. London: Duke University Press.

Stricherz, G. (2002). *Americans in Kodachrome, 1945–65*. Santa Fe: Twin Palms Publishers.

Sumiala, J. and Tikka, M. (2011). Reality on Circulation: School Shootings, Ritualised Communication, and the Dark Side of the Sacred. *Journal for Communication Studies* 4(2): 145–59.

Taïeb, E. (2016). Rumeurs complotistes: de la croyance à la défiance. *INA Global*. https://halshs.archives-ouvertes.fr/halshs-01311149

Taylor, C. (1989). *Sources of the Self: The Making of the Modern Identity*. Harvard: Harvard University Press.

Thomas, E., McGarty, C., Lala, G., Stuart, A., Hall, L. J., and Goddard, A. (2015). Whatever Happened to Kony 2012? Understanding a Global

Internet Phenomenon as an Emergent Social Identity. *European Journal of Social Psychology* 45: 356–67.

Thomson, D. (2018). *The Returned: They Left to Wage Jihad, Now They're Back*. Cambridge: Polity Press.

Thrift, N. (2011). Lifeworld Inc – and What to Do about It. *Environment and Planning D: Society and Space* 29(1): 5–26.

Tomkins, S. (1991). *Affect, Imagery, Consciousness, vol. 3: The Negative Affects: Anger and Fear*. New York: Springer.

Tonkin, E. (1979). Masks and Powers. *Man* 14(2): 237–48.

Touraine, A. (2007). *A New Paradigm for Understanding Today's World*. Cambridge: Polity Press.

Tufekci, Z. (2013). 'Not This One': Social Movements, the Attention Economy, and Microcelebrity Networked Activism. *American Behavioral Scientist* 57(5): 848–70.

Tufekci, Z. (2017). *Twitter and Tear Gas: The Power and Fragility of Networked Protest*. New Haven: Yale University Press.

Uribe, V. (2004). Dismembering and Expelling: Semantics of Political Terror in Colombia. *Public Culture* 16(1): 79–95.

van Dijck, J. (2007). *Mediated Memories in the Digital Age*. Palo Alto, CA: Stanford University Press.

Vidino, L. and Hughes, S. (2015). *ISIS in America: From Retweets to Raqqa*. Washington: George Washington University Program on Extremism.

Vincent, E. (2015). Ce que les services belges savaient d'Abdelhamid Abaaoud. *Le Monde*, 20 November.

Vincent, E. (2016). Salah Abdeslam, le caïd insaisissable. *Le Monde*, 19 March.

Wagner, R. (2012). First-Person Shooter Religion: Algorithmic Culture and Inter-Religious Encounter. *CrossCurrents* 62(2): 181–203.

Walzer, M. (2015). Islamism and the Left. *Dissent*, Winter.

Weber, M. (1991 [1948]). *From Max Weber: Essays in Sociology*, trans. H. Gerth and C. Wright Mills. London: Routledge.

Weiskel, T. (1976). *The Romantic Sublime: Studies in the Structure and Psychology of Transcendence*. Baltimore: Johns Hopkins University Press.

Wetherell, M. (2012). *Affect and Emotion: A New Social Science Understanding*. London: Sage.

Wieviorka, M. (2004). *La violence*. Paris: Balland.

Williams, R. (1977). *Marxism and Literature*. Oxford: Oxford University Press.

Windle, J. and Briggs, D. (2015). Going Solo: The Social Organisation of Drug Dealers within a London Street Gang. *Journal of Youth Studies* 18(9): 1170–85.

Index